CW00690384

WASTE MANAGEMENT LAW— A PRACTICAL HANDBOOK

AUSTRALIA
Law Book Co.
Sydney

CANADA and USA
Carswell
Toronto

HONG KONG
Sweet & Maxwell Asia

NEW ZEALAND
Brookers
Wellington

SINGAPORE and MALAYSIA
Sweet & Maxwell Asia
Singapore and Kuala Lumpur

WASTE MANAGEMENT LAW

A Practical Handbook

Fourth Edition

John Garbutt

*Consultant, Nicholson Graham & Jones,
London*

First Edition published 1992
Second Edition published 1995
Third Edition published 2000

Fourth Edition published in 2005 by
Sweet & Maxwell Limited of
100 Avenue Road, London NW3 3PF
Typeset by LBJ Typesetting Ltd of Kingsclere
Printed and bound by T.J. International, Padstow, Cornwall

No natural forests were destroyed to make this product;
only farmed timber was used and replanted

ISBN 0 421 895 306

CONTENTS

PART IV HEALTH AND SAFETY ISSUES, EU LEGISLATION,
    COMMON LAW LAND AND REMEDIES

PREFACE TO THE FOURTH EDITION

Nicholson Graham & Jones is a leading City of London law firm, founded in 1858. Its strengths are in company law, litigation, tax, construction and engineering, intellectual property, and new technologies. In recent years it has developed a number of specialisms, including a Planning and Environment Law Group.

The pace of change in environmental law has been fast, but that related to the control of waste management has, if anything, been faster. To the extent that it is frequently difficult to keep up with change and counterchange, the reaction of the waste management industry has been remarkable. In the main it has transformed itself from a somewhat resistible collection of businesses, some forward-looking with high standards and others with extremely low standards, into a coherent and cohesive industry. Some of its members are household names, or divisions of them, and demonstrate the highest sense of responsibility in the operation of their businesses and in the protection of the public environment. As for the stragglers, increasingly the trade associations are insisting on significant improvements in performance, otherwise excommunication will follow. In the public sector, both central and local government agencies, particularly the Environment Agency, have greatly advanced their knowledge and expertise, often in the face of much difficulty associated with ongoing reorganisation and under-resourced struggles to meet demands for increasing regulatory action. The European Union and other international agencies, such OECD and the United Nations, are themselves taking important initiatives not only in the international trade in waste, but also in regard to environmental protection standards, particularly in relation to water and air.

To the waste manager and his or her various professional advisers, all this government activity manifests itself in what may sometimes seem to be a never-ending range of new legislation, imposing itself on almost every individual, but mostly on the waste manager and his advisers. This book is aimed at them but also at regulators and those that have to operate this important legal regime. The success of earlier editions has confirmed that there is a need for a short guide to the range of new and existing legal provisions affecting waste management. I have concentrated on town and country planning, environmental control and health and safety. The intention is to assist readers with an overview of the present state of the law and to equip them to deal with questions and problems which will arise frequently. The aim is to help to reduce the time which is taken up for research.

This fourth edition is required because the pace of change has not relented. Most importantly, the waste on land provisions of Part II of the Environmental Protection Act 1990 are not only mature but are now subject to further adjustment under the Pollution Prevention and Control Act 1999. Besides providing the legal base for the establishment and operation of the Environment Agency, the Environment Act 1995 has generated new producer responsibility obligations on business as a whole, giving effect to EU requirements regarding recycling and reuse of waste. The 1995 Act has also established an entirely new regime of contaminated land control, an area now having some influence on strategies for dealing with closed waste management sites. The 1999 Act is in force, updating and considerably changing integrated pollution, protection and control measures and providing greater powers and responsibilities to the Environment Agency and local government as regulators of polluting processes. The Landfill Directive further complicates the IPPC regime. The EU continues to have a major influence; the section on health and safety at work has been almost completely rewritten as a result of major changes to regulations implementing a considerable number of directives. The opportunity has been taken to update the water resources and pollution control sections and throughout new judicial interpretations have been provided. The town and country planning section has needed updating, taking into account new procedures for dealing with development plans and recent modification to inquiry procedures.

I wish to enter two main caveats. The first is that this handbook is no more than a short guide. The limits on its size and length prevent its being an exhaustive treatise on all the law which affects waste management. For example, I have not dealt (except briefly concerning planning issues) with road traffic or public highway law, mainly because these are more general topics. I have identified where further investigation and study is required.

The second caveat confirms the obvious, that the law relating to the environment continues to change. Provisions of the Pollution Prevention and Control Act 1999 are only starting to take effect in any practical way. I have set June 30, 2004 as the appropriate date for the purposes of this work and it will be noted that in some cases new initiatives have been incorporated.

As with previous editions, I have not worked alone. My partners are to be thanked for their considerable help and support in continuing to promote the idea of the handbook. Sarah Taylor gave useful assistance in checking and updating the health and safety section and in research. I am particularly grateful to Fiona Nicholas who has been responsible for word processing the major changes of this fourth edition, with her usual commitment.

For the sake of clarity, note that only "he", "his" and "him" are used in the text; such references also refer to the feminine pronoun.

John Garbutt
September 2004

ABOUT THE AUTHOR

John Garbutt has been a solicitor for 40 years. He is a former partner and Head of the Planning and Environment Group and is now a consultant at city solicitors, Nicholson Graham & Jones; has been employed in local government; and subsequently was chief executive of both the waste management and industrial minerals divisions of Blue Circle Industries. He also set up and ran their environmental affairs office. He is a former member of the Landfill and Treatment Committee of the Environmental Services Association and has served on the Health and Safety Executive Advisory Committee on Major Hazards. He is a member of the UK Environmental Law Association. He speaks and writes extensively on planning and environment matters from a legal and managerial perspective.

TABLE OF CASES

TABLE OF STATUTES

TABLE OF STATUTORY INSTRUMENTS

TABLE OF EUROPEAN LEGISLATION

REGULATIONS

DECISIONS

TABLE OF ABBREVIATIONS

BAT	best available techniques
BATNEEC	best available techniques not entailing excessive cost
BC	Borough Council
BPEO	best practicable environmental option
CC	County Council
CFCs	chlorofluorocarbons
CHP	combined heat and power
COPA	Control of Pollution Act
DC	District Council
DEFRA	Department for the Environment, Food and Rural Affairs
DETR	Department of the Environment, Transport and the Regions
DoE	Department of the Environment (now DETR)
EA	Environment Agency
EC	European Community
EU	European Union
EPA	Environmental Protection Act
GDPO	Town and Country Planning (General Development Procedure) Order
GPDO	Town and Country Planning (General Permitted Development) Order
HRA	Human Rights Act
HSC	Health and Safety Commission
HSE	Health and Safety Executive
IPC	integrated pollution control
IPPC	integrated pollution prevention and control
LAWDC	local authority waste disposal company
LBC	London Borough Council
MBC	Metropolitan Borough Council
MPG	mineral planning guidance
NCC	Nature Conservancy Council
NRA	National Rivers Authority
PCA	Planning and Compensation Act
PCBs	polychlorinated biphenyls
PCTs	polychlorinated terphenyls
PPCA	Planning Prevention and Control Act
PPG	planning policy guidance
SEPA	Scottish Environmental Protection Agency
SSSI	site of special scientific interest
TCPA	Town and Country Planning Act
UKCIP	UK Climate Impacts Programme
VOC	volatile organic compounds
WIA	Water Industy Act
WMP	waste management paper
WRA	Water Resources Act

PART I

STATUTES AND STRUCTURE OF CONTROL

CHAPTER 1

THE STATUTORY FRAMEWORK OF CONTROL

NOTE ON DEVOLUTION

In this book the law is stated as it applies to England and Wales. A wide **1–001** range of environmental control and regulation functions has been devolved to the National Assembly of Wales. In many cases the National Assembly has taken on the responsibilities in Wales of the Deputy Prime Minister (mainly planning), Secretaries of State both for the Environment, Food and Rural Affairs (environment and other matters) and for Wales. In almost all cases the responsibilities of local authorities and the Environment Agency in the Principality remain the same. For the transfer of functions under the various Acts mentioned in this book, see the National Assembly of Wales (Transfer of Functions) Order 1999.[1]

THE EARLY CONTROLS

Given the sophisticated systems of controls now in existence, it is difficult to **1–002** recall that some 30 years ago specific statutory requirements hardly existed for the control of waste and the operation of sites for the disposal and treatment of waste. Until 1972, control existed primarily on the basis of the Public Health Act 1936, in particular the provisions relating to statutory nuisance, and the Town and Country Planning Acts. The former tended to operate in a reactive way, relying upon local public health authority action following complaint. The latter suffered from a number of difficulties, in particular the lack of flexibility of many planning consents, difficulties of enforcement and of the limitations placed on planning authorities by the law relating to planning conditions.

DEPOSIT OF POISONOUS WASTE ACT 1972

Pollution of water, whether surface or underground, could be controlled **1–003** under the Rivers Prevention of Pollution Acts 1951 and 1961 and the Water Resources Act 1963, but environmental waste hazards, in the specific sense, were not grappled with until the Deposit of Poisonous Waste Act

---

[1] SI 1999/672.

1972. This Act was hurriedly ushered through Parliament following a newspaper campaign and some notorious incidents, sometimes involving children trespassing dangerously on waste tips. However, the 1972 Act could only be regarded as a stopgap provision, in that the system of control was very limited. Thus, the combination of increased public awareness of environmental factors and the growing need for, and impact of, waste disposal, coupled with a rapidly accelerating demand for waste facilities from an affluent society, led to the Control of Pollution Act 1974. For the first time, legislation specifically required county-wide waste disposal plans, together with a system of licensing of waste facilities and landfill sites.

CONTROL OF POLLUTION ACT 1974 AND ENVIRONMENTAL PROTECTION ACT 1990

1–004 Until 1994, the Control of Pollution Act 1974 remained the basis for most waste disposal control. However, the waste on land provisions of Pt II of the Environmental Protection Act (EPA) 1990 were brought into force progressively between 1991 and 1994. The 1990 Act replaced the 1974 Act with a similar regime of control, but supplemented by three main further duties:

(a) The scope of responsibility was widened beyond merely the disposer of waste, to include the producer of waste and all those along the waste chain until final disposal.

(b) A new duty of care was placed on any person importing, producing, carrying, keeping, treating or disposing of controlled waste or who, as a broker, has control of such waste, to take all reasonable measures to prevent the escape of waste from his control or that of any other person, to ensure that any other person obeys the prohibition on unauthorised or harmful deposit, treatment or disposal of waste and to undertake certain other obligations where the waste is transferred.[2]

(c) A continuing liability rests upon the holder of a waste management licence which may not be relinquished, surrendered or transferred without the Environment Agency's approval.

See further below regarding EPA 1990.

CONTROL OF POLLUTION (AMENDMENT) ACT 1989

1–005 The Control of Pollution (Amendment) Act 1989 created a new offence of transporting controlled waste without registering with the local authority.

ENVIRONMENTAL PROTECTION ACT 1990

1–006 The UK Government is bound to comply with Directives and other legislation approved by the European Community. In particular, UK legislation must comply with the Framework Directive on Waste, as

---

[2] See paras 10–032 and 10–044 in Ch.10.
[3] 75/442/EEC.

modified and updated by the 1991 Council Directive on Hazardous Waste,[4] Council Directive 96/61/EC concerning integrated pollution, prevention and control, Council Directive 1999/31/EC on the landfill of waste and the European Parliament and Council Directive 2000/76/EC on the incineration of waste.[5] The combined effect of this European legislation has been to require significant modifications to EPA 1990, which are presently achieved by the Waste Management Licensing Regulations 1994,[6] as amended,[7] the Landfill (England and Wales) Regulations 2002,[8] and the Waste Incineration (England and Wales) Regulations 2002.[9]

Part I of EPA 1990 deals with integrated pollution control and air pollution control by local authorities. The regime of control replaced the Alkali etc. Works Regulation Act 1906. The Act provides for two separate pollution control systems. For the processes regarded as being significant potential polluters an entirely new system of integrated pollution control (IPC) replaced what have been distinct systems according to the particular type of impact on the environment. IPC provides that all persons undertaking "prescribed processes" must have an authorisation from the Environment Agency which provides that any pollution, whether of air, water or land, is adequately controlled. Certain waste disposal installations and processes are caught by the IPC system. The less polluting processes are the subject of a system controlled by the local public health authority. Here the only part of the process controlled by Part I is pollution of the atmosphere. Any pollution of water and land continues to be the subject of other regimes.

Part I of EPA 1990 is intended to be repealed progressively by the Pollution Prevention and Control Act (PPCA) 1999 (see below). Part II of EPA 1990 will be the subject of significant amendment. For further details see Ch.9.

(a) Statutory nuisance

The long-standing Public Health Act 1936, supplemented at a later stage by   **1–007** the Public Health (Recurring Nuisances) Act 1969, was repealed and replaced by Pt III of EPA 1990—with only limited alterations. The public health authority is placed under a duty to ensure that action is taken to prevent nuisances and this can, of course, affect waste production and disposal sites, particularly those which are closed.[10]

(b) Litter

Part IV of EPA 1990 has also been instrumental in bringing into force new,   **1–008** more comprehensive controls over litter.

[4] 91/689/EEC.
[5] see Ch.15.
[6] SI 1994/1056.
[7] see Ch.10.
[8] SI 2002/1559.
[9] SI 2002/2980.
[10] See Ch.12.

ENVIRONMENT ACT 1995

1-009 The main function of the Environment Act 1995 was to establish, for England and Wales, the Environment Agency (EA). This body, which came into being on April 1, 1996, assumed the responsibilities of HM Inspectorate of Pollution, the National Rivers Authority and the local waste regulation authorities. A separate body for Scotland, the Scottish Environmental Protection Agency, was given similar responsibilities. From the waste industry's viewpoint the main effect was that the day-to-day regulation ceased to be with local authorities, although they do still retain the functions of local planning authority.[11] The Act also provided a new regime for the control of contaminated land.[12] Of some importance to the waste industry were provisions in Pt V of the Act, which make provision for a national waste strategy and introduce producer responsibility requirements, particularly with regard to recycling and reuse. Part V also brought into force further requirements for the review of mineral planning permissions which potentially can have an effect upon reclamation by landfill operations.

Special waste control

1-010 Waste of a particularly dangerous kind is the subject of a special regime, set out currently in the Special Waste Regulations 1996,[13] as amended by the Special Waste (Amendment) (England and Wales) Regulations 2001.[14] The essence of the regulations is the requirement that in its journey from production to final and safe disposal, the special waste should be accompanied by consignment notes which identify precisely the type of waste, its characterisation, quantity and type and information about containers, as well as the processes from which the waste originated. The intention is that the journey of the waste from start to finish should be documented and reported to the EA.

OTHER WASTE MANAGEMENT LEGISLATION

1-011 The most important other statutes affecting the operation of the waste management business are the Town and Country Planning Act 1990 and the Health and Safety at Work etc. Act 1974. The former requires that all development (whether operational or a material change of use) requires planning permission. The Act, together with other town and country planning legislation, was consolidated, in 1990, into four separate acts, dealt with in detail in Pt II.

---

[11] See Ch.4.
[12] See Ch.11.
[13] SI 1996/972.
[14] SI 2001/3148. See Ch.10.

The Health and Safety at Work etc. Act 1974 forms the framework of a comprehensive system of control administered by the Health and Safety Executive, imposing on most employers, as well as employees and others, a wide range of duties to maintain healthy and safe premises, materials and systems of work.[15]

WATER RESOURCES ACT 1991

The Water Resources Act (WRA) 1991 came about as a result of the consolidation of most of the legislation relating to water and land drainage, as well as the administration of water. The effect of the Act, which came into force on December 1, 1991, was to consolidate all the water pollution control provisions of the Rivers Prevention of Pollution Acts 1951 and 1961, the Water Resources Act 1963 and the Water Act 1989. The 1991 Act also controls the abstraction of water for most purposes.[16] **1–012**

WATER INDUSTRY ACT 1991

Part of the consolidation exercise mentioned above, the Water Industry Act (WIA) 1991 gives effect to the control of discharges to sewers.[17] **1–013**

POLLUTION PREVENTION AND CONTROL ACT 1999

This Act, which received royal assent on July 27, 1999, makes provision for implementing EU Council Directive 96/61/EC concerning integrated pollution, prevention and control. Supplementary objectives are the regulation of other activities capable of causing any environmental pollution and the provision of powers to prevent or control emissions capable of causing any such pollution. It is intended that the Act will replace Pt I of EPA 1990, but in respect of existing processes this will be a gradual transition, extending at least into 2007. The intention is also that landfill and other waste management activities presently controlled under Pt II (waste on land) of EPA 1990 ultimately will be administered under the 1999 Act regime. For further detail, see Ch.9. **1–014**

HUMAN RIGHTS ACT 1998

The Human Rights Act (HRA) 1998 came into force in the UK on October 2, 2000. While it is of considerable significance to the UK's largely unwritten constitution, its impact in relation to planning, environment and **1–015**

---

[15] See Ch.14.
[16] See Ch.7.
[17] See Ch.7.

health and safety controls on the waste management industry seems likely to be limited.

Effect of the Act

1–016 Hitherto, the UK's specific human rights responsibilities have been by reference to the European Convention on Human Rights 1950. Procedurally, the Convention allows those seeking protection and relief to make application to the European Court of Human Rights, based in Strasbourg; however, the procedures are slow and expensive. The effect of the 1998 Act is to overlay UK legislation with the obligations, duties and protections contained within the Convention. However, the right remains to make application to Strasbourg.

The Act's main provisions

1–017 The five main provisions of the Act are:

    (a) the incorporation into domestic law of Convention rights;
    (b) the requirement that all legislation shall be administered and interpreted so that it is compatible with Convention rights and the emanations of the European Court, as well as the European Commission of Human Rights;
    (c) the courts have powers to make a declaration that legislation is incompatible with the Convention—at that stage there is an obligation on the Government to introduce legislation to rectify the situation;
    (d) there are rights for any victims of action taken by public authorities in a way contrary to the Convention—public authorities include central and local government, the EA and the Planning Inspectorate; and
    (e) any legislation introduced must be accompanied by an assurance from the Government that it is compatible with Convention rights.

The Convention

1–018 Most of the Convention is to be found in Sch.1 to HRA 1998. The following Articles may have some relevance to waste management operations.

Convention rights and freedoms (Part I)

1–019   ● Article 2—right to life.

- Article 5—right to liberty and security.
- Article 6—right to a fair trial.
- Article 7—no punishment without law.
- Article 8—right to respect for private and family life.
- Article 10—freedom of expression.
- Article 14—prohibition of discrimination.

The first protocol (Part II)

- Article 1—protection of property.   **1–020**

Application to waste management law

It seems likely that the main effect of the Act will be to call into question **1–021** rights of third parties to participate in statutorily controlled democratic processes. For example, it has been claimed that current arrangements for dealing with structure and local plan representations may be objectionable because of the right of local planning authorities to overrule or disregard inspectors' recommendations (see para.3–006). Of more importance may be the rights of individuals under Art.5 (liberty and security), Art.8 (respect for private and family life) and Art.10 (freedom of expression). Very often third party complaints about failures on the part of industry to properly comply with obligations under the law (*e.g.* breaches of planning consent, waste management licence, etc.) are not dealt with by regulators as justice might normally require. Frequently the regulators will exercise a discretion which hitherto has not been open to third parties to challenge successfully in the courts. The Act can be expected to have some effect on the pressures that third parties can apply to regulators, who risk admonition by the courts and possible liability directly to compensate the injured parties. There is no doubt that strategies and policies not only of the waste management industry but also of regulators need to be reassessed carefully in the light of the Act's provisions.

For the application of the Convention in cases of environmental pollution, see *Lopez Ostra v Spain*,[18] and the British judgment, *Power and Rayner v UK*.[19] As to the relationship between planning control and the human rights legislation see the House of Lords judgment in *R. v Secretary of State, Ex p. Holding & Barnes*,[20] *County Properties Limited v The Scottish Ministers*,[21] and *Friends Provident v Secretary of State and Others*.[22]

---

[18] Council of Europe December 19, 1994.
[19] [1990] 12 E.H.R.R. 355.
[20] [2001] 2 All E.R. 929.
[21] Unreported, August 16, 2001.
[22] Unreported, Administrative Court, October 16, 2001.

CHAPTER 2

THE STRUCTURE OF CONTROL IN ENGLAND AND WALES

Central government

Primary responsibilities for the control and the environmental effects of **2–001** waste rest with the Secretary of State for the Environment Food and Rural Affairs. He oversees not only the duties and responsibilities of the department, but also those of the EA, and, with the Deputy Prime Minister, has a supervisory role so far as the system of local government in England is concerned. In regard to Wales, other duties rest upon the Secretary of State for that principality. However, a wide range of environmental control and regulation functions has been devolved to the National Assembly of Wales. In many cases the National Assembly has taken on the responsibilities of the Secretaries of State. In almost all cases the responsibilities of local authorities and the EA in the principality remain the same. For the transfer of functions under the various Acts mentioned in this book, see the National Assembly of Wales (Transfer of Functions) Order 1999.[1] Elsewhere, the reference to the Secretary of State for the Environment Food and Rural Affairs, particularly in relation to appeals and similar powers, should be read, in relation to Wales, as the Welsh Assembly.

An important government responsibility in relation to the management of waste is the production of a waste strategy. "Waste Strategy 2000" is in two parts and deals with a number of topics including:

- proposals to comply with EU Landfill Directive (see paras 10–073 and 15–010) setting targets for the reduction of the amount of waste going to landfill;
- targets for preventing waste;
- strategies for recycling, composting or uses of fuel;
- landfill tax commitments;
- a target, by 2005, to reduce industrial and commercial waste sent to landfill, to 85 per cent of 1998 levels;
- targets for recycling of household waste (see paras 10–084 and 10–090);

[1] SI 1999/672.

- statutory performance standards for local authorities;
- stimulation of markets for recycled materials.

Part II of the strategy provides information on waste management options, dealing with hazardous waste and packaging waste and reports on progress with various waste streams.

Other government departments

2–002   Other government departments have responsibilities in respect of waste management, including the Office of the Deputy Prime Minister (planning, regions, local government), the Department of Trade and Industry (incineration of waste for energy purposes, landfill gas exploitation, administration of the Pipelines Act 1962, promotion of trade and research in waste management, including alternative energy, recycling and waste minimisation), the Department for Education and Employment (supervision of Health and Safety Executive and the Health and Safety at Work etc. Act 1974), the Department of Transport (highways and traffic, including the regulation of construction of use of vehicles for the transport of waste and rail transport). The duties of the former Ministry of Agriculture, Fisheries and Food (general supervision of the development and restoration of land used for waste management purposes) have now been subsumed in the responsibilities of the Department of the Environment, Food and Rural Affairs (see above).

Regional government

2–003   Part 1 of the Planning and Compulsory Purchase Act 2004 establishes a new system of regional development planning in England. The provisions of this Act are not yet fully in force but see below para.3–002.

Local government

2–004   Subject to the provisions of the 2004 Act concerning regional government, in England and Wales all the tiers of local government have a role to play in waste disposal, regulation and collection. In most of the shire counties of England, where the two tiers of county and district council continue to apply, the county councils have responsibility under the Town and Country Planning legislation for the development control of waste management. Where unitary authorities have been set up (in the main conurbations and throughout Wales), all local government responsibilities devolve to those single authorities.

   With regard to waste regulation, local government no longer has any direct role, as a result of the devolution of most of their duties to the EA, by virtue of the Environment Act 1995. This change took place on April 1, 1996.

County councils and unitary authorities continue to have overall responsibility for waste disposal although, as a result of s.32 of EPA 1990, the operational aspects of waste disposal are now separated from administrative duties (see the discussion on LAWDCs below). In the shire counties, where separate district councils remain, those district council duties are limited to waste collection, a function which they may delegate elsewhere, notably to the private sector.

In Greater London and some metropolitan areas, the position is different. In London, the planning and operational roles devolve to the various London boroughs, subject again to the operational constraints now imposed by s.32. Waste collection is also devolved to the London boroughs. In London and some metropolitan areas there are combined waste disposal authorities.[2] Significant changes to the strategic administration of London came about as a result of the Greater London Authority Act 1999, when the Mayor and the Greater London Assembly assumed executive functions. Their functions include the following:

(a) Production of an integrated transport strategy for London.
(b) A London Development Agency to foster economic development.
(c) A general responsibility for assessing and reporting on the state of London's environment and for preparing and publishing strategies on air quality and waste. The Mayor will also have supervisory duties for local authority waste recycling plans, air quality management plans and in relation to biodiversity and ambient noise.
(d) In planning, the preparation of a spatial development strategy, some development control of a strategic nature, where the Mayor and Assembly will be consulted on specific developments. For procedures see the Town and Country Planning (London Spatial Development Strategy) Regulations 2000.[3] These developments are expected to apply to:

- buildings in excess of 15,000m^2 of floor space (20,000m^2 in central London and 30,000m^2 in the City);
- high buildings more than 25m adjacent to the Thames (more than 75m in the City or more than 30m elsewhere);
- mining operations on more than 10 hectares; and
- waste development of more than 50,000 tonnes per year.

See the Town and Country Planning (Mayor of London) Order 2000.[4]

For further guidance see Government of London Circular 1/2000, "Strategic Planning In London". As to national parks, see para.3–001 below.

[2] See the Waste Regulation and Disposal (Authorities) Order 1985 (SI 1985/1884), as amended).
[3] SI 2000/1491.
[4] SI 2000/1493.

OTHER BODIES

The Environment Agency

2–005   Until April 1, 1996, HM Inspectorate of Pollution was charged with the administration and enforcement of Pt I of EPA 1990 (integrated pollution control). The National Rivers Authority had responsibility for the control of abstraction and pollution of water resources under the Water Resources Act 1991. However, the effect of the Environment Act 1995 was to establish an all-embracing Environment Agency which, from April 1, 1996, assumed the responsibilities of the Inspectorate and the National Rivers Authority. It also took on all waste regulation duties of local government. The EA's extensive powers include those which relate to enforcement and prosecution, particularly offences related to WRA 1991, PPCA 1999 and Pts I and II of EPA 1990. The EA published in 1998 a written statement in regard to enforcement and prosecution, adopting principles of proportionality, consistency, transparency and targeting (see "Environment Agency. Enforcement and Prosecution Policy").

Water

2–006   While the control of water pollution, etc. is now with the EA, the regional water companies remain responsible for the supervision and enforcement of controls for the discharge of trade and sewage effluent to sewers under WIA 1991.

Health and safety

2–007   The Health and Safety Executive has consultation and liaison responsibilities under Pt I of EPA 1990. Relating to these, other inspectorates such as the Mines Inspectorate, the Quarries Inspectorate and the Pipelines Inspectorate also have functions in connection with ancillary matters.

Interface between collection and disposal of waste

2–008   It follows from the above requirements of EPA 1990 that the collection of waste devolves primarily upon the district councils and unitary authorities in England and Wales (EPA 1990, s.30). There is an obligation to accept, free of charge, all household waste in their areas, except where the location is too isolated or inaccessible, or where the authority is satisfied that adequate arrangements for disposal have been made by the person controlling the waste. The collection authority is also responsible, if requested by the occupier of the premises, to collect any commercial waste, but it has no obligations in respect of the collection of industrial waste (for the definitions of household, commercial and domestic waste, see EPA 1990, s.75). Except in very special cases the collection of household waste cannot incur any charge, but there is liability to pay a reasonable rate in respect of other wastes.

Once collected it is the duty of the collection authority in England to deliver the waste at such places as the disposal authority directs (EPA 1990, s.48).

Under s.49 of EPA 1990, the waste collection authorities have various responsibilities in respect of waste recycling, in particular to provide for a plan for dealing with waste by separation, baling or otherwise packaging it for recycling purposes. Waste collection authorities have powers to establish arrangements for recycling waste themselves or to provide for others to undertake the role. Other parties may include the waste disposal authority or the private sector (EPA 1990, s.48). Under s.52, the waste collection authority is entitled to receive payments from the waste disposal authority in respect of waste retained for recycling. The payments represent the net saving of expenditure on the disposal of waste as the authority may determine. Conversely, payments may be made by the waste collection authority to the waste disposal authority in circumstances where the latter makes alternative arrangements, rendering it unnecessary for collection to take place. Note that whereas payments for material retained for recycling by the waste collection authority are mandatory, this is not so where a third party undertakes recycling. In these circumstances the obligation on the waste disposal authority or waste collection authority to make payments is merely discretionary. The amounts of payments are to be calculated in accordance with the Environmental Protection (Waste Recycling Payments) Regulations 1992,[5] as amended from time to time.

Refuse Disposal (Amenity) Act 1978

Further duties are visited primarily on the unitary and district councils in **2–009** England and Wales by the Refuse Disposal (Amenity) Act 1978. The Act replaces the Civic Amenities Act 1967, which not only imposed sanctions against unauthorised dumping of waste (including abandoned vehicles), but also required authorities to provide what had come to be known as "civic amenity sites" (*i.e.* places where the public may at all reasonable times and free of charge get rid of their waste). Payment can only be imposed on non-residents of the area or in respect of non-household waste.

LAWDCs and private arrangements

It will be appreciated that collection and disposal of waste is also **2–010** undertaken by the private sector. Many major companies have subsidiaries or divisions engaged in the collection of household waste (usually by

[5] SI 1992/462.

contract with the collection authority), but they will also operate independently in the industrial and commercial sectors. All types of waste may be disposed of or recycled at various private sector installations, including landfill sites and waste treatment and incineration facilities.

Besides the public and private sectors, Parliament created what can amount to a hybrid entity, responsible for both collection and disposal of waste. This has come about by virtue of s.32 of and Sch.2 to EPA 1990. The legislation gives effect to the policy that waste regulation and waste disposal functions should, so far as possible, be separated. During the course of 1991 and 1992 the Secretary of State for the Environment gave directions to existing disposal authorities, requiring them, within a specified time period, to form or participate in forming a waste disposal company (known as a local authority waste disposal company, or LAWDC) and transfer to those companies all parts of their undertakings relevant to operational waste disposal. There is no obligation on the part of the disposal authority to form a waste disposal company, but there are limited options. The only alternatives available are to make arrangements for the private sector to take over waste disposal. DoE Circulars 8/91 and 10/91 provide useful guidance on the arrangements made both in formation and subsequent administration.

PART II

TOWN AND COUNTRY PLANNING:
THE LEGISLATION

Planning control is absolutely fundamental to all activities affecting land in the United Kingdom. Very little in the way of the development of land may be undertaken without going through the sometimes complex procedures of planning applications. From small beginnings, where a very limited number of activities were under control and, even then, not to any detailed extent, the system has developed through the latter part of the twentieth century into one of the most complex codes of law affecting equally the great and the small, the public and private sectors, from the massive industrial complex down to the garden shed. In certain circumstances one cannot prune one's garden trees without specific permission. The previous chapter discusses how the town and country planning system is administered. This Part examines the system of development plans, how development control works and is enforced, special controls for conservation of land and buildings, trees and amenities, and finally the application of town and country planning to hazardous substances.

THE LEGISLATION FROM 1990

From a diversity of different acts there emerged, in 1990, a set of consolidating statutes bringing a large proportion of planning legislation into a much simpler form. These acts are the Town and Country Planning Act (TCPA) 1990, the Planning (Listed Buildings and Conservation Areas) Act 1990, the Planning (Hazardous Substances) Act 1990, and the Planning (Consequential Provisions) Act 1990. However, no sooner was the ink dry than Parliament moved on and the whole system of modification and counter-modification was started again through the Planning and Compensation Act (PCA) 1991. The Transport and Works Act 1992 introduces procedures for authorising major projects particularly relating to railway, water and other transport systems. The Act was a parliamentary response to criticisms of procedures which had been widely made, where major projects were authorised by way of parliamentary approval under the Member's Private Bill procedure. Such a procedure was regarded as unnecessarily slow and complex, where the rights of the individual were often severely curtailed by the very nature of those procedures and the cost of taking part in them.

Subsequently Parliament approved the Environment Act 1995, altering arrangements for the establishment and administration of national parks, the modification of certain mineral planning permissions and altering the law relating to hedgerows.

Further changes, both to development planning and control are fore-shadowed in the Planning and Compulsory Purchase Act 2004. At time of writing, most of the provisions are not in force. For further details, see the relevant text (below).

Mention should be made of the Human Rights Act (HRA) 1998, which effectively came into force on October 2, 2000. The Act formally incorporates into UK law the provisions the 1950 European Convention on Human Rights. The Regional Development Agencies Act 1998 may have some future relevance to waste management. The Act establishes from April 1, 1999 regional development agencies for nine English regions (which take their place alongside similar bodies which have existed for some time in Scotland and Wales). While the agencies will have no planning powers as such, their functions are strongly related to development, particularly in "brown field" areas. These functions include furthering the economic development and regeneration of an area, promotion of business efficiency, investment and competitiveness along with employment, and contributing to the achievement of sustainable development in the UK (see *e.g.* UK government policy "Sustainable Development. A Better Quality of Life"). Flowing from these Acts (and their predecessors) is a mass of statutory instruments (subsidiary legislation) to which reference is made from time to time. Furthermore, and illustrating that town and country planning practice is an art as much as a science, account must be taken of a whole range of circulars, guidance notes and other documents published on behalf of the Deputy Prime Minister, Secretary of State for the Environment, Food and Rural Affairs, their predecessors, as well as subsidiary agencies. Town and country planning is as much about government policy as it is about the law. This is why departmental circulars and information, development control, policy and other guidance notes are referred to and interpreted so frequently in planning inquiries and High Court actions.

CHAPTER 3

THE DEVELOPMENT PLAN SYSTEM

INTRODUCTION

The 1990s has seen a period of considerable change in the procedures for **3–001** the establishment of development plans throughout England and Wales. The Town and Country Planning Act 1968 had introduced between 1971 and 1974 a two-tier system of structure and local plans. In London and other metropolitan areas, structure plans were the responsibility of the Greater London Council and metropolitan counties, while local plans were usually dealt with by the London borough and metropolitan district councils. The responsibility for making structure plans in shire counties was usually with the county council, and for local plans with the district council. There were special arrangements in respect of areas of the Peak and Lake District National Parks, where joint planning boards had their own structural plan, notwithstanding that their areas were made up of parts of other administrative areas.

The Local Government Act 1985 was the catalyst for a new and emerging system of unitary development plans. The 1985 Act saw the abolition of the Greater London Council and the metropolitan counties. The surviving London boroughs and metropolitan districts were required to prepare unitary development plans in two parts, the first having the character of the structure plan and the second a local plan. This was the position at the time of the consolidating TCPA 1990.

Major changes flowed from a combination of PCA 1991 and the Local Government Act 1992. The effect of the latter Act was to introduce progressively in England a system of unitary local government, largely based upon urban areas. However, sometimes entire counties have been transformed into individual unitary authorities, examples being Berkshire, Herefordshire and the Isle of Wight. Elsewhere in England the two-tier county and district councils remain, having respective responsibility for structure and local plans. The 1991 Act required district councils to prepare district-wide development plans; the county councils retained separate minerals development plan responsibilities (and also have duties related to waste plans). Unitary authorities prepare all of these plans, as appropriate.

Some special arrangements apply. In Wales, the Local Government (Wales) Act 1994 established a system of unitary authorities, each required to prepare a unitary development plan. The Environment Act 1995 brought about changes in the administration of national parks in England and

Wales. The National Park Authorities (Wales) Order 1995,[1] as amended, set up the three national park authorities where all functions of the local planning authority are assumed. Unitary plans are to be prepared for these national parks. In England, the seven national park authorities must prepare structure and local plans for their areas.[2] Special arrangements also apply to the Broads, enterprise zones, urban development areas, and those areas designated under the Leasehold Reform, Housing and Urban Development Act 1993, where the Urban Regeneration Agency becomes the local planning authority (see TCPA 1990, ss.5–8A).

THE PLANNING AND COMPULSORY PURCHASE ACT 2004

3–002   At the time of writing, this Act is not yet fully in force. However, it makes significant changes to the current development plan processes, including a more formal regional strategy and what are intended to be simpler and speedier local plan procedures.

Regional spatial strategy

3–003   Section 1 of the 2004 Act provides for a regional spatial strategy (RSS). The RSS must set out the Secretary of State's policies for the development and use of land in each region. In effect, the RSS replaces regional planning guidance. Regional planning bodies (RPBs) are to be set up under s.2 of the Act and are expected to have a membership made up of councillors of constituent authorities, *e.g.* county, district and unitary councils.

The RSS will be a statutory document, with which other plans must conform, usually prepared by the RPB, but requiring the approval of the Secretary of State. Processes for public participation and consultation are the subject of regulations and generally follow those applying to structure plans (see below para.3–006). The Town and Country Planning (Regional Planning) (England) Regulations 2004[3] will act as the basis for the setting up of regional planning bodies. The regulations, which came into force on September 28, 2004, establish criteria for recognition of regional planning bodies, prescribe the form and content of draft revisions of regional spatial strategy and procedures for their preparation. During the transitional period before the strategies are completed under the new regulations, various regional planning guidance documents will be treated as the regional spatial strategies. The Town and Country Planning (Initial Regional Spatial Strategy) (England) Regulations 2004[4] provide that

[1] SI 1995/2803.
[2] See the National Park Authorities (England) Order 1996 (SI 1996/1243); see also DoE Circular 12/96, "Environment Act 1995. National Parks".
[3] SI 2004/2203.
[4] SI 2004/2206.

various regional planning guidance documents (the RPG series) for all regions of England will be treated as the regional spatial strategy from a date to be prescribed. See also the Town and Country Planning (Regional Planning Guidance as Revision of Regional Spatial Strategy) Order 2004.[5] This order fixes the date and circumstances for the changeover of reliance on regional planning guidance to regional spatial strategies. Each English region is dealt with separately.

DEVELOPMENT PLAN PROCEDURES[6]

Regulations prescribing the form and content of structure plans, unitary development plans, waste local plans and mineral local plans are consolidated in the Town and Country Planning (Development Plan) (England) Regulations 1999,[7] which came into force on January 4, 2000. **3–004**

Unitary development plans

In preparing for a unitary plan, local planning authorities are obliged to keep under review the matters affecting the development of their area or its planning. They are empowered to institute surveys and to review or keep up-to-date with planning matters. Among the matters to be considered in the review are the principal physical and economic characteristics of the area and neighbouring areas, population, communications and any other matters of relevance including those prescribed or directed to be considered by the Secretary of State. Local planning authorities must also take into account any prospective changes.[8] Thereafter they must prepare the development plan in two parts. First, a written statement must formulate the authority's general policies in respect of development and use of land in its area. Secondly, the plan must contain a written statement containing proposals for development and other use of land in more specific form, including a map. A reasoned justification of Pt 2 policies must also be included. Note that Pt 1 must include policies in respect of suitable waste disposal sites or installations.[9] **3–005**

The plan must take into account a considerable amount of local and regional policy advice, notably the RSS.[10] The plan must also review and generally be in conformity with central government guidance on available resources to carry out general policy set out in the plan, housing policy,

---

[5] SI 2004/2208.
[6] The Planning and Compulsory Purchase Act 2004 makes a number of changes to development plan processes—see Pt II of the Act which at time of writing is not yet fully in force. See below para.3–016.
[7] SI 1999/3280.
[8] TCPA 1990, s.11.
[9] See Waste Management Licensing Regulations 1994 (SI 1994/1056) and PPG10, "Planning and Waste Management".
[10] See above para.3–003.

green belts and a wide range of economic considerations. Advice on mineral working policies and waste treatment and disposal matters must also be taken into account. Increasingly, environment policies at European and central government level need to be incorporated into plans. Of special note are the waste plans prepared by the EA strategy.[11] More internationally based policies are also the subject of guidance which needs to be taken account of in development planning and development control.[12]

Public participation

3–006   The local planning authority which prepares a unitary development plan has a range of public participation obligations set down in s.13 of TCPA 1990; the procedure is dealt with in detail in the Town and Country Planning (Development Plan) (England) Regulations 1999.[13] The Regulations require that prior to formally putting the proposals on deposit for public inspection, a limited consultation exercise must take place, largely confined to public sector bodies such as the Secretary of State, other relevant local authorities including parish councils, the EA, the Countryside Commission, etc. Wider consultation at this stage (*e.g.* with members of the public) is discretionary. However, any responses or representations made at this stage must be taken into account.

Once the unitary development plan has been deposited, wide-ranging consultation and publicity requirements follow (reg.11). Objections and other representations are usually required to be made in writing and to be lodged within six weeks, beginning with the date of the first publication of a local newspaper notice (reg.12). Where objections have been made, the authority is required to hold a public local inquiry unless all the parties agree that this is not necessary. It is often the case that the authority will prepare modifications to its plan to meet any objections.

Following the inquiry, the appointed inspector will prepare his report and recommendations which are then considered by the authority. In the event that the inspector proposes changes, but the authority does not intend to accept these, it is obliged to give public notice and consider any further objections or representations. A further local inquiry may be held (reg.16). Where the authority wishes to modify the plan, either in accordance with the inspector's recommendations or for some other reason, the list of proposed modifications and reasons for proposing them must be published and, again, objections taken into account. A further inquiry may be held where this is seen to be necessary.

It will be apparent that, by and large, the procedure following the inquiry is a matter for the discretion of the authority and challenge to the Secretary of State by dissatisfied parties is usually not available. However, there have

---

[11] See Ch.10, para.10–075.
[12] See, for example, DETR guide, "Planning for Sustainable Development: Towards Better Practice".
[13] SI 1999/3280.

been a number of cases where challenges to the High Court are pursued, under s.287 of TCPA 1990. The High Court has not been slow to quash decisions of local authorities where it is concluded that the wide discretions available to the authority have not been exercised in a rational, reasonable and lawful way.

Notice of final adoption of the plan is required to be given and the authority must place the plan on deposit for inspection,[14] A unitary development plan may not be adopted by a London borough council unless Pts I and II of the plan are in general conformity with the spacial development strategy—a document which it is the responsibility of the Greater London Authority to prepare.

Note that the Secretary of State has wide powers to intervene in the unitary development plan process. He may give directions,[15] call in the plan for his own approval[16] and conduct his own local inquiry or other examination.[17] Alterations to unitary plans proceed under s.21. The procedure is essentially the same as for the making of a new plan.[18]

Structure plans

In the shire counties (*i.e.* counties outside London and areas where unitary authorities are not responsible) the development plan system operates on a two-tier basis with (1) a structure plan and (2) local plans. The responsibility for making structure plans in shire counties is usually with the county council, although subject to exceptions (*e.g.* for national parks—see para.3–001 above).   **3–007**

Section 31 of TCPA 1990 spells out what is required in a structure plan. Effectively, it is not a plan at all in the graphic sense, but is a written statement of the authority's policy and general proposals in respect of the development and other use of land in its area (including measures for the improvement of the physical environment and the management of traffic). It also contains such other matters as the Secretary of State may require. While, primarily, the structure plan is a statement of policies, it is usually illustrated by a range of diagrams and plans. Fundamentally, its function is to prescribe broad policy, but not to focus in detail on the use of specific areas of land. The Secretary of State's guidance note PPG12, "Development Plans", lists the following as appropriate[19]:

(a) new housing, including figures for housing provision in each district;
(b) green belts and conservation in town and country;

---

[14] TCPA 1990, s.15 and reg.17.
[15] *ibid.*, s.17.
[16] *ibid.*, ss.18 and 19.
[17] *ibid.*, s.20.
[18] For further guidance see PPG12, "Development Plans and Regional Planning Guidance 1992" and PPG12 (Wales), "Development Plans in Wales (1992)".
[19] Note, however, that PPG12 is now replaced by PPS12, "Local Development Frameworks".

(c) the rural economy;
(d) major industrial, business, retail and other employment-generating development;
(e) strategic transport, highway and other infrastructure;
 (f) mineral working (including disposal of mineral waste) and protection of mineral resources;
(g) waste disposal, land reclamation and reuse;
(h) tourism, leisure and recreation; and
 (i) energy generation.

Other provisions as to the content of the plan are set out in the Town and Country Planning (Development Plan) (England) Regulations 1999.[20] A structure plan will take into account central government policies both national and regional. For example, the Government has developed a range of regional policy guidance in the RPG series, now covering all English regions. Similar advice applies also to Wales. Also to be taken into account are policies in respect of suitable waste disposal sites and installations (see Waste Management Licensing Regulations 1994[21]; and DoE Circular 11/94, "EPA 1990: Pt II. Waste Management Licensing. The Framework Directive on Waste"; see also PPG23, "Planning and Pollution Control" (1994) which also provides advice on the approach in a plan to waste disposal and other environmental policies, and PPG10, "Planning and Waste Management"). PPG23 and PPG10 are not applicable in Wales.

Alterations to or replacement of structure plans

3–008 Not only is the whole of England outside the metropolitan areas now the subject of operative structure plans, but many have already been the subject of alteration or replacement, provided for by s.32 of TCPA 1990. The procedures for alterations or replacement follow a similar course to those for a unitary plan. In short, these procedures involve:

(a) a review and, if necessary, a further survey (s.30);
(b) proposals for draft alterations or replacement (s.32);
(c) publicity and consultation (s.33);
(d) the firming up of policies and proposals in a further draft plan and formal deposit for public inspection and objection (s.33);
(e) review of objections at an examination in public (an informal inquiry) (s.35B);
 (f) publication of proposed modifications and review by the authority of objections; and
(g) final adoption with public notification.

[20] SI 1999/3280.
[21] SI 1994/1056.

For further details of procedures see the Town and Country Planning (Development Plan) (England) Regulations 1999.[22] There is no statutory requirement for the regularity of assessment of structure plans, but in practice these tend to be dealt with on roughly a five-yearly sequence. PPG12 gives further advice, but this has been replaced by PPS12, "Local Development Frameworks".

The effect of structure and unitary plans

Although the structure plan is, by its nature, a document which provides **3–009** broad general policy, it is no less important for that reason.

Structure and unitary plans have statutory basis and represent one of the primary documents of policy to which the planning authority must refer on any application for planning permission for development. Indeed, by virtue of s.26 of PCA 1991, the structure and unitary plans (and the local plan—see below) are given a primary status by providing that "where in making any determination under the planning acts regard is to be had to the development plan the determination shall be made in accordance with the plan unless material considerations indicate otherwise". Section 26 has been incorporated into TCPA 1990 as s.54A. In simple terms this means that a planning authority may not go against the statutory plans without the identification of special reasons for doing so. This is particularly important in regard to waste management, as will be seen. Structure plans are, in practice, the basis upon which local plans are prepared. Indeed, s.36 of TCPA 1990 requires that a local plan shall be in general conformity with the structure plan. It is usual, where local plans attempt to step outside the policies of the structure plan, for objection to be made either by the county council or by the Secretary of State. However, primarily to take account of the fact that in some cases a local plan may need to be more up to date and appropriate to changing circumstances than the structure plan can be, it is provided by s.46 of TCPA 1990 that, in the case of conflict, the local plan usually prevails.

Local plans

The local plan represents the second tier of the development planning **3–010** system. Its main purpose is to "clothe" the strategy document represented by the structure plan. It goes into a good deal of detail about an area and may well (by reference to an ordnance survey-based map) designate land uses for the whole of the area within the plan document. It represents the day-to-day reference point for developers and planning authorities and is the basis upon which development control is undertaken. Nonetheless, planning decisions contrary to the local plan may be made by the local planning authority within the terms of s.54A of TCPA 1990 (see above).

[22] SI 1999/3280.

Types of local plan

3–011 Despite its name, the local plan may not always be limited to a specific part of a county area—usually this will be the case, but there are two other types: mineral and waste subject plans. Until PCA 1991, a subject plan offered "consideration of a particular description or descriptions of development or other use of land in the area to which it relates". Thus, a subject plan might deal with mineral extraction or waste management which it usually deals with on a county-wide basis. However, since the 1991 Act, specific provisions for minerals local plans and waste policies have been provided by ss.37 and 38 of TCPA 1990. Minerals or waste plans and policies are prepared only by the authority which is allocated the development control responsibility, usually the county council. In the case of waste local plans it is important to bear in mind that these are distinguished from the disposal plan required under EPA 1990.[23] However, there is an obligation that the local planning authority should have regard to the interrelationship between the two types of plan. Some minerals and waste subject plans still exist and will do so until replaced by the new local plans.

Less regularly encountered is the action area plan. Such plans are often designed to deal with areas where there have been large-scale dereliction or major structural changes arising, perhaps from the termination of a significant previous use such as the closure of a steelworks. However, again the 1991 Act reforms have procured that action area plans should be incorporated into the normal district plan for the area in question. Local plans, except minerals or waste disposal plans where there is a county council or unitary authority, will be the responsibility of the district council.

A local plan's content

3–012 Section 36 of TCPA 1990 sets out the content and requires that a local plan shall consist of a written statement formulating, in such detail as it thinks appropriate, the local planning authority's proposals for the development and other use of land in its area or for any description of development or other use of such land, including such measures as the authority thinks fit for the improvement of the physical environment. The plan must be accompanied by such diagrams, illustrations or other descriptive material as may be prescribed or in the authority's discretion, the purpose being to explain or illustrate the proposals. Section 36 provides specifically that a local plan shall not contain policies in respect of minerals or the deposit of mineral waste, refuse or waste materials unless it is a plan for a national park.

Under earlier arrangements, local plans could be prepared for part of an authority's area, but s.36(2) now requires a district-wide plan.

Procedures for local plans

3–013 Procedures for local plans are different from those relating to structure plans. A public participation exercise is much reduced and the procedure is controlled by the Town and Country Planning (Development Plan)

---

[23] See para.10–026 below.

(England) Regulations 1999.[24] During the plan's preparation the local planning authority must consult the appropriate Secretary of State, any other planning authority in the area which is the subject of the proposals, as well as authorities for adjacent areas, parish councils, the EA and other public bodies concerned with nature conservation, historic buildings and the like. Following consultation, the authority is then required to serve a copy of its proposals on any relevant county council which is required to issue a statement about whether the proposals are in general conformity with the structure plan. If it is unable to confirm this, then that acts as an objection to the plan.

The plan is then sent to the Secretary of State and copies are made available for inspection by the public. Notice of the deposit is required to be given by advertisement.[25]

Public inquiry

It is usual for the planning authority to undertake a public local inquiry to deal with any objections which have been made, but it does not need to do this if all objectors indicate in writing that they do not wish to appear at an inquiry. An inspector is appointed to hold the inquiry and his responsibility is to report not to the Secretary of State, but to the local planning authority. His report is a public document. The authority must decide on any action to be taken in respect of the report and must produce a statement of its reasons, again available for public inspection. It will prepare any proposed modifications and await any objections. If necessary, a further inquiry is held. Court of Appeal guidance on the responsibilities of local planning authorities in adopting local plans is set out in *Stirk v Bridgenorth DC*.[26] On any decision by the authority to adopt the plan, whether modified or not, a further public notice is required and the Secretary of State must be notified that it has done this. After a further 28 days, assuming that the Secretary of State has not indicated that he wishes to intervene, usually the authority adopts the plan and gives public notice that it has done so.

3–014

Effect of a local plan

Like the structure plan, the local plan once approved is the basis upon which development control is undertaken and planning applications, appeals, enforcement notices and other matters are considered. Since the passing of PCA 1991, such plans have had their status increased. Section 54A of TCPA 1990 (inserted by the 1991 Act) provides that, "where in making any determination under the planning acts, regard is to be had to the development plan, the determination shall be made in accordance with the plan unless material considerations indicate otherwise".

3–015

---

[24] SI 1999/3280.
[25] TCPA 1990, s.40.
[26] [1996] EGCS 159.

Planning and Compulsory Purchase Act 2004 Part II

3–016   Part II of this Act provides for the replacement of the above procedures with what the government describes as a simpler process for development planning. However, these provisions are not yet fully in force (at time of writing). The main provisions are:

(a) the local planning authority will be required to make a survey of their area taking into account relevant characteristics of the area, land use, population, communications and existing development. Both district and county councils will have these duties for matters within their responsibility;

(b) the main document will be a local development scheme to be prepared by appropriate local planning authorities, following the regional plans and directions by the Secretary of State;

(c) separate schemes will be provided in respect of minerals and waste development;

(d) the development plan document will be submitted to the Secretary of State for independent examination, along with representations made as a result of a range of public participation exercises;

(e) once approved, the document will be part of the development plan for development control purposes.

The Town and Country Planning (Local Development) (England) Regulation 2004[27] were made under the provisions of the 2004 Act and came into force on September 28, 2004. These regulations establish the form and content of the local development scheme and procedures to be followed to bring such schemes into force. The two forms of local development document, supplementary planning documents and development plan documents are dealt with separately in the regulations. The development plan document procedure involves the publication of proposals and consultation with prescribed bodies, submission of the document to the Secretary of State followed by a further period of consultation and consideration of representations. The Secretary of State may appoint a person to undertake an independent examination and to make recommendations. At that stage, the development plan document will be adopted by the local planning authority. The supplementary planning document procedure is simpler, involving only the publication and consultation of the document and consideration of representations. Thereafter, the document may be adopted by the local planning authority. The regulations apply to county councils for the purposes of minerals and waste development planning, otherwise to local planning authorities.

For provisions dealing with the arrangements for changeover from the present system of structure plans, unitary development plans and local plans, to the new documents provided under the 2004 Act, see the Town

[27] SI 2004/2204.

and Country Planning Act (Transitional Arrangements) (England) Regulations 2004.[28]

INFORMAL POLICIES

There is nothing to prevent a local planning authority, whether at county or **3–017** district level, from introducing and publishing informal policies designed to give developers guidance on the authority's likely views in regard to a wide range of different subjects; for example, planning authorities publish guidelines on design of buildings, car parking provision and housing standards. The authority is free to take these policies and guidance notes into account in making planning decisions and pursuing its responsibilities. However, in the case of disputes (*e.g.* through appeals) an informal policy which has not gone through the rigours of public examination, inquiries and, possibly, approval by the Secretary of State risks carrying less weight and is open to much more stringent examination than formal structure or local plan policies which have been approved. It follows that in any planning appeal the local authority may well have to justify fully its informal policy by evidence and argument. Nonetheless, the Secretary of State or his inspector frequently disregard untested informal policies, especially if such a policy is produced for reasons of expediency.

HIGH COURT PROCEDURES

Decisions made in conclusions reached by the Secretary of State, the Welsh **3–018** Assembly or the relevant planning authority, as the case may be, are usually final and there is only a limited basis upon which challenge to development plans may be pursued. However, the limited methods of challenge are provided for in s.287 of TCPA 1990. The challenge can only be made by a "person aggrieved" by the plan or by any alterations or replacements. Grounds of challenge are only that:

(a) the plan is not within the powers conferred by Pt II of TCPA 1990, or

(b) any requirement of that Part or of regulations made under it has not been complied with in relation to the plan's approval or adoption, or, as the case may be, its alteration or replacement.

An application must be made within six weeks of the date of publication of the first notice of approval or adoption of the plan or alteration or replacement and must be entered at the Administrative (High) Court.

The grounds of challenge are restricted and normally result from some fundamentally unlawful policy or a breach of procedural requirements. For example, applications to the High Court may be made where:

---

[28] SI 2004/2205.

(a) the reasons given by a local planning authority for rejecting an inspector's recommendation are not coherent or adequate;
(b) the inspector's report is flawed;
(c) the planning authority had not given rational consideration to the inspector's report; or
(d) the local planning authority has cut short further procedures (*e.g.* by rejecting a second or subsequent local inquiry).

A successful application will normally result in the quashing of the plan or some part of it. Sometimes the court may make an interim order suspending the plan wholly or in part, pending detailed consideration of the application.

Appeals from the High Court to the Court of Appeal and subsequently to the House of Lords are only allowed if leave is granted by those courts.

CHAPTER 4

DEVELOPMENT CONTROL

INTRODUCTION

Very little development may take place without the grant of planning **4–001** permission. This is especially true of waste management projects where government and public perception is that reconciliation of development, environmental and economic considerations must be the subject of careful assessment in the context of development control.

All "development", as defined by s.55 of TCPA 1990, requires planning permission. There are two parts to the definition: first, the carrying out of building, engineering, mining or other operations in, on, over or under land, and secondly, the making of any material change in the use of any buildings or other land.

Section 55(2) prescribes a list of uses and operations which are excluded from the definition and no planning permission is, therefore, required. These include:

(a) maintenance, improvement or other alteration of any building or works which affect the building's interior only or do not materially affect its external appearance—this usually covers interior alterations, external painting and minor modifications;

(b) maintenance and improvement of a road by a highway authority but excluding works which may have a significant adverse effect on the environment;

(c) certain works carried out by a local authority or statutory undertaker for repair or renewal of sewers, pipes, cables etc.;

(d) the use of buildings or other land forming part of a dwelling-house (*e.g.* a garden) for any purpose incidental to the enjoyment of the dwelling-house;

(e) agriculture and forestry, including the use of any building for that purpose;

(f) changes of use within the Use Classes Order (see para.4–006 below); and

(g) most demolition, except houses.

It is important to note that whilst planning permission may not be required for some of the activities noted above, there may still be a need for listed building consent (see para.5–017 below).

Section 55 specifically identifies the deposit of refuse or waste materials on land as involving a material change of use even if the land is comprised in a site already used for that purpose, provided that:

(a) the superficial area of the deposit is extended; or
(b) the height of the deposit is extended and exceeds the level of the land adjoining the site.

BUILDING OPERATIONS ETC.

4–002   The definitions of "building", "engineering", "mining" or other operations have exercised the courts on many occasions. In respect of "building operations", confusion exists particularly in regard to demolition. The confusion has been overcome largely by a change in the definition brought about by PCA 1991, which defines the term as including demolition, rebuilding, structural alterations or additions, and other operations normally undertaken by a person carrying on business as a builder. A "building" is defined by s.336 as including "any structure or erection and any part of a building as so defined but does not include plant or machinery comprised in a building". The courts have often had to consider to what extent a structure represents a building. The characteristics were identified in *Cardiff Rating Authority v Guest Keen Baldwin's Iron and Steel Co. Ltd.*[1] Three main factors are:

(a) size
(b) permanence (*i.e.* a building normally constructed on site as opposed to being transported); and
(c) physical attachment to the land.

Prefabricated buildings, such as a portakabin (particularly one fitted with services such as drains etc. and left on the land for a particular purpose and for some time), will normally require planning permission. The same will apply normally to operations such as the provision of fixed plant, weighbridges etc.

An engineering operation is not defined in the Act except to incorporate "the formation or laying out of a means of access to highways". The best interpretation appeared in *Fayrewood Fish Farms Ltd v Secretary of State*,[2] where the court expressed the view that an engineering operation would be an operation which generally would be supervised by an engineer. Pipelines are not usually development if the works involved include inspection, maintenance, adjustment, repair, alteration or renewal. It follows that the installation of a new pipeline would normally require planning permission.

Mining operations are not defined in TCPA 1990, but the term is defined under the Town and Country Planning (General Permitted Development)

[1] [1949] K.B. 385.
[2] [1984] J.P.L. 267.

Order 1995[3] as "the winning and working of minerals in, on or under land, whether by surface or underground working". Under s.55(4) of the Act the definition is extended to include:

(a) the removal of any material of any description from a mineral working deposit, from a deposit of pulverised fuel ash or other furnace ash or clinker, or from a deposit of iron, steel or other metallic slags; and

(b) the extraction of minerals from a disused railway embankment.

"Mineral working deposit" is defined by s.336 of TCPA 1990 as meaning "any deposit of material remaining after minerals have been extracted from land or otherwise deriving from the carrying out of operations for the winning and working of minerals in, on or under land".

MATERIAL CHANGE OF USE

A mere change of use does not of itself require planning permission unless **4–003** it is "material". An assessment of what is material depends very much on individual circumstances and it is impossible in a work of this kind to supply detailed guidance exhaustively. Nonetheless, it is important to focus on the concepts of primary and ancillary uses. For example, if the primary use is a landfill site, then buildings thereon and used for landfill purposes normally will be ancillary. Thus, the change of the use of a building (*e.g.* from weighbridge office to mess room) will normally not require planning permission.

Note that where permission has been granted for the erection of a building and no use was specified, there is a right to use the building for the purpose for which it was designed. It is important to bear in mind that the exemption from the need for planning permission in respect of the change of an ancillary use may disappear in certain circumstances. For example, where an ancillary use grows to a point where it can no longer be said to be ancillary, there may be a material change of use. This might arise at a transfer station where a small amount of recycling is undertaken. However, if the recycling operation achieves significance subsequently, perhaps incorporating trading of recycled material, then the character of the use may have changed to the extent that the ancillary description is no longer valid. In these circumstances, it will probably be necessary for a fresh planning permission to be obtained.

The planning unit

A major component of a judgment whether a material change of use has **4–004** occurred is the consideration of the planning unit. This might arise in the case of a larger site with a combination of different uses, whether ancillary

---

[3] SI 1995/418.

to the main use or otherwise. The courts have accepted that a small unit may be regarded as the planning unit for the purposes of considering whether a material change of use has occurred. In *Burdle v Secretary of State for the Environment*,[4] the court identified three general tests:

(a) Where the court can recognise a single main purpose of the occupier's use of land to which other activities are incidental or ancillary, the whole unit of occupation should be considered.

(b) It may be appropriate to consider the entire unit of occupation, even though a variety of activities is carried on and it is not possible to identify one which is incidental or ancillary (*e.g.* in a multi-use site where the various activities increase and decrease in intensity from time to time but different activities do not have separate and physical identities in the land).

(c) A single unit of occupation may arise, with a range of physically separate and distinct areas occupied for different and unrelated purposes. In these circumstances it would be proper normally to consider each as a separate planning unit.

The court has made clear that the assessment is a matter of fact and degree in each case and more specific guidelines are not usually available. An assessment for the purposes of establishing a planning unit is a matter of fact and degree. Bridge J. in *Burdle* (above) suggested that the most useful guideline would be that the unit of occupation is the appropriate planning unit unless and until some smaller unit can be recognised as the site of activities which amount, in substance, to a separate use, both physically and functionally.

Waste disposal installations

4–005 The Town and Country Planning (Environmental Impact Assessment) (England and Wales) Regulations 1999[5] serve to confirm that a change in the use of land or buildings to a use for the purposes of a waste disposal installation for the incineration, chemical treatment or landfill of hazardous waste is deemed to involve a material change in use for the purposes of s.55.

Use Classes Order 1987, as amended

4–006 Excluded from the definition of material change of use are changes which take place within particular classes of use which are identified by the Town and Country Planning (Use Classes) Order 1987.[6] The Order, which has

---

[4] [1972] 3 All E.R. 240.
[5] SI 1999/293.
[6] SI 1987/764.

been amended from time to time, sets out 16 use classes, divided between four groups, categorised as follows:

(a) shops, financial and professional services premises, and food and drink premises;
(b) business premises, including offices, research and development uses, industrial processes, storage and distribution;
(c) hotels, residential institutions and dwelling-houses;
(d) non-residential institutions (*e.g.* nursery or day centre), museums, places of assembly, cinemas, dance halls etc.

Changes within the specific subcategories are not normally development for which planning permission is required.

Advertisements

The display of advertisements is within the definition of development. The **4–007** use for their display on any external part of a building not used for that purpose is treated as involving a material change of use in that part of the building and may, therefore, require planning permission. The display of advertisements is, nonetheless, subject to detailed control by virtue of the Town and Country Planning (Control of Advertisements) Regulations 1992.[7]

REQUIREMENT FOR PLANNING PERMISSION

Having arrived at the conclusion that the specific operation or material **4–008** change of use constitutes development, the next stage in the process is to consider how that development may be permitted. There are four main ways:

(a) by development order;
(b) by the specific grant of planning permission;
(c) by simplified planning zone scheme; and
(d) by designation of an enterprise zone.

Without the grant of permission, the operation or use is potentially unlawful and liable to enforcement.[8]

Permission by development order

There are two main types of development order: general and special. **4–009**

General development orders: General Permitted Development Order 1995

A substantial number of relatively minor developments are specifically granted planning permission, usually without any requirement for an

---

[7] SI 1992/666), as amended (see para.5–006 below).
[8] See para.4–094 below.

application. There are presently 33 classes of such development. The Town and County Planning (General Permitted Development) Order (GPDO) 1995,[9] as amended, has the effect of granting planning permission for these classes. GPDO 1995 has been amended regularly and any relevant modifications are incorporated in the following. It should be borne in mind that a GPDO permission is normally the subject of general and specific limitations and conditions which need to be examined carefully. The order may not apply at all or may be restricted in its application, where such disapplication or restriction is the subject of a condition of a planning permission relating to the land in question. This situation is often found with minerals and waste management activities. In certain circumstances, the local planning authority may withdraw GPDO rights by making a direction under art.4 of the Order (known as an art.4 direction). Those GPDO permissions having relevance to the waste management industry are as follows.

Minor operations

4–010   Minor operations are permitted. These include:

  (a) the provision or replacement of gates, fences, walls or other enclosures, subject to height restrictions;
  (b) certain accesses to a highway; and
  (c) the external painting of the building or work, except for advertisement, announcement or direction.

Changes of use

4–011   The following changes of use relate only to a building and not to any open air storage:

  (a) from general industrial or storage/distribution to business use;
  (b) of not more than 235m² of storage and distribution space to business use;
  (c) from business or general industrial to storage and distribution use (up to 235m²).

Other changes are those from one use permitted by a planning permission granted on an application, to another use which that permission would have specifically authorised, provided:

  (a) that the application for planning permission was not made before the date the order came into force (December 5, 1988);
  (b) it would not be carried out more than 10 years after the grant of planning permission; and
  (c) it would not result in the breach of any condition, limitation or specification in the original planning permission.

[9] SI 1995/418.

It is intended that GPDO 1995 should allow the change to take place once only. It does not permit a return to the original use except in special circumstances.

Temporary buildings and uses

The provision of buildings, moveable structures, works, plant or machinery **4-012** required temporarily in connection with and during the currency of operations (excluding mining operations) on land or on adjoining land is permitted, provided that the operations have planning permission. Conditions of this GPDO consent include requirements for the removal of the building, structure etc. and the reinstatement to the original condition of the land in question when the operations have been completed.

Caravans

Certain temporary uses of caravans are permitted. **4-013**

Agriculture and forestry

The provision of certain buildings and works required for agricultural **4-014** purposes is permitted, subject to a range of conditions and limitations. These rights may be appropriate in circumstances where landfill sites are restored to agriculture. Similar rights exist in connection with forestry operations.

Industrial and warehouse development

A number of developments are permitted under this heading including: **4-015**

    (a) certain restricted extensions or alterations of an industrial building or warehouse, up to 25 per cent of the cubic content and 1,000m^2 in floor space, but subject to a range of conditions and other limits;

    (b) installation of plant and machinery, and the provision, rearrangement or replacement of services including roadways, railways and conveyors, subject to conditions including a height restriction;

    (c) the creation of hard surfaces associated with certain buildings;

    (d) the deposit of waste material resulting from an industrial process on any land used for that purpose on July 1, 1948, regardless of whether the superficial area or the height of the deposit is extended as a result. However, permission is not granted if either the waste material includes any material resulting from the winning and working of minerals (but see below), or the use in 1948 was then for that purpose. For Court of Appeal guidance on the interpretation of this provision, see *Kent CC v Secretary of State*[10]

---

[10] [1997] J.P.L. 1115.

Development by local and other authorities and statutory undertakers

4–016 There is a wide range of development rights available under GPDO 1995 to public and similar bodies (*e.g.* the privatised water companies) which relate to their normal operations and the maintenance of these.

Development ancillary to mining operations

4–017 GPDO rights here include certain permissions to install, rearrange, replace, repair or alter plant and machinery, buildings, private ways, railways or sidings and other services at a mine or quarry or land which is adjacent to or occupied with such mine or quarry. The exercise of some of the rights requires prior approval of the mineral planning authority. However, such rights may be useful to waste managers in circumstances where their operation incorporates the refilling/reclamation of an ongoing mineral operation.

Waste tipping into mines

4–018 A separate category of GPDO 1995 permits waste disposal at a mine or quarry or ancillary land provided that it takes place on that land and the waste derives from the winning and working of the minerals or its subsequent preparation for sale or use. There are height restrictions and, in certain circumstances, a scheme of disposal must be submitted to the mineral planning authority.

Telecommunications development

4–019 Certain rights exist to install (subject to height restrictions and other conditions) microwave antennae and ancillary equipment. Since July 31, 1991, the installation, alteration or replacement of system apparatus by or on behalf of a driver information system operator may be undertaken subject to certain conditions.[11]

Demolition of buildings

4–020 Any building operation consisting of the demolition of a building is permitted with effect from July 1992. However, again there are a number of conditions which must first be complied with. For further guidance see the Town and Country Planning (Demolition—Description of Buildings) Direction 1995 and DoE Circular 10/95, "Planning Controls over Demolition".

Closed circuit television cameras

4–021 The installation, alteration or replacement on a building of a closed circuit television camera to be used for security purposes is conditionally permitted. The dimensions of the camera, including its housing, must not exceed 75cm x 25cm x 25cm and it must not be located more than 250cm above

---

[11] See PPG8, "Telecommunications".

ground. There are further conditions on location and the number of cameras which may be permitted.

Limitations on the application of the GPDO

While GPDO 1995 provides quite extensive, albeit conditional planning **4–022** permissions for a wide range of mainly ancillary development, the rights are limited in a number of ways.

Restrictions in the original planning permission can be imposed. It is quite common in the case of minerals or waste management operations for a condition to be imposed upon the original consent that GPDO rights should not be available either wholly or in part. This is a legitimate condition provided that it can be justified by the planning authority on good planning grounds, for example that the operation is in an area of sensitive countryside and that there should be detailed control on location and design of buildings, plant and machinery. The effect is that all development normally the subject of a GPDO permission will require a specific planning application.

GPDO 1995 provides by art.4 that a local planning authority or the Secretary of State may withdraw a GPDO permission by a direction made under that Article. In these circumstances, compensation may be awarded where a planning application, made necessary by an art.4 direction, is refused or granted subject to conditions.[12]

A developer may not take advantage of the GPDO permission if it is granted in connection with an existing building or use which was itself unlawful in some way. Thus, if a building had been constructed without planning permission and was present unlawfully, its extension, while within GPDO tolerances, would not benefit from the GPDO permission.

GPDO 1995 will not authorise any development which requires or involves the formation, laying out or material widening of an access to a trunk or classified road or obstructs the view of persons using the highway to a potentially dangerous extent.

Permission is not granted by GPDO 1995 in respect of certain pipelines which contain hazardous substances.

In the case of land in national parks, areas of outstanding natural beauty and conservation areas, as well as the Broads, certain GPDO rights are either reduced or removed altogether.

Normally development is not granted by GPDO 1995 if it involves the demolition of a building.

Any development which, despite being noted as permitted by GPDO 1995, nonetheless requires an environmental assessment under the terms of the Town and Country Planning (Environmental Impact Assessment) (England and Wales) Regulations 1999[13] is not permitted development except in special circumstances noted in art.3 of GPDO 1995.

As noted above, most GPDO permissions are individually limited by conditions.

---

[12] TCPA 1990, s.108.
[13] SI 1999/293.

Special development orders

4–023   Section 59 of TCPA 1990 has effect to provide not only for general development orders, but also special orders which may be made by the Secretary of State to apply only to specific land or descriptions of land. Originally reserved for development having a national importance or significance (*e.g.* Town and Country Planning (Atomic Energy Establishments) Special Development Order 1954),[14] in recent years the procedure has been made use of by central government to establish urban development areas, mainly for the rehabilitation and redevelopment of run down inner city land. An urban development area is designated by the Secretary of State under the Local Government Planning and Land Act 1980, whereby an urban development corporation (separate from and independent of the local authority) is established for a limited period pending the rehabilitation and redevelopment exercise. Like an enterprise and simplified planning zone scheme (see below), the special development order for the area in question grants permission for the development in accordance with the approved scheme, usually subject only to limited conditions. Thus, an application for that development within the scheme is avoided during the currency of the special development order.

Development outside the scheme needs to be the subject of an application to the urban development corporation which, during the period of its appointment, acts as the local planning authority.

It is intended that all urban development corporations should have a limited life, at the end of which the policy is to return their land and interests to the local authority concerned. At that stage planning control reverts to the normal system, although any consents granted under the special development order remain valid.

Local development orders

4–024   It should be noted that the provisions of TCPA 1990 are intended to be extended by Pt IV of the Planning and Compulsory Purchase Act 2004. However, the provisions are not yet in force at time of writing. A new s.61A will be inserted into the TCPA 1990. This will provide that local planning authorities will have power to make local development orders, primarily to implement policies in development plan documents made under Pt II of the 2004 Act. A local development order may grant planning permission either for a specific development or for a class of development. There are reserve powers for the Secretary of State or the National Assembly for Wales to intervene at any time before a local development order is adopted by the local planning authority. Planning permission granted by a local development order may be unconditional or subject to conditions or limitations as specified.

[14] SI 1954/982.

Enterprise zones and simplified planning zone schemes

These schemes were prompted by the Government's desire to give an **4–025**
impetus to the development in particular of derelict or degraded areas of
land or other property such as docks, where uses have become largely
obsolete.

An enterprise zone is set up under the Local Government and Planning
Act 1980 and gives developers a wide range of incentives designed to
generate economic activity. One of these incentives is that the zone scheme,
once approved, provides for a development to take place without any
further application for planning permission, provided that it is in accordance with the scheme. The scheme may specify a development or merely
identify a class or classes of development.[15]

A simplified planning zone scheme is similar to an enterprise zone but
with a more restrictive set of incentives.[16] A scheme may specify a
development or class of development for a particular part or all of the
simplified planning zone and it may impose conditions, limitations or
exceptions. Provided that the development proposed is within the terms of
the scheme, no further planning permission is required. Enterprise zones
and simplified planning zones are set up for a specified period of time at
the end of which normal control is imposed, although any development
taking place within the terms of the scheme before the end of that period
remains valid. It should be noted that procedures for the making of
simplified planning zone schemes are intended to be amended by s.45 of
the Planning and Compulsory Purchase Act 2004. These provisions are not
yet in force.

Determination whether planning permission required

There are occasions when there will be uncertainty over whether the **4–026**
proposed use of land for waste management purposes or the development
of building and other works actually requires planning permission. Normally, discussion with the local planning authority will overcome the
problem. In the case of the determination whether a use of land is already
permitted, s.191 of TCPA 1990 provided a statutory means whereby the
facts could be put to the planning authority by formal application and an
"established use certificate" obtained. Any certificate was then conclusive
evidence according to the extent of the determination by the planning
authority (or on appeal by the Secretary of State). However, with effect
from July 27, 1992 the provisions of s.191 were replaced as a result of PCA
1991, which provides two new forms of certificate. The first is a certificate
of lawfulness of existing use or development, and is an improvement on the
established use certificate in that planning authorities can be asked to give

---

[15] TCPA 1990, s.88.
[16] ibid., ss.82 et seq.

an authoritative view on the existence or otherwise of planning permission not only for a use of land, but also for operational development. The second certificate is of the lawfulness of a proposed use or development. This is particularly useful not only for the present owner or operator of a site, but also for a prospective purchaser, in that it can provide the authoritative answer to the question, "Is my proposed development lawful?"[17] In the case of applications for both certificates, a formal procedure must be followed, in accordance with the revised sections inserted in TCPA 1990 by the 1991 Act (ss.191–193). The procedures for applications are set out in the Town and Country Planning (General Development Procedure) Order 1995,[18] as amended. Advice is contained in Annex 8 to DoE Circular 10/97, "Enforcing Planning Control: Legislative Provisions and Procedural Requirements". In the event that certificates are refused, there is a right of appeal to the Secretary of State.

THE PLANNING APPLICATION[19]

4–027   On the assumption that it is concluded that the proposals represent development and that there is no planning consent in force in respect of those proposals, it will be necessary for a formal application for planning permission to be made. Developments comprising waste management are nowadays frequently complex, have a high profile in environmental terms and can arouse vociferous and emotive opposition in any given locality. Such developments can, potentially, cause air, land and water pollution, and can give rise to numerous amenity objections on grounds of traffic, noise, visual harm and smell. In the case of landfills, the long-term effects of surface settlement, leachate and gas pollution are also significant factors.

Besides their usual responsibilities, local planning authorities are obliged by Sch.2 to the Landfill (England and Wales) Regulations 2002,[20] to take into account a range of rules. These cover locational, water resources, geological, physiological, natural and heritage factors, so that no serious environmental risk is proposed, oblige the operators to comply with specific water pollution and other environmental controls, including, if necessary, protective geological and other barriers, coupled with leachate collection and sealing systems, gas and other air pollution controls etc.—see also the EU Landfill Directive and the Landfill Regulations (para.7–027).

Taking all these matters into account, there are almost no occasions in the case of a waste management development where careful preparation and consultation is unnecessary. Such consultation will need to be made not only with the planning authority and the other responsible regulatory

---

[17] For a useful case on the proper approach to an application for such a certificate see *R. v Thanet DC Ex p. Tapp and Britton* [2001] EWCA Civ 559.

[18] SI 1995/419.

[19] It should be noted that modifications to procedures for planning applications are made in the Planning and Compulsory Purchase Act 2004. At time of writing, these modifications are not yet in force but see ss.42 to 44 of the 2004 Act.

[20] SI 2002/1559.

agencies, but also with a wide range of environmental and other similar bodies and not least residents and other members of the public. Preparatory to consultation (and probably contemporaneously with it), a wide range of baseline geological, engineering and other studies will need to be undertaken to provide the evidence upon which the design of the development and the amelioration of its impact can be judged. It frequently will be the case that an environmental assessment needs to be an integral part of any planning application (see below). Pre-application consultations develop an understanding, particularly by the planning authority, of the developer's intentions and will identify policies and requirements, in particular development plan arrangements for waste management, anticipated changes of policy, and the implications of any development on current uses and plans for nearby land and vice versa.

Environmental assessment

While it has always been necessary to provide all reasonable information to **4–028**
enable a planning authority properly to determine an application, no detailed rules for this were established until the approval of the Town and Country Planning (Assessment of Environmental Effects) Regulations 1988.[21] Following various amendments, the 1988 Regulations were replaced by the Town and Country Planning (Environmental Impact Assessment) (England and Wales) Regulations 1999.[22]

The original regulations in England and Wales were intended to apply the requirements of European Council Directive 85/337/EEC on the assessment of the effects of certain public and private projects on the environment. This Directive was amended by Council Directive 97/11/EEC. The new Regulations came into force on March 14, 1999. The Regulations are underpinned by s.71A of TCPA 1990, inserted by PCA 1991. Guidance is obtained from DETR Circular 02/99, "Environmental Impact Assessment" and, for Wales, in Welsh Office Circular 11/99. For special applications involving modification of minerals permissions, see also the Town and Country Planning (Environmental Impact Assessment) (England and Wales) (Amendment) Regulations 2000[23] which amend the 1999 Regulations mentioned above.

An environmental assessment has a formal content laid down by Sch.4 to the Regulations. Information required includes a full description of the development, including land use requirements during construction and operational phases. Details must be given of any production processes and their consequences in terms of wastes and emissions, an outline of the main alternatives considered and reasons for the choice made, descriptions of the environmental elements likely to be significantly affected by the existence of the development, the use of natural resources and the emission of

[21] SI 1988/1199.
[22] SI 1999/293.
[23] SI 2000/2867.

pollutants. A description of the measures to prevent, reduce and offset effects on the environment is also required. A non-technical summary of such matters needs to be supplied together with an indication of any technical deficiencies or lack of know-how encountered by the applicant in compiling the environmental statement. How far do the planning authority need to take remedial measures into consideration where these measures are extensive and their implementation is likely to be complicated? In *R. (on the application of PPG11 Limited) v Dorset County Council and Viridor Waste Management Ltd*[24] an action group sort an order quashing the decision of the County Council to grant planning permission to use a partially worked quarry as a landfill site. The permission had included a condition prohibiting the felling of any trees and imposing other environmental clean-up requirements. The court held that the extent to which a local planning authority would need to take remedial measures into account depended on the nature of the proposed measures. If they were limited in scope and relatively simple to put in place, the implications of the environmental impact would not need to be included in the assessment prior to the grant of permission.

The environmental statement accompanies the planning application and is part of it. As such it is available for examination by any member of the public. A grant of planning permission cannot be made without proper consideration of the statement.

When is an environmental assessment required?

4–029   The 1999 Regulations specify in two schedules the descriptions of development for which an assessment may be required. Schedule 1 describes the development where an assessment is compulsory. Included in the descriptions of development are:

>   (a) waste disposal installations for the incineration, chemical treatment or landfill of hazardous or non-hazardous waste, with a capacity exceeding 100 tonnes per day;
>   (b) large waste water treatment plants, as defined in the Regulations; and
>   (c) quarries and open cast mining, where the site's surface exceeds 25 hectares.

Schedule 2 is reserved for types of development which require an environmental statement only if they are likely to have significant effects on the environment by virtue of factors such as their nature, size or location. Where the planning authority and the developer are unable to agree on the need for a statement in Sch.2 cases, the dispute may be referred to the Secretary of State for his direction. The descriptions of development which fall within Sch.2 include:

>   (a) quarries, open cast mining and peat extraction (unless included in Sch.1);

---

[24] Unreported, 2003.

(b) industrial installations for the production of electricity, steam and hot water where the area of the development exceeds 0.5 hectare;

(c) construction of railways or roads where the area of the works exceeds one hectare;

(d) oil and gas pipeline installations where the area of the works exceeds one hectare;

(e) installations for the disposal of waste (unless included in Sch.1) where the disposal is by incineration or the area of the development exceeds 0.5 hectare or the installation is to be sited within 100m of any controlled waters[25]; and

(f) installations for the recovery or destruction of explosive substances where the area of new floor space exceeds 1,000m².

In most cases modification of a development listed in Schedules 1 and 2 will require an environment statement where the change or extension may have significant adverse effects on the environment.

Absence of environmental statement

Normally the absence of an environmental statement, where one is required, will be fatal to an application for planning permission. Indeed, the failure of the planning authority (or the Secretary of State on any appeal) to consider whether an environmental statement is needed will also have the effect of rendering any subsequent planning permission vulnerable to being quashed by the court.[26]   **4–030**

The application process

Most planning applications are required to comply with the Town and Country Planning (General Development Procedure) Order (GDPO) 1995[27] as amended. This contains the provisions relating to procedures, including certificates of ownership, consultation, notification of applications, registers of applications and notices, appeals, directions by the Secretary of State in relation to call-in and applications for certificates of lawfulness.   **4–031**

Applications are made by the completion of a form obtainable from the planning authority. In Greater London and the unitary and metropolitan areas the application is made to the borough or unitary authority, respectively. Elsewhere, applications are forwarded normally to the district council, but in almost all waste management cases outside metropolitan and unitary areas the responsibility for the decision is with the county planning authority; in these circumstances the application is made to the county

---

[25] This term has the same meaning as in WRA 1991.
[26] See *Berkeley v Secretary of State and Another* [2001] 2 A.C. 603. See also *R. v Lewisham LBC Ex p. Goodman Hedges* (unreported, February 14, 2003) and *Bellway v Gillespie*, March 27, 2003.
[27] SI 1995/419.

council. There are special rules for national parks, urban development areas and enterprise zones.

Outline applications

4–032   Outline applications may be made only in respect of the erection of a building (which does not include plant or machinery). As such they are of limited value to the waste management industry. The essence of an outline permission is to gain a formal decision in principle, usually as to the siting and use of the land. If the decision is favourable, then a permission will impose various conditions concerning such matters as siting, design, external appearance, access and so on. The planning authority will often be reluctant to deal with an application in outline and is entitled to call for further details before reaching a decision, hence its limited use in waste management cases. For limits on the power of a local planning authority to impose conditions on an outline planning permission, see *R. v Newbury DC, Ex p. Chieveley Parish Council.*[28]

Where development, the subject of an outline application falls within the categories normally requiring an environmental assessment, the appropriate time for this assessment is at the time of the outline application, rather than in relation to the subsequent approval of conditions and/or details—in relation to the subsequent approval of conditions and/or details—see *Bromley LBC Ex p. Diane Barker.*[29]

Fees[30]

4–033   Since 1981, most planning applications require the payment of a fee, as set out in the Town and Country Planning (Fees for Applications and Deemed Applications) Regulations 1989.[31] These Regulations are amended from time to time mainly to keep fees up to date with inflation. The most recent amendments were made by the Town and Country Planning (Fees for Applications and Deemed Applications) (Amendment) Regulations 2002.[32] In most waste management cases it will be desirable to undertake pre-application discussions with the planning authority. The authority has no right to charge any fee for these discussions. In *R. v Richmond upon Thames BC, Ex p. McCarthy & Stone,*[33] the council had attempted to charge for each planning consultation. The House of Lords held that local authorities are creatures of statute and, as such, can only exercise powers given to them by law. There is no provision enabling them expressly to charge for giving planning advice. The case hinged on the construction of a well-used provision of the Local Government Act 1972, which gives local authorities power to do anything that might facilitate, or be incidental to,

[28] (1998) 10 Admin. L.R. 676.
[29] Unreported, November 23, 2001, CA.
[30] Changes to the arrangements for the imposition of fees and charges are made in s.53 of the Planning and Compulsory Purchase Act 2004. However, the provisions are not yet in force.
[31] SI 1989/193.
[32] SI 2002/768.
[33] [1991] 4 All E.R. 897.

the discharge of their functions. It was held that if authorities used this provision to enable them to charge for pre-planning application advice, they could use the provision to charge for the performance of almost every other of their functions. Such a construction could not possibly be justified.

Certificate of ownership

Under TCPA 1990, a planning application for most waste management **4–034** activities must be accompanied by a certificate that the applicant is the site owner or has given notice to that owner. In cases where the owner cannot be found or is difficult to trace, special arrangements apply. This certificate must also confirm that notice has been given to any agricultural tenant.

Publicity for applications

Adequate consultation is important; in its absence, there is a risk that any **4–035** subsequent decision will be quashed—see *R. v Bolsover DC Ex p. Paterson*.[34]

Before July 1992 it was necessary for an applicant for most planning permissions involving waste operations to submit a certificate that notice had been posted on the site and advertised in a local newspaper. However, since July 1992 publicity requirements are now imposed on the local planning authority (see GDPO 1995). To some extent the nature of publicity is left to the authority's discretion, but in the case of certain types of development (including waste management) there is a statutory require- ment for the authority to advertise in a local newspaper and to post a notice on the site which is capable of being read by passing members of the public. Furthermore, there will be a requirement that neighbours likely to be affected by the development should also be sent formal notification of the application.[35] Where a local planning authority has received an application for planning permission for any development of land affecting the setting of a listed building or the character or appearance of a conservation area, they are required to publish notice of the application in a local newspaper and display a notice on or near the land.[36]

While publicity for the application will be undertaken by the planning authority, the prudent applicant will already have undertaken consultation on an informal basis, with as wide an audience as feasible.

Plans and other details

The legislation requires that a planning application should include such **4–036** particulars and be verified by such evidence as may be required to enable the planning authority to understand the proposals. In these circumstances, particularly in the case of major waste management activities, a consider- able amount of information will need to be provided concerning the

[34] Unreported, June 26, 2000, High Court.
[35] Further guidance is available in DoE Circular 15/92, "Publicity for Planning Applications".
[36] For further details, see the Planning (Listed Buildings and Conservation Areas) (Amend- ment) (England) Regulations 2004 (SI 2004/2210).

proposals for the operation of the site, baseline information and details regarding environmental effects. It is usual for detailed plans to be submitted describing the status quo, the changes to be effected, phasing, landscaping, restoration etc. Detailed design drawings of buildings and operational facilities may be required at the time the application is submitted, but are more regularly reserved for decision at a later stage.

Consultation

4–037 Once the planning application has been received the planning authority is required:

(a) to acknowledge the application and to give a receipt for the submitted fee (if correctly calculated);

(b) to insert details of the application in a public register and to put details on deposit for public inspection;

(c) to undertake a wide range of consultations with various organisations and bodies likely to be affected. However, consultation may be dispensed with where the development is already subject to standing advice provided by a consultee or where the development is the subject of an environmental impact assessment.

The organisations and bodies in (c) above include the county or district planning authority (as the case may be), the Health and Safety Executive (hazardous substances), the highway authority (traffic and access), rail operating companies (developments affecting railways), the Coal Authority (buildings or pipelines in an area of coal working), English Heritage (ancient monument), the EA (developments affecting a river or stream, deposit of refuse or waste, dealing with sewage or trade waste), the Nature Conservancy Council (sites of special scientific interest), the Department of the Environment Food and Rural Affairs (agricultural land) and the waste disposal authority (developments by the deposit of refuse or waste). Certain major and strategic developments may also be required to be the subject of consultation with the Regional Development Agency for the area in question. Occasionally, other consultations have to be made in respect of development affecting aerodromes and caravan sites.[37] Parish and community councils are entitled to be advised of each application and are usually sent a copy.

Planning authorities have obligations, which are non-statutory, to consult other bodies in certain circumstances. These include a sports council, water and drainage boards, water and sewage companies and those who have an interest in rights of way.

Applications affecting mineral rights

4–038 Where the development involves winning and working of minerals, certain statutory mineral owners must also be given notice of an application. These are the Coal Authority (coal), the Secretary of State for Trade and Industry

---

[37] See ODPM Circular 1/2003, "Safeguarding Aerodromes, Technical Sites and Military Explosives Storage Areas: The Town and Country Planning (Safeguarding Aerodromes, Technical Sites and Military Explosives Storage Areas) Direction 2002".

(gas or oil) and the Crown Estates Commissioners (silver or gold). The notice is given by the planning authority.

Time scales

As a general rule, a planning application must be determined within eight   **4–039**
weeks from its receipt unless the applicant agrees with the authority that a longer period is acceptable. In the case of an application subject to an environmental assessment, the period is extended to 16 weeks. Even in the case of applications allowing a 16-week period, it is rare for an application to be determined within that period. The applicant has a choice whether to agree to extend that period or to appeal on the grounds of non-determination.[38]

Development by local planning authority

On occasions, land used by a local authority for a waste management   **4–040**
activity may be acquired by a private operator. Quite often, and particularly since July 1992, the development will be authorised by a formal planning permission, which would normally apply in the private sector. However, prior to that date there were procedures whereby local planning authorities could grant themselves planning permission, subject to compliance with certain rules. On passing the resolution to grant permission there is a deemed consent. That resolution is normally evidence (in the same way as an ordinary planning permission) of the matters consented by the planning authority and may be relied upon by a subsequent owner.

There are exceptions which arise where a planning authority has benefited from the grant of planning permission to itself (see the Town and Country Planning General Regulations 1992).[39] As a general rule the permission then enures only for the benefit of the authority. However, by the Town and Country Planning (General) (Amendment) Regulations 1998,[40] there is an exclusion from the above control under the 1992 Regulations which applies to those planning authorities which are the sole local authority for their area. In those circumstances the planning permission runs with the land.

Call-in powers

The Secretary of State has power to call in an application for his own   **4–041**
decision. This is a rare occurrence but will happen where the application departs from the provisions of a development plan, is highly significant, or (in some cases) where there is a major public controversy.

Determination of planning application

Once the local planning authority has completed the examination of the   **4–042**
application and the various consultations, it is free to proceed to a determination of the application. In making its determination various

---

[38] See "Planning appeals" at para.4–076 below.
[39] SI 1992/1492.
[40] SI 1998/2800.

matters need to be taken into account. Since PCA 1991 the primary matter is the development plan, including, as appropriate, structure, local or unitary plans. The duty as laid down by s.54A (inserted into TCPA 1990 by the 1991 Act) is as follows:

> "Where in making any determination under the Planning Acts, regard is to be had to the development plan, the determination shall be made in accordance with the plan unless material considerations indicate otherwise."

Parliament's apparent intention is to give primacy to the development plan, to encourage all such plans to be up to date and to indicate the appropriate development to be permitted in a given area. Section 54A does not prevent the planning authority from going against its development plan, but there must be material considerations justifying this. The local planning authority must demonstrate that it has complied with the requirements of s.54A, either expressly or by implication. This will best be demonstrated either by dealing with the s.54A exercise in the officer's report on the application, or in the resolution of the council or its delegated committee or, since August 1, 2000, in the decision notice.[41] Public concern and fear about the possible implications of a development can be a material consideration to be taken into account by a local planning authority, provided the concern is based on reasonable grounds (see *West Midlands Probation Committee v Secretary of State for the Environment*.[42]

Other matters to be taken into account include any environmental impact assessment (sometimes the planning authority will seek professional advice on the content and quality of this). The planning authority must also take into account representations made by the public, owners of land and consultees. It should also give consideration to the desirability of retaining existing uses (examples of this would be in the case of high-quality agricultural land or landscape or where nature conservation is important). The development's effects so far as traffic and general environmental considerations are concerned should be taken into account. It is also important that the authority should have regard to the arguments for the need for the development, particularly in circumstances where waste management facilities are either not available or are in short supply in a given area. By the same token, public advantage from the development (in terms of employment, local economy, etc.) are matters material to any decision. The effects of the interrelationship of new development and existing hazardous or neighbour-sensitive installations, such as incinerators and landfills, should also be taken into account.[43]

---

[41] See the Town and Country Planning (General Development Procedure) (England) (Amendment) Order 2000 (SI 2000/1627). For further requirements as to decision notices see below para.4–047 Guidance on the operation of the regulations and the changes brought about by them have now been given in an ODPM Circular 08/2003: "Amendments to the GDPO and Listed Buildings Regulations".

[42] [1998] J.P.L. 388).

[43] For Court of Appeal guidance on the proper application of s.54A, see *Loup and others v Secretary of State and Salisbury DC* [1996] J.P.L. 22.

Matters not appropriate to a planning authority's consideration

   (a) Financial considerations are not normally relevant.   **4–043**
   (b) A permission may not be refused to achieve a different purpose (*e.g.* to depress the value of the land, to enable a cheap acquisition).
   (c) Personal hardship is usually not appropriate to be taken into account except in very special circumstances.
   (d) It is no part of a planning authority's responsibility to distinguish between different occupiers. It must consider each application on its merits and deal with it according to planning law. This may mean that applications by different people can each be granted.
   (e) Discrimination on grounds of race or sex is forbidden.

Presumption in favour

It is particularly valuable to bear in mind that "there is always a   **4–044** presumption in favour of allowing applications for development having regard to all material considerations, unless that development would cause demonstrable harm to interests of acknowledged importance". In only very rare cases (*e.g.* green belt land), must the developer prove the case for his development. It is normally up to the planning authority to establish why the development should not be granted permission.

However, the presumption needs to be read with the s.54A requirements (see para.4–042 above) which will require normally that the proposals are in accordance with the development plan. It will be recognised that there is some importance in ensuring that such development plans are formulated in a way that subsequent planning applications do, in fact, make proposals which comply either wholly or in a significant part.

Refusal to deal with applications

A power for the local planning authority to decline to determine appli-   **4–045** cations was inserted into TCPA 1990 as s.70A by PCA 1991. The intention is to stop the practice of repeated applications which impose a strain on the resources both of local planning authorities and objectors. Section 70A provides that a local planning authority may decline to determine an application for planning permission if in the preceding two years the Secretary of State has refused a similar application and in the authority's opinion there has been no significant change. There is no right of appeal against this decision, but in the case of an irrational or unreasonable opinion it may be possible to refer the matter for judicial review by a High Court judge (see para.4–090).

Policy guidance notes

Planning authorities and developers are provided with a very wide range of   **4–046** guidance notes, a selection of which is set out in Appendix 1 below. While pollution and potential pollution issues are material matters in development planning and control the planning authority should not attempt to use the planning system to secure controls which can be achieved by pollution legislation such as EPA 1990 and WRA 1991.[44]

Notice of decision or determination

4–047 Once the local planning authority has reached a conclusion about a planning application, it is required to give written notice of its decision or determination. In circumstances where the permission is to be granted, conditions will be imposed and the planning authority must give reasons for the imposition of those conditions. Where an application is rejected, the planning authority must specify reasons for refusal. Since August 1, 2000, art.22 of GDPO 1995 has been amended by the Town and Country Planning (General Development Procedure) (England) (Amendment) Order 2000[45]; the effect of which is that reasons for refusal or the imposition of a condition must also specify all policies and proposals in the development plan which are relevant to the decision. From December 5, 2003 notices of planning decisions issued three months after that date must comply with further obligations set out in the Town and Country Planning (General Development Procedure) (England) (Amendment) Order 2003.[46] In short, the notice of the decision must include a summary of the reasons for any grant of the permission and a summary of the policies and proposals in the development plan regarded as relevant. Where permission is granted subject to conditions, the notice is required to state clearly and precisely the full reasons for each condition imposed, noting relevant policies and proposals. Where planning permission is refused, the notice must state clearly and precisely the full reasons for refusal, again specifying development plan policy and proposals.

PLANNING CONDITIONS

4–048 Section 70 of TCPA 1990 authorises a local planning authority to grant permission subject to such conditions as it thinks fit. Section 72 permits the imposition of conditions regulating the development or use of any land under the applicant's control or requiring the carrying out of any works on that land, whether or not it is part of the application, provided it is expedient for the purposes of or in connection with the development authorised. There is also power to require the removal or reinstatement of buildings or works or the discontinuance or reinstatement of any use. There

---

[44] See *Gateshead MBC v Secretary of State for the Environment and Northumbrian Water plc* [1994] EGCS 92, and DoE guidance notes PPG23, "Planning and Pollution Control" and PPG10, "Planning and Waste Management". A corresponding guidance document for Wales is "Technical Advice Note TAN21".

[45] SI 2000/1627.

[46] SI 2003/2047.

are now special rules relating to conditions for mineral development and, since PCA 1991, the depositing of refuse or waste (for details see para.4–056 *et seq.* below).

Restrictions on imposing planning conditions

Notwithstanding the apparently wide discretion to impose conditions, the **4–049** planning authority is subject to a number of constraints as to its powers, which have been set down by the courts and adopted subsequently by the Secretary of State in policy advice and in Circular 11/95, "The Use of Conditions in Planning Permissions". The leading case on these powers is *Newbury DC v Secretary of State for the Environment*,[47] which set down some fundamental rules.

First, the condition must fulfil some planning purpose. Secondly, it should fairly and reasonably relate to the permitted development. This includes a condition in respect of land outside the area covered by the application, even if not under the applicant's control, provided that it has a fair and reasonable relationship to the application land. A condition is not invalid if it forbids development pending a future event occurring (*Grampian Regional Council v City of Aberdeen*.[48] "Grampian conditions" (as they are known) are useful devices to ensure the grant of permission while the applicant is still in negotiation, say, for a new access. The *Grampian* decision was reviewed in the House of Lords' judgment in *British Railways Board v Secretary of State for the Environment*.[49] Prior to that case it was believed that a condition would be invalid if there was no reasonable prospect that it would be fulfilled within the time limit imposed. The *British Railways* case made clear that the existence of "no reasonable prospect" does not mean necessarily that the grant of planning permission would be wrong.

Thirdly, the conditions should not be manifestly unreasonable. Examples of unreasonableness are requirements for payment of money or in kind in exchange for the consent, interference with private land ownership, uncertain conditions or conditions which would have the effect of blocking the right to compensation. Note, however, that some of these constraints may be capable of being overcome by the device of a planning agreement or obligation under s.106 of TCPA 1990.

Matters controlled by other legislation

In general, planning conditions should not be imposed in respect of matters **4–050** which are controlled by other, more detailed legislation. For example, conditions would not be appropriate normally where authorisation for the

---

[47] [1981] A.C. 578.
[48] [1984] J.P.L. 590.
[49] [1994] J.P.L. 32.

development in question will also be needed under Pt I (integrated pollution control) or Pt II (waste on land) of EPA 1990, or under the Pollution Prevention and Control Act 1999. (PPC). Guidance is available in DoE guidance note PPG23, "Planning and Pollution Control".

Effect of invalid condition

4–051 What if the condition is found to be invalid? Does this destroy the whole planning permission? The answer to this is "Yes", if the condition goes to the root of the permission.[50] If the deletion of the offending condition does not have any real significance to the development permitted then the consent will stand with the condition excised.

Planning permissions with time scale conditions

Start of development

4–052 Since TCPA 1968 came into force, all planning permissions granted on an application are subjected to a condition which normally requires the development to start within five years of the grant.[51] Outline permissions are usually subject both to a commencement time scale and to a require-ment that other details ("reserved matters") shall be submitted within three years of the date of grant and that the development must be started within five years of the grant or two years from the final approval of the reserved matters, whichever is the later of those dates.[52] In the event that a permission, whether outline or full, is silent as to these matters, it is deemed to have been subject to these conditions. Different periods may be imposed by the planning authority in its reasonable discretion. It should be noted that s.51 of the Planning and Compulsory Purchase Act 2004 reduces the normal period within which the development must start after planning permission to three years, instead of five years. These provisions are not yet in force.

For waste management consents—particularly landfill approvals—it is perfectly proper for a long commencement date to be inserted in the consent. This would be appropriate in circumstances where the site's availability is uncertain (e.g. because prior mineral workings will be conducted for an indeterminate period). Thus, a condition on the landfill operation could provide for a period which allows sufficient time for the mineral working to be completed.

In the event that development is not started within the relevant time in accordance with conditions imposed, the planning permission lapses auto-matically. The local planning authority has no power to informally waive time limits in planning permissions.[53]

---

[50] *Kingsway Investment (Kent) Ltd v Kent CC* [1971] A.C. 72.
[51] TCPA 1990, s.91.
[52] *ibid.*, s.92.
[53] See the cases of *R. v East Sussex County Council Ex p. Reprotech* [2003] 1 W.L.R. 348 and *Henry Boot Homes Ltd v Bassetlaw District Council* (unreported, November 28, 2002).

Commencement of development

Development is begun when a "material operation" takes place. This term **4–053** is defined in s.56 of TCPA 1990 as the start of operations or as the date of the change in use. Operations recognised by the section as representing a commencement of the development include work of construction or demolition, digging foundation trenches, laying of underground facilities or any operation in the course of laying out or constructing a road or part of it. Section 56 is modified in the case of minerals development by the Town and Country (Minerals) Regulations 1995.[54] Under the Regulations, development consisting of the winning and working of minerals is taken to be begun on the earliest date on which the winning and working of minerals to which the relevant grant of planning permission relates begins.[55] There is a power in the Act to resolve a problem which arises when a development is started but not finished. In these circumstances the planning authority may serve a "completion notice" under s.94 of TCPA 1990. Failure to comply with the notice, which must allow at least 12 months for compliance, means that the permission ceases to have effect. A completion notice must be confirmed by the Secretary of State.

Temporary permissions

Local planning authorities are permitted to grant planning permission for a **4–054** limited period, but Government policy is generally against using such permissions merely as a compromise when refusal of a permanent permission would be appropriate. There are special rules which apply to minerals and waste management permissions, but other consents can be temporary in special circumstances (*e.g.* where the building has a short-term life or a use is intended only for a limited period). In the case of certain uses which might have a deleterious effect on local amenities, there are sometimes circumstances where a temporary consent may be granted to provide a trial period to test local reaction and impact.

Time limits for minerals permissions

Under Sch.5 to TCPA 1990, all permissions consisting of the winning and **4–055** working of minerals are subject automatically to a condition relating to duration. The Town and Country Planning (Minerals) Act 1981 (now substituted by TCPA 1990) provided that permissions already granted by February 22, 1982 must cease within 60 years of that date. All new permissions will normally impose a time limit. Otherwise they carry a condition imposing a 60-year period. There is a right to allow a longer or shorter period. A duration condition applies not only to a consent for the winning and working of minerals, but also one involving the deposit of mineral waste (added by PCA 1991). It follows that if a waste management

---

[54] SI 1995/2863.
[55] For a case in the implementation of mineral permissions see *Staffordshire CC v Riley* (unreported, February 21, 2001, CA).

operation succeeds a minerals operation and relies upon the same planning permission, then the waste management operation itself will also be subject to the duration provisions. It will, therefore, be important for the waste manager to ensure that adequate time has been allowed for him to realise his investment and comply with his obligations.

Interim development order permissions

4–056   Section 22 of and Sch.2 to PCA 1991 introduced new procedures for dealing with permissions for the winning and working of minerals (which might incorporate landfilling as an after use) which had originally been granted under an interim development order (IDO). These were permissions granted before July 1948 which nonetheless remained valid. In an attempt to bring these permissions up to date, particularly with regard to their conditions, certain provisions applied:

(a) applications for registration of IDO permissions had to be made by March 25, 1992, otherwise the permission became invalid;

(b) where no working had taken place between July 1948 and the beginning of April 1979, the permission would cease to have effect;

(c) challenges to the permission's validity by the mineral planning authority are referred to the Secretary of State;

(d) valid permissions, if dormant (no working in the two years to the end of April 1991), may not be exercised until a scheme of operation or restoration is agreed by the planning authority;

(e) in any other case, application for determination of conditions should be made within 12 months of approval of registration, otherwise the permission ceases to have effect.

It is important that waste managers should check the position carefully if they believe that operations were previously based on an IDO permission.[56]

Old mineral permissions

4–057   Following the establishment of the procedure for interim development order permissions mentioned above, the DoE turned its attention to other mineral permissions. Provisions similar to those applying for IDO mineral permissions are to be found in s.96 of and Schs 13 and 14 to the Environment Act 1995. Guidance on the law and procedures is provided in MPG14, "Environment Act 1995: Review of Mineral Planning Permissions". The provisions apply both in England and Wales.

Schedule 13 deals with the review of old mineral planning permissions. The first stage is an initial review which applies to sites where the main

---

[56] Further guidance is available in the DoE guidance note MPG8, "PCA 1991: Interim Development Order Permissions—Statutory Provisions and Procedures".

minerals permission was granted before February 22, 1982. "Dormant" sites are sites where no minerals development may lawfully be carried out pending the agreement of the mineral planning authority to a new scheme of conditions. Active sites are being reviewed in two successive phases each of three years. The first phase covers active sites where the predominant minerals permission was granted after July 30, 1948 and before April 1, 1969. Phase II sites relate to the period after March 31, 1969 and before February 22, 1982. Notwithstanding the provision of two phases, all initial review sites where any part is within a national park, area of outstanding natural beauty or site of special scientific interest are treated as Phase I sites.

By January 31, 1996, each mineral planning authority was required to prepare a list of all sites of the three types within their areas. There was a requirement to publish this list and secure that the land and mineral owners' attention was drawn to it. A failure to include a site in the list was intended to be overcome by giving a right for a land or mineral owner to apply for inclusion. Any qualifying site not on the list after three months from the date of first publication of the list loses the benefit of the planning permission. Once sites are registered then all Phase I sites must be the subject of an application for the authority's approval to a new scheme of conditions. A similar procedure applies for Phase II sites where the list of such sites must be prepared by the authority no later than October 31, 1998. Similar publicity provisions are required. Again, land or mineral owners must submit new schemes of conditions for the authority's approval, otherwise the permission ceases to have effect. As with IDO permissions, the overall intention is to provide "modern standards of environmental control". The authority will normally have three months within which to decide whether to accept the scheme put forward or to require a different set of conditions. In the event that no response is made by the authority within the three-month period (or such other period as may be agreed with the applicant), the conditions as submitted by the applicant will automatically come into effect.

Once conditions have been agreed, or the issues have been dealt with by the Secretary of State on appeal, the new conditions apply from the date of determination.

It is also important that waste managers should check carefully that the Sch.13 procedures have been followed correctly.

MPG14 makes clear that while separate planning permissions for landfill are not subject to review if they do not constitute development involving the deposit of mineral waste, the position is different if conditions imposed on the permission for winning and working of minerals also provided for restoration by landfilling. In these circumstances the original mineral consent is liable to review in accordance with the 1995 Act provisions.

Periodic reviews

All mineral sites will be the subject of periodic reviews, whether or not they **4–058** have qualified for review under the 1991 or 1995 Acts. Such reviews will take place every 15 years from the date of either a previous review or, where no such review has taken place, from the date of the latest mineral permission relating to the site in question. The procedure involves at least 12 months' notice being given by authorities to land and mineral owners of the date by which applications for approval of new conditions must be submitted. In default of the submission of new conditions, the permissions in question will cease to have effect.[57]

On receipt of a valid application the authority has three months to determine whether the submitted conditions are acceptable or to decide on modifications. The period may be extended by agreement with the applicant. If no notice of determination is served within the three months or an agreed longer period, then the conditions submitted are deemed to be approved from that date. In the case of dispute, appeals lie to the Secretary of State for the Environment, Transport and the Regions or the Welsh Assembly.

Environmental assessment

4–059   It will invariably be the case that an application for approval of new conditions should be accompanied by an environmental assessment, prepared in accordance with the Town and Country Planning (Environmental Impact Assessment) (England and Wales) Regulations 1999.[58]

Compensation

4–060   In some cases (*e.g.* where modification of a permission has resulted in significant potential loss to the operator) there will be a right to compensation.[59]

Restoration

4–061   Since the early years of development control, it has been common practice to require restoration and after-use issues on mineral permissions to be resolved at some stage in the life of the operation. Experience shows that even with the wide range of ministerial consents granted in the early 1950s, restoration requirements were somewhat rudimentary. However, the modern permission for minerals operations and waste management will inevitably carry conditions of some sophistication. Conditions will require either that a scheme of restoration be worked out, usually in phases, with the planning authority during the life of the operation, or that there must be a detailed scheme before consent is granted. The usual practice is to require a combination of these two approaches.

---

[57] See Environment Act 1995, Sch.14.
[58] SI 1999/293, as amended. See also *R. v North Yorkshire CC Ex p. Brown* [1999] 2 W.L.R. 452; and para.4–028 above.
[59] See Environment Act 1995, Sch.13, para.15 and Sch.14, para.13.

When he plans his landfill or other waste management project, the operator will often find that the underlying mineral consent will already contain a regime for the control of restoration/after use which may or may not be appropriate to the development he plans.

Aftercare

It has come to be recognised that a requirement simply for restoration is usually not sufficient, because restored land, tree planting etc. will require attention, husbandry, renewal and so on. Powers to impose aftercare conditions in respect of mineral land are set out in Sch.5, Pt I to TCPA 1990 and, since the coming into force of PCA 1991, aftercare requirements may also be imposed in respect of development involving a deposit of refuse or waste materials.

4–062

TCPA 1990 specifies five years as the aftercare period during which the required steps must be carried out, but the Secretary of State may prescribe a longer period. The time starts once restoration is completed and, in the case of phased restoration, at the end of the final phase. The aftercare condition requires that the use of the land must be specified as either agriculture, forestry or amenity and should then identify the steps required to bring the land to the required standard for the specified use or, alternatively, require the applicant to put forward a scheme.[60] Any person with an interest in the land subsequently may seek a certificate from the authority that an aftercare condition has been complied with.

Since the coming into force of Pt II of EPA 1990 there are additional obligations under the terms of a waste management licence which may apply post-closure (see para.10–055 below).

Applications to discharge planning conditions

Occasionally an operator may find his planning consent has obsolete conditions or that they are unduly onerous. Section 73 of TCPA 1990 provides a remedy. An application may be made to develop land without complying with conditions under a previous planning permission. Such an application cannot relate to a consent which is time expired. The authority, if it decides to grant the application, may impose alternative conditions or may refuse the application. It may consider only the question of the condition subject to which the original permission was granted, and may not consider extraneous matters. Section 73 is a useful provision, enabling retrospective correction of consents where conditions may have been breached. The application is similar to the ordinary planning application but somewhat modified.[61]

4–063

[60] MPG7, "The Reclamation of Mineral Workings", provides further information.
[61] For requirements in relation to decision notices, see above, para.4–047.

Retrospective planning permission

4–064 PCA 1991 inserted a new s.73A into TCPA 1990, enabling a planning authority to grant planning permission with retrospective effect. The provision applies to development carried out without planning permission, in accordance with planning permission granted for a limited period or without complying with some condition subject to which planning permission was granted originally. It is important to bear in mind that unlike an application under s.73 (above), an application under s.73A requires the local authority not only to consider whether the condition had been wrongly imposed but also to consider all the planning circumstances applying at the time of the decision. In effect the decision maker is required to consider the development *de novo*.[62]

EFFECT OF A PLANNING PERMISSION

4–065 Section 75 of TCPA 1990 spells out the effect of a grant of planning permission. The main principles are:

(a) that any grant to develop land shall enure for the benefit of the land and any person interested in it (except if the permission otherwise provides)—this means essentially that the permission will run with the land and will seldom be reserved to any particular person; and

(b) where planning permission is granted for the erection of a building the permission may specify the purposes for which the building is to be used—if no purpose is specified the permission is to be construed as including permission to use the building for the purpose for which it is designed.

A local planning authority owes no duty of care to any person who might be affected detrimentally by the exercise of a power to grant planning permission. In *Lam v Brennan and Torbay BC*,[63] the Court of Appeal rejected the contention that the council had breached its duty to take care to avoid the effects of permitted development on local residents. It was held that the law did not recognise a private right of action for breach of statutory duty in respect of regulatory systems for the benefit of the public at large which involves the exercise of administrative discretion and the carrying out of general administrative functions by public bodies. The town and country planning regime was held to be such a system. However, there can be exceptions to this rule—see *Kane v New Forest DC*.[64]

Can a planning permission be abandoned?

4–066 Subject to the conditions relating to the time scale of a permission (see para.4–052 above), it would not appear that a planning consent can be abandoned except, perhaps, where there is a clear and unequivocal agree-

---

[62] See *Sevenoaks DC v Secretary of State for the Environment* [1994] 69 P. & C.R. 87. For requirements in relation to decision notices, see above, para.4–047.
[63] [1998] P.L.C.R. 30.
[64] [2001] 3 All E.R. 914.

ment to do so or the permission provides for this specifically. The leading case on this question of abandonment is *Pioneer Aggregates Ltd v Secretary of State for the Environment.*[65] The House of Lords held that the appellants could recommence mineral extraction under a 1950 permission even though there had been a notification to the authority that quarrying would cease in 1966, and no work had taken place since that date. It follows that probably some fresh act of new development is required before abandonment can be construed. For example, consider a material change of use of the land. The previous use/development would come to an end once the change has been made and, in these circumstances, it is usual that an attempt to change to the original use is not allowed without formal reapplication and consent. By the same token the exhaustion of a mineral or landfill consent by the completion of the activities permitted could lead to a conclusion of abandonment, although longer-term supplementary work, such as restoration and aftercare, would need to be taken into account.

PLANNING AGREEMENTS AND OBLIGATIONS[66]

Since TCPA 1932, the power has existed for planning authorities, developers and landowners to enter into agreements for the purpose of restricting or regulating the development or use of land. Practitioners no doubt will come across such agreements, made, for example, under s.37 of the 1962 Act, or s.52 of the 1971 Act. Upon the consolidation of planning legislation, the appropriate provision is now s.106 of TCPA 1990, but significant changes were made by PCA 1991. The usual function of such an agreement has been to provide for obligations, usually on the part of the developer, which could not be the subject of planning conditions because of the restrictive rules relating to the type of conditions that might be imposed. A secondary advantage is that other parties, such as landowners, could covenant with the planning authority to undertake or co-operate in some improvements or "planning gain", whether in respect of the land the subject of development or other land.

Characteristics of planning agreements

The typical planning agreement has a number of features which should be noted. First, a local planning authority can enter into covenants but not so as to fetter its powers, particularly in relation to the exercise of discretion. Thus, an authority could not commit itself to grant planning permission or

4–067

4–068

[65] [1985] A.C. 132.
[66] The Planning and Compulsory Purchase Act 2004 makes provision in ss.46–48 for the repeal of ss.106–106B of the TCPA 1990. However, these provisions are not yet in force. The replacement provisions anticipate regulations to be made by the Secretary of State which will lay down a system of planning contribution *i.e.* by developers and others, in exchange for which a planning permission will be granted.

approve other authorisations where, for example, it needs to take into account a range of material considerations, including the views of consultees. Nor may it enter into an agreement in respect of land outside its area. Secondly, the agreement can be effective to bind only the estate or interest of the covenantor and is enforceable usually against successors in title.

Thirdly, the agreement will usually be a land charge, registrable under the Local Land Charges Act 1975. Fourthly, the agreement can be enforced as though it was an ordinary contract in relation to land (*i.e.* by an action in the courts for an injunction and/or damages).

Finally, an agreement may be varied or discharged by the consent of the parties and there is a procedure in the event of the absence of consent to seek the order of the Lands Tribunal for discharge or modification.[67] The basis of an order is usually on the grounds that the covenant in question is out of date. For a description of the criteria, see *Abbey Homesteads (Developments) Application*.[68]

Planning agreements made before the new PCA 1991 provisions came into force remain unaffected.

Planning obligations

4–069   By s.12 of PCA 1991, which came into force on October 25 of that year, the arrangements for planning agreements were significantly changed. This arose by the introduction in the legislation of a new planning instrument— the planning obligation. The main changes are:

(a) a planning obligation may be entered into either bilaterally or unilaterally;

(b) there are wider provisions than for planning agreements;

(c) there is greater detail as to the formal requirements;

(d) modification and discharge of agreements and covenants are more easily effected; and

(e) variation or discharge by order of the Lands Tribunal under the Law of Property Act 1925 is not available (but see new procedures at para.4–072 below).

One of the difficulties for a developer under the old planning agreement regime arose if he wished to enter into an agreement with the planning authority to overcome some objection which could not be dealt with by a planning condition. If he was unable to obtain the planning authority's co-operation there was very little more he could do. He could appeal to the Secretary of State, but there was essentially no power for the latter or his inspector to impose any requirement as to a planning agreement on the

---

[67] Law of Property Act 1925, s.84.
[68] [1986] J.P.L. 683.

authority, to complement any planning permission granted on appeal. Now it is possible for the developer and/or landowner to offer a planning obligation, either in the form of an agreement with the authority and any other relevant parties or by way of a unilateral instrument executed as a deed. This may be offered to the planning authority or, on appeal, to the Secretary of State, probably conditionally on the grant of the required planning permission.

However, some care is needed in drafting unilateral obligations, particularly if undertakings are being given which may not be enforceable.[69]

Content of a planning obligation

By s.106 of TCPA 1990, as amended, a planning obligation may restrict the development or use of land, require specified operations, activities or use of land and may involve the payment of money to the authority, either on a specified date or periodically. It may be unconditional or subject to conditions and may impose restrictions etc, indefinitely or for limited periods. Any payments required to be made under the agreement may be indefinite or for a specified period. **4–070**

Enforcement

The document is enforceable in the same way as an ordinary deed containing contractual obligations (*i.e.* by action in the courts for damages and/or injunction), but, by s.106(6), the planning authority is given further powers in the event of a breach of an obligation to enter the land in question and carry out any covenanted operations and recover the costs of doing so from the person against whom the obligation is enforceable. Under the Contracts (Rights of Third Parties) Act 1999, third parties may have rights under planning agreements. It will be important to consider whether such rights ought to be excluded in any planning obligation/agreement. **4–071**

The planning obligation will:

(a) identify itself as an obligation for the purposes of s.106;
(b) specify the land in question;
(c) identify the person accepting the obligation and his interest in the land; and
(d) identify the planning authority.

The planning obligation is a local land charge.

---

[69] See *Wimpey Homes Holdings Ltd v Secretary of State for the Environment* [1993] J.P.L. 919 and *South Oxfordshire DC v Secretary of State for the Environment and others* [1994] E.G.C.S. 80.

Modification and discharge of planning obligations

4–072   In a new s.106A of TCPA 1990 (inserted by PCA 1991), provisions are
made for modifying or discharging a planning obligation. This may be done
by agreement with the authority and the other persons against whom the
obligation is enforceable, or by means of a formal application.

Application for discharge

4–073   Any person against whom a planning obligation is enforceable may apply to
the local planning authority to modify or discharge. However, this application may not be made until the expiry of the "relevant period". This is
defined in s.106A(4) as a period of five years after the obligation is entered
into or such other period as may be prescribed. No other period has yet
been prescribed.

   The authority is required by s.106A(6) to determine that the application
shall be refused or that the obligation shall be discharged (but only if the
obligation no longer serves a useful purpose) or be modified (but only if the
obligation continues to serve a useful purpose and could serve that purpose
equally well if modified). Detailed application procedures are now set out
in the Town and Country Planning (Modification and Discharge of
Planning Obligations) Regulations 1992.[70] These Regulations also provide
for notice to be given to other persons against whom the obligation is
enforceable and for the local planning authority to give publicity to the
application. There is a right of appeal to the Secretary of State in the event
that the local authority does not give its decision within eight weeks or such
extended period as may be agreed or where it determines that the planning
obligation shall not be modified. Curiously, there seems to be no right to
appeal if the obligation is modified in a way unsatisfactory to the applicant.

The difficulties of planning gain

4–074   In the past there has been considerable difficulty in determining the proper
scope and extent of a local planning authority's powers to require a
developer's commitment to planning agreements. The DoE has made a
number of attempts to provide advice and recommendations.[71] The difficulty has frequently been that the planning authority has seen a developer's
need for a permission as an ideal bargaining opportunity to gain advantages
which it would not otherwise achieve. Many of these advantages may have
nothing to do with the development which is the subject of the application.
There is no doubt that the discretion available to the planning authority
under s.106 is much wider than that available in the imposition of planning

---

[70] SI 1992/2832.
[71] See DoE Circular 1/97, "Planning Obligations".

conditions.[72] Nonetheless, the courts are entitled to review the exercise of the authority's discretion in the use of s.106 powers.[73]

Other powers for statutory agreements

Besides the s.106 agreement provisions, there are other powers in alterna- **4–075** tive legislation which may be appropriate in the case of certain developments. See, for example:

(a) the Greater London Council (General Powers) Act 1974, s.16 (now exercisable by any London borough);

(b) the Highways Act 1980, s.278 (as replaced by the New Roads and Street Works Act 1991, s.19) (relating to highway works);

(c) the Housing Act 1985, s.609 (relating to the enforcement of covenants against an owner for the time being); and

(d) various local acts, usually promoted by the local planning authority to deal with a particular local matter.

For guidance on highways matters see DTLR Circular 04/2001, "Control of development affecting trunk roads and agreements with developers under s.278 of the Highways Act 1980".

PLANNING APPEALS[74]

There is a right to appeal against planning decisions and failures to take **4–076** decisions, such appeal usually being made to the Secretary of State. The right arises where a local planning authority has refused an application or granted it subject to unacceptable conditions, or has refused an application for any consent, agreement or approval required under a condition of an earlier consent or has imposed unacceptable conditions, or has refused an application for an approval required under a development order, or has granted it subject to unacceptable conditions. By the same token, an appeal may lie to the Secretary of State where the local planning authority has failed to take a decision within certain time limits (usually eight weeks, but longer in the case of mineral operations and other development, *e.g.* those

---

[72] See para.4–049.

[73] See, for example, *R. v Gillingham BC Ex p. Parham Ltd* [1988] J.P.L. 336 and *R. v Wealden DC Ex p. Charles Church South East Ltd* [1989] 3 P.L.R. 42. The cases of *R. v Plymouth City Council Ex p. Plymouth and South Devon Co-operative Society Ltd* [1994] 67 P. & C.R. 78 and *Tesco Stores Ltd v Secretary of State for the Environment* [1995] 2 All E.R. 636, a House of Lords decision, also deal with the limits to the validity of planning obligations, especially where what is offered has little or no relationship with the proposed development. Similar circumstances arose in the case of *R. v South Holland DC Ex p. Lincoln Cooperative Society Ltd* [2001] J.P.L. 675.

[74] It should be noted that the Planning and Compulsory Purchase Act 2004 modifies the functions of local planning authorities in relation to appeals made under s.78 of the TCPA 1990. However, these provisions are not yet in force.

subject to a requirement for an environmental assessment (see para.4–028)).

Time for appeal

4–077 Notice of appeal must be given within three months of the notice of the decision or, in the case of non-determination, of the date by which the decision should have been made. The Secretary of State has reserved a power to allow longer time, but this is used very rarely. There is a form for appeal which may be obtained from the Planning Inspectorate.

Who may appeal?

4–078 Note that TCPA 1990 allows only the applicant the right to appeal and as already discussed above the applicant does not have to have any interest in the land. As a result there is no right of any other party to appeal, whether that party is the fee simple owner or a third party, unless the appellant is a successor to the applicant's interest.

Documents required for the appeal

4–079 Besides the completion of the form, the appellant is also required to send to the Planning Inspectorate copies of the following documents:

(a) the original application;
(b) all plans, drawings and other documents submitted with the application including any environment impact statement (see para.4–028);
(c) all correspondence with the authority concerning the application;
(d) the certificates relating to ownership and any notices given relating to these matters (see para.4–034 above);
(e) any other relevant plans or drawings, even if not sent to the authority with the application;
(f) notice of the authority's decision, if any;
(g) if the appeal relates to an application for approval of reserved matters, the original application for outline planning permission, the plans and the permission which was granted; and
(h) fresh ownership certificates will also be required and notices of the appeal must also be given to persons who have an interest in the land.

Notice of the appeal must be served on the local planning authority, together with any plans, documents etc. not previously sent to it.

Note that the Secretary of State is entitled to refuse to accept a notice of appeal if documentation has not been served on him within the time limits specified.[75]

---

[75] See the Town and Country Planning (General Development Procedure) (England) (Amendment) Order 2000 (SI 2000/1627).

Powers of the Secretary of State on appeal

By s.79 of TCPA 1990, the Secretary of State is empowered to either allow **4–080** or dismiss the appeal or reverse or vary any part of the authority's decision. Effectively, he deals with the application as if it had been made to him in the first instance. It is to be noted that if an appellant fails to proceed with his appeal promptly and without due delay the Secretary of State has power to dismiss the appeal at any time before it is determined. Notice of the intention to use this power must be given to the appellant, with an opportunity for him to take any specified steps.

Section 79 requires that the Secretary of State provides the appellant and/or the local planning authority with an opportunity of appearing before, and being heard by, an inspector appointed for the purpose. Jurisdiction to deal with all appeals is now transferred to inspectors under the Town and Country Planning (Determination of Appeals by Appointed Persons) (Prescribed Classes) Regulations 1997,[76] but with a few exceptions. However, the Secretary of State has a right to claw back significant appeals for his own decision if there is a good reason, for example the size of the development, the complexity of the issues or where the proposals give rise to significant public controversy. In the case of appeals to be determined by the Secretary of State inquiry procedures are governed by the Town and Country Planning (Inquiries Procedure) (England) Rules 2000.[77]

A large proportion of appeals is now dealt with by written representations (*i.e.* there is no hearing or inquiry). However, it will be unusual for an appeal relating to waste management matters to be dealt with by written representations. The more normal procedure would entail the calling of a public local inquiry.

For further guidance on policy and practice see DETR Circular 05/2000, Planning Appeals: Procedures (Including Inquiries into Called in Planning Applications).

Procedure at public local inquiry

The procedure varies depending upon the significance and complexity of **4–081** the inquiry and the issues to be considered. The main components are as follows.

First, the Secretary of State notifies the local planning authority of an intention to hold an inquiry. The authority must respond by informing him and the appellant of the details of any persons having an interest in the land who made representations on the original application, and the Secretary of State must then notify these persons. The authority is also required to notify certain public agencies, including government departments, where they have made representations concerning the application.

---

[76] SI 1997/420.
[77] SI 2000/1624. Corresponding procedures for Wales are to be found at SI 2003/1267.

In important cases, a pre-inquiry meeting will be held to consider what may be done with a view to securing that the inquiry is conducted efficiently and expeditiously. Parties will be asked to make available an outline statement of their case. In major inquiries, there is a non-statutory code of practice set out in DETR Circular 05/2000.

A statement of case (known as the r.6 statement) must be served by the local planning authority six weeks from the "starting date" (a specific date set by the DETR, to which the pre-inquiry timetable is linked) or four weeks from the pre-inquiry meeting. This statement must be served on the Secretary of State and the appellant, and certain interested parties who have made representations. The statement is an indication of the case which the planning authority will advance at the inquiry. It will usually contain reasons for the decision and the policies which were the basis of that decision, and it will indicate documents intended to be relied upon.

The appellant must serve a statement of case, within the same timetable, which statement must be sent to the same parties. Other parties who have notified the Secretary of State of an intention or wish to appear at the inquiry may also be required at the Secretary of State's discretion to submit a statement of case.

Meanwhile, the Planning Inspectorate will have notified all the parties of the date of the inquiry, usually not later than 22 weeks from the starting date. The inquiry will be held at a suitable place in the vicinity of the appeal site. The appellant will usually be asked to post notices of the inquiry date and the authority will also be invited to notify local people.

The inspector appointed to conduct the inquiry is obliged by the rules to arrange an inquiry timetable where either a pre-inquiry meeting is held or it appears that the inquiry is likely to last for eight days or more.

Appeals determined by inspectors

4–082   Separate rules apply where the decision on any appeal is delegated by the Secretary of State to his inspector. Here the rules are to be found in the Town and Country Planning Appeals (Determination by Inspectors) (Inquiries Procedure) (England) Rules 2000.[78] The procedures up to the date of the inquiry are largely the same as noted above, although pre-inquiry meetings are less likely to be held; an outline statement of case is usually dispensed with, the parties relying upon the r.6 statement. In "inspector" cases, notification of the inquiry must be made 20 weeks from the starting date.

Conduct of the appeal inquiry

4–083   Depending on whether the appeal decision is to be made by the Secretary of State or by his delegated inspector, the rules for the conduct of the inquiry are those mentioned above.

[78] SI 2000/1625.

Subject to the rules, the inspector is given a wide discretion about the way in which the inquiry will be conducted, but the general principles are that the main parties and third parties are to be given all reasonable opportunities to make their case and to have the opportunity to question the principal parties. Any proofs of evidence are required to be sent to the inspector not later than three weeks before the inquiry, with copies to the other side and any other relevant parties. Proofs with more than 1,500 words are required to be summarised. It is now usual for only the summaries to be read, although the shorter proofs may be taken in full. The inquiry will press on with supplementary matters, cross-examination etc. Statements of "common ground" between the parties are invariably required to be exchanged.

The inquiry is usually conducted as a contentious exercise and there are, therefore, some similarities with a court of law. However, rules of evidence are relaxed and the exercise is mainly an investigation of the soundness of the reasons for refusal of permission. Note that generally the appellant is not under any burden of proof to establish his case; it is for the planning authority to establish that its reasons for refusal are justifiable. Nonetheless, in particularly contentious cases where, as with waste management, a high-potential environmental profile will exist, some element of justification will be required from the appellant, if only to refute the argument that on balance the status quo is to be preferred on amenity and environment grounds.

After the inquiry

Once the inquiry is completed and the inspector has undertaken an **4–084** examination of the appeal site and all other areas which are appropriate, he will make his written report to the Secretary of State or will issue his decision to the parties. The report will include decisions as to the facts, conclusions and recommendations or, where the decision is delegated to the inspector, the actual decision, together with reasons for those. Reasons for the decision have to be clear and coherent.[79] Once final conclusions are reached, all the parties are notified of the decision. Sometimes, where there has been a significant period of time between the close of the inquiry and the issue of the decision, the Secretary of State will issue a "minded to" letter. As its name implies, such letter will disclose the decision which the Secretary of State is "minded to" reach. However, it may well be that there have been changes in the factual position underlying the appeal or modifications to policy or other developments which justify giving the parties a further opportunity to make more representations. In appropriate cases the main parties may take the opportunity of seeking a re-opening of the inquiry. If that happens then the inquiry rules apply afresh. At the

---

[79] For examples, see the cases, *Runnymede Borough Council v Secretary of State* (unreported, November 14, 2000, Administrative Court) and *Thurrock Borough Council v Secretary of State and Holding* (unreported, February 22, 2001, Administrative Court.

conclusion of the exchange of further comments and/or a re-opened inquiry, the inspector will prepare a supplementary report with recommendations and the Secretary of State will then make a final decision.

Costs

4–085   Usually, costs are not awarded following public local inquiries, but the major exception to this arises where one or more of the parties has behaved unreasonably. This may arise where the local planning authority has withdrawn one of its grounds of appeal at a late stage or the appellant or another party has changed his ground of appeal or made significant changes to his case, putting opponents in difficulty and to extra expense. Costs may also be awarded for unreasonable conduct in written representations and "hearing" cases. For more information see DoE Circular 8/93.

Written representations

4–086   While it is reported that the written representation procedure is now used in 85 per cent of planning appeals, its application in the case of waste management appeals is likely to be much more limited, perhaps to the occasional formal contest of simple issues relating, for example, to the proper form of conditions of consent. The procedure is governed by the Town and Country Planning (Appeals) (Written Representations Procedure) (England) Regulations 2000.[80]

Procedure for written representations appeals

4–087   The Secretary of State, through the Planning Inspectorate, advises the parties of the appeal and the "starting date" of this.

The local planning authority is required to give written notice of the appeal within two weeks of the starting date to persons consulted in connection with the application and others who made representations, giving information in its notice concerning the application and securing any further representations to be made within six weeks of the starting date. The authority must also provide further information to the Secretary of State and the appellant.

The notice of appeal normally comprises the appellant's representations. The local planning authority may either elect to treat the above information as its representations or submit more formal representations within six weeks of the starting date. Once the initial representations have been made there is an option for the appellant or the local planning authority to make

---

[80] SI 2000/1628. Further information is available in DETR Circular 05/2000. Corresponding procedures in Wales are to be found in SI 2003/390.

further comments within nine weeks of the starting date. Anything submitted late may be disregarded by the Secretary of State or his inspector, but time limits may be extended. Third parties are enabled to make representations within the above timetables.

The Secretary of State, usually through his inspector, will make the decision, which invariably will follow a visit to the site with the parties, but there are no formalities for this.

Appeal hearings

In comparatively simple cases it is open to the Secretary of State to provide **4–088** for a hearing before an inspector. This is intended to be a more informal exercise, without the procedural rigours of an inquiry. Nonetheless, there are now formal rules which apply to appeals dealt with by a hearing.[81] The Rules require preliminary information to be supplied by the local planning authority and the exchange of statements, impose time scales for date and notification of hearing and lay down simple methods of procedure. Arrangements for site inspections are also provided for. The inspector usually takes the lead in conducting the proceedings, which can be more in the nature of a discussion about the issues than a matter of examination and cross-examination of witnesses. Such proceedings are inappropriate for large-scale development and/or where complex issues arise, or, indeed, where third parties wish to be heard.[82]

FURTHER CHALLENGES IN THE HIGH COURT

Decisions on appeal and a range of other orders may be the subject of a **4–089** challenge to the High Court under s.288 of TCPA 1990. The grounds for challenge are limited, normally to questioning the validity of the action taken by the Secretary of State or other parties on the grounds that the order or action is not within the powers of the Act or that relevant requirements, usually as to procedure, have not been complied with. An application under s.288 must be made within six weeks of the date on which any order is confirmed or the action is taken (*e.g.* the decision on appeal). Applications may only be made by persons aggrieved (*i.e.* those who have a direct interest in the decision or order or, usually, the local authority).

The most common challenge in respect of decisions of the Secretary of State or his delegated inspector tends to be on the basis that facts or legal

---

[81] See the Town and Country Planning (Hearings Procedure) (England) Rules 2000 (SI 2000/1626).

[82] A code of practice can be found in Annex 2 to DETR Circular 05/2000. High Court guidance can be found in *Rydon Homes Ltd v Secretary of State for the Environment and Sevenoaks DC* [1997] J.P.L. 145. See also the Court of Appeal judgment in *Dyason v Secretary of State for the Environment* [1998] J.P.L. 778, where the High Court judge drew attention to the danger that the informality of hearings could lead to inadequate examination of the relevant issues and prevent a full and fair hearing from taking place. Corresponding procedures for Wales are to be found in SI 2003/1271.

principles have not been taken into account sufficiently or at all; alternatively, the challenge may be on the basis that factors have been taken into account which should not have been regarded as relevant or appropriate.

The usual order of the High Court is to quash the decision or order and the matter then reverts to the decision-making body for reconsideration. There are certain rights to appeal further to the Court of Appeal and to the House of Lords, but only after leave has been granted.

Judicial review

4–090   Third parties materially affected by decisions on planning applications, appeals and other matters may have a right to refer the decision by application to the High Court for judicial review. The High Court requires that the claim for judicial review must be filed on the appropriate form promptly and in any event not later than three months after the grounds to make the claim first arose. The emphasis is on promptness and if the court is of the view that a claim has not been made without undue delay there is power to refuse to grant permission for making an application for judicial review or any relief sought under the terms of the application.[83]

OTHER METHODS OF PLANNING CONTROL ONCE PLANNING PERMISSION GRANTED

4–091   The effect of a planning permission and the rights of a holder of such permission are described at para.4–065 above. It will be only on rare occasions that a holder of a planning permission can lose the development rights associated with it. However, there are some little used provisions of TCPA 1990 which, subject to certain limitations and conditions, can be applied by planning authorities to alter those rights.

Discontinuance orders

4–092   By s.102 of TCPA 1990, a local planning authority can make an order requiring the discontinuance of any use of land, regardless of whether it is a lawful or unlawful use. Note that the power is effective only against the use of land and not against building or other operations. Other powers exist in this regard (see below). The authority that makes an order is liable to pay compensation for any loss arising from the order, which does not take effect unless confirmed by the Secretary of State.

There are special provisions for discontinuance orders to be used in respect of the development of land for the winning and working of minerals

---

[83] For the court's approach to the question of delay see the House of Lords' judgment in *R. v London Borough of Hammersmith and Fulham Ex p. Burkett* [2002] UKHL 23.

or the depositing of refuse or waste materials (the second of these was added by PCA 1991). The procedures are complex and are contained in Sch.9 to TCPA 1990. Schedule 9 can also be used by the planning authority to impose new conditions in respect of the operations, to require the alteration or removal of buildings or works, plant or machinery. Aftercare conditions can be imposed. However, it is more likely that the provisions of Sch.14 to the Environment Act 1995 will be used to provide for the modification of conditions and general updating of mineral consents (see para.4–056 above).

Revocation or modification of planning permission

Section 97 of TCPA 1990 provides a procedure whereby extant planning permissions can be revoked or modified by order of the planning authority, but it may only be exercised up to the date that the development which has been permitted has been achieved (*i.e.* once the building or operation is completed or the change of use is effected). Orders require confirmation by the Secretary of State and compensation is payable for any losses suffered. Sch.5 to TCPA 1990 provides for modification of permissions for the winning and working of minerals or (since PCA 1991) involving the deposit of refuse or waste materials. The modifications, dealt with by Sch.5, can permit the retrospective imposition of aftercare requirements. **4–093**

Compensation for revocation or modification can be paid by virtue of s.107 of TCPA 1990, but there are modifications to the rules in the case of mineral working, brought about by the Town and Country Planning (Minerals) Regulations 1995.[84] It should be added that modification of planning permissions is now more likely to be dealt with under Sch.14 to the Environment Act 1995 (see para.4–056 above).

ENFORCEMENT OF PLANNING CONTROL

The enforcement of planning control is aimed primarily at the developers of land who undertake their activities either without a required planning permission or in contravention of the conditions or limitations of existing permissions. The enforcement notice may relate to an unlawful use of land or an operational activity such as the erection or alteration of buildings. Local planning authorities need a simple and speedy procedure for ensuring compliance with planning law, but what has been achieved over the last 40 years or so is very far removed from that. Despite many legislative attempts to clarify and speed up the law and its procedures, the subject still remains somewhat complex and hedged about with difficult procedural requirements. Following a very careful review of the legal position, undertaken by Robert Carnwath Q.C., further modifications and **4–094**

[84] SI 1995/2863.

simplifications were provided for in PCA 1991 (which made amendments to TCPA 1990). There is little evidence that the legislation has curbed the ingenuity of recalcitrant developers and their advisers in the evasion of planning controls.[85]

Time limits

4–095   Enforcement action has to be taken within certain time limits and these are different depending upon the type of development complained of. Section 171B of TCPA 1990 provides that no enforcement action may be taken after the end of a period of four years from the completion of building, engineering, mining or other operations. The four-year rule also applies where a breach of planning control is alleged, which consists of the change of use of any building to a single dwelling-house. A 10-year rule applies in all other cases.

If enforcement action is not taken within the time limits there is no further right to do so and any uses and operations then become lawful by virtue of s.191 of TCPA 1990. The 10-year rule is an innovation of PCA 1991 and means that immunity from enforcement action is conferred automatically on all breaches of planning control which occurred between 1964 and July 1982. Immunity from that time will accrue on a rolling basis. Prior to 1964, the four-year rule applied to all development.

Special attention should be paid to time limits appropriate to continuing operations, of which the extraction of minerals and the deposit of waste are examples. The view of Lord Denning in the mineral case of *Thomas David (Porthcawl) Ltd v Penybont RDC*[86] was that time would start to run again continually with every shovel-full of material extracted.

It would appear to follow that the principle would also apply to similar continuous operations, such as landfill.

Planning contravention notices

4–096   Government policy has always been to try to encourage local planning authorities and developers to co-operate in unravelling and resolving breaches of planning control. No doubt this has been engendered by the considerable difficulties in finding a water-tight regime of law to resolve disputes. PCA 1991 introduced into TCPA 1990 a new notice, called a "planning contravention notice" (s.171C). This notice may be served by the authority on owners and other persons with an interest in land. It seeks information about activities on land and the individuals or organisations

---

[85] Guidance on enforcement procedures is available in PPG18,"Enforcing Planning Control" and in a comprehensive DoE Circular 10/97, "Enforcing Planning Control: Legislative Provisions and Procedural Requirements". The DETR has also published in 1997 "Enforcing Planning Control: Good Practice Guide for Local Authorities".

[86] [1972] 1 W.L.R. 1526.

involved. It may enquire about the existence of any planning permissions or reasons for alleging that no such permission exists. It asks for details of the interest held in the land and of any interest held by any other person. There is scope for the notice to require the person served to apply for planning permission, to stop carrying out the operations complained of or to undertake remedial works. On receipt, the addressee may make representations to be considered by the authority. These notices are important because a criminal liability arises if they are not complied with during a period of 21 days of the service of the notice. The recipient of a notice is only required to comply with it as far as he can and to provide information within his knowledge.

Enforcement notice procedures

Assuming that the planning authority decides to bypass the contravention **4–097** notice procedure or is dissatisfied with its result, it will often want to issue an enforcement notice or serve a breach of condition notice (see para.4–111 below). There are strict statutory requirements for the contents of an enforcement notice and the documents which must accompany it (TCPA 1990, s.173). The notice must:

(a) include a clear statement specifying the alleged breach;
(b) provide a specification of the steps which the authority requires to be taken to comply with the notice, which might include ceasing a use, altering or removing buildings or other works, carrying out buildings or works or contouring the deposit of refuse or waste materials;
(c) specify the date on which it is to take effect;
(d) specify the period within which it is required to be complied with (*i.e.* the periods when steps must be taken)—note that separate periods may apply to different aspects of the development complained of;
(e) specify the authority's reasons for issuing the notice;
(f) specify the land; and
(g) provide an explanatory note, including a specification of all policies and proposals in a development plan relevant to the decision to issue the notice.

The notice must be served on the owner and occupier of the land in question and on any other person having an interest in the land which, in the authority's opinion, is materially affected by it. Service must be effected not more than 28 days after its issue, and at least the same period must elapse between date of service and the date on which it takes effect. Each party served must be sent a list of the names and addresses of all recipients of the notice.

Note that there is no obligation imposed on the authority to issue an enforcement notice where there are apparent breaches of planning law.

PPG18, "Enforcing Planning Control", issued in December 1991, makes clear that while local authorities have a primary responsibility for pursuing enforcement action as necessary in the public interest, they must avoid doing so where the matter complained of is trivial, where there is no harm to amenity or where the development is acceptable on its planning merits. If such a development would be acceptable if conditions were imposed then the notice may be restricted simply to requiring the removal or limitation of the matter complained of.

Enforcement notice appeals

4–098   All enforcement notices must contain a statement, comprising ss.172–177 of TCPA 1990, which identifies the rights of appeal. The Planning Inspectorate will make available to potential appellants its explanatory booklet "Enforcement Notice Appeals—A Guide to Procedure".

Those who may appeal against an enforcement notice include persons having an interest in the land to which such notice relates or a relevant occupier (*i.e.* usually a person who has a licence to occupy). This means effectively that freeholders and leaseholders will have rights of appeal.

Grounds of appeal

4–099   An appeal may be brought on various grounds as follows:

    (a) that in respect of the matters complained of, planning permission ought to be granted or a condition or limitation of a consent ought to be discharged—this ground is considered automatically on any appeal, whether or not it is pleaded specifically;
    (b) that the matters alleged in the notice have not occurred;
    (c) that the matters alleged in the notice do not constitute a breach of planning control;
    (d) that the time limits for a notice have expired;
    (e) that there was a defect in the service of the notice;
    (f) that steps required by the notice are excessive; and/or
    (g) that the time for compliance with the notice is unreasonably short.

A notice of appeal must be lodged with the Secretary of State within the period specified as the date on which it is to take effect (usually 28 days). Notice must be in writing on a specific form available from the Planning Inspectorate. The notice of appeal should specify the grounds of appeal and provide a brief statement of the facts to be relied upon. If these are not provided, they may subsequently be requested by the Secretary of State and must be given within 14 days. Fees, payable separately to the Secretary of State and the local planning authority, must accompany the appeal and are usually equivalent to that which would be appropriate to an application for planning permission in respect of the development in question. The fees are payable by all appellants notwithstanding that they relate to the same development, but such fees are not payable if the appellant has already made a planning application which is undetermined at the date when the enforcement notice was served. The fees are refunded on withdrawal of the appeal at least 21 days before the inquiry, if the local planning authority withdraws the notice, if the Secretary of State decides that it is a nullity, or if the appeal is allowed on most of the grounds (other than (a) above).

The procedures for appeals are set down in the Town and Country Planning (Enforcement Notices and Appeals) (England) Regulations 2002.[87] In some cases development the subject of an enforcement notice falls into a category which requires an environmental assessment (see para.4–028 above). In those circumstances where a planning application has not been made, invariably it will be the case that there is no environmental assessment. These circumstances are dealt with in the Town and Country Planning (Environmental Impact Assessment) (England and Wales) Regulations 1999[88] as amended; these provide that the Secretary of State may not grant planning permission on any appeal unless he has first taken into account the environmental statement and any representations made by any party on that statement. The Regulations contain procedures which enable the Secretary of State to demand an environmental statement and to arrange for consultation. DETR Circular 02/99 describes the details of the regulations, their applicability and the procedures to be adopted by local planning authorities.

The Office of the Deputy Prime Minister has issued an explanatory Circular 02/2002, "Enforcement Appeal Procedures".

Local authority statement before inquiry

The Secretary of State will have identified a "starting date" which is usually **4–100** the date by which he has received all the documents required to enable him to entertain the appeal. Within six weeks of the starting date the local planning authority is required to submit to the Secretary of State and any other person on whom the enforcement notice had been served a statement indicating the submissions proposed to be put forward on the appeal. This will include a summary response to each of the grounds of appeal, together with a statement as to whether the authority would be prepared to grant planning permission in respect of the development the subject of the enforcement notice, the statement will specify what conditions they would wish to impose on the permission.

Enforcement appeal inquiry

It is likely that most waste management enforcement appeal cases will **4–101** proceed by way of a public local inquiry. However, it is open to the parties to agree either to make use of the hearings procedure or to deal with the

[87] SI 2002/2682. Corresponding regulations for Wales are set out in SI 2003/394.
[88] SI 1999/293.

matter on the basis of written representations. There are separate rules for each type of procedure. In the case of an inquiry, there are separate rules depending on whether the determination of the appeal is allocated to the Secretary of State or to his inspector.

In the former case, the applicable rules are the Town and Country Planning (Enforcement) (Inquiries Procedure) (England) Rules 2002.[89] The rules require the Secretary of State, the local planning authority and any appellant to be responsible for certain specified activities, including:

(a) the local planning authority must provide the Secretary of State and any appellant with a completed questionnaire and a copy of the documents referred to, to notify relevant parties that an appeal has been made and giving the opportunity for representations to be made to the Secretary of State;

(b) the Secretary of State will set up the arrangements for the inquiry and appoint an inspector. Where he anticipates that the inquiry might last for four days or more, he will often arrange for a pre-inquiry meeting to be held to decide on the arrangements for the conduct of the inquiry. He will require the local planning authority and the appellant to serve a reasonably detailed statement of their case. Statements of case may also be required from other interested parties, where appropriate;

(c) the parties will provide proofs of evidence to the Secretary of State and to any person upon whom a copy of the enforcement notice has been served. Where the proof of evidence is longer than 1500 words a summary

(d) the parties are required to produce an agreed statement of common (r)the parties are required to produce an agreed statement of common ground for the Secretary of State and any other person upon whom the enforcement notice has been served.

The procedure at the inquiry and subsequently follows that applicable to normal planning appeals (see para.4–081).

Some enforcement decisions may be delegated to an inspector. In this case, the applicable rules are the Town and Country Planning (Enforcement) (Determination by Inspectors) (Inquiries Procedure) (England) Rules 2002.[90] The procedures are much the same as those noted above, except that the roles of the Secretary of State are largely taken by the Inspector himself, although certain notices and requirements particularly as to the provision of preliminary statements are reserved as a responsibility of the Secretary of State.

Enforcement appeal hearings

4–102　Where the parties agree that the enforcement appeal may be dealt with by informal hearing, the applicable rules are the Town and Country Planning (Enforcement) (Hearings Procedures) (England) Rules 2002.[91] Preliminary

---

[89] SI 2002/2686. Corresponding Rules for Wales are set out in SI 2003/1269.
[90] SI 2002/2685. Corresponding Rules for Wales are set out in SI 2003/1270.
[91] SI 2002/2684. Corresponding Rules for Wales are set out in SI 2003/1271.

procedures are largely the same as apply in the case of a full inquiry, but there is a greater discretion available to the inspector as to the method of proceeding, proofs of evidence and so on. A case involving a hearing will usually be for decision by the inspector himself. However, the procedure is equally applicable in cases where the Secretary of State reserves the obligation to make the decision.[92]

Written representations

The parties may agree that an enforcement appeal can be determined on   **4–103** the basis of written representations. In this case, the procedures are governed by the Town and Country Planning (Enforcement) (Written Representations Procedure) (England) Regulations 2002.[93] In these cases, the responsibility for the decision on the appeal is with the Secretary of State. As may be expected, the procedures involve the exchange of written statements by the parties, with an opportunity to comment on the opponent's statements. Timescales are set for each part of the process.

Secretary of State's powers on appeal

The Secretary of State or his inspector may quash, correct or vary the   **4–104** notice and he is also empowered to grant planning permission for the unauthorised development, either wholly or in part. He may discharge any condition or limitation which is the subject of the dispute. Note also that he has power to correct any defect, error or misdescription in the enforcement notice and may vary its terms if he is satisfied that this action will not cause injustice to the appellant or the local planning authority.[94]

Further appeal to the High Court

A dissatisfied party to an appeal inquiry who has an interest in the land may   **4–105** (with the court's permission) appeal to the High Court, but only on a point of law. There is a limited right to argue that the Secretary of State has insufficiently taken into account matters which were before him. The High Court may only remit the matter to the Secretary of State for reconsideration in the light of their guidance, but remission can open up the whole range of issues previously before the inquiry. Each of the sets of procedure rules (above) provide for these matters.

Enforcement notice pending appeal

Once an appeal has been made, and until it is finally determined, an   **4–106** enforcement notice is suspended unless the High Court or other Court of Appeal requires that interim effect be given to the notice, to an extent which the court will decide.

[92] Corresponding Rules for Wales are set out in SI 2003/395.
[93] SI 2002/2683.
[94] TCPA 1990, s.176.

Costs

4–107   The Secretary of State may make an order for costs in relation to an enforcement appeal inquiry on essentially the same basis as he may do in relation to an ordinary planning inquiry (see para.4–085 above).

Compliance with a valid enforcement notice

4–108   Assuming that the recipients or the appeal tribunal, High Court, etc. accept that an enforcement notice is valid, either wholly or in part, then compliance must be achieved within the time limits. Failure to comply is a criminal offence unless the defendant can show that he did everything reasonable to secure compliance. Non-compliance carries a fine not exceeding £20,000 in the magistrates' court but, on conviction on indictment, the fine can be unlimited. In imposing a penalty, the court can take into account the financial benefit achieved by the offender through non-compliance. In any prosecution for failure to comply with an enforcement notice, it is not open to the defendant to raise any issue concerning the validity of the notice if he did not raise this on any appeal against the notice.[95]

It is additionally open to the local planning authority to enter the land and itself carry out the steps required by the enforcement notice. The expenses of doing so may then be recovered from the landowner or the person who caused the breach of the planning control.[96]

Stop notices

4–109   Sometimes, a local planning authority may be faced with a breach of planning control which has serious consequences and this might well arise in the case of an unlawful waste management activity. It may not be sensible to await the delayed result of any appeal process. Section 183 of TCPA 1990 provides a remedy in the form of a stop notice. The notice may be served at any time either with the enforcement notice or subsequently, but not later than four years from the date when the activity started. The notice does not have a prescribed form but TCPA 1990 requires that it must:

   (a) refer to the relevant enforcement notice;
   (b) have a copy of that notice annexed to it; and
   (c) specify the date on which it is to take effect, which must not be earlier than three days from service (unless the local planning authority has special reasons for an earlier date) and not be later than 28 days from date of service.

[95] See *Vale of the White Horse v Treble-Parker* [1996] EGCS 40; see also the House of Lords supporting judgment in *R. v Wicks* [1997] J.P.L. 1049).
[96] TCPA 1990, s.178.

The notice will normally require cessation within a specific time limit. Failure to comply with the stop notice is a criminal offence, but there are special cases where compensation is payable in the event that the enforcement notice in question is discharged. However, such compensation is not available if the notice is simply quashed on the ground that planning permission should be granted. In certain circumstances compensation also follows the variation of an enforcement notice or the withdrawal of either notice.[97]

Penalties for failure to comply with a stop notice are set out in s.187. Note that there is no right of appeal against a stop notice. However, it may be appropriate to challenge the service of the notice by way of judicial review (*i.e.* reference to the court as to the validity of the notice or its procedures). Nonetheless, this is a limited basis of challenge (see para.4–084–90 above).

Temporary stop notice

Section 52 of the Planning and Compulsory Purchase Act 2004 provides **4–110** new powers to issue temporary stop notices where a local planning authority thinks that there has been a breach of planning control and that it is expedient that the activity in question is stopped immediately. New ss.171E–H are inserted by the Act and these provide for procedures, restrictions, offences and compensation. It should be noted that these provisions are not yet in force.

Breach of condition notice

PCA 1991 inserted s.187A into TCPA 1990 to provide for a new procedure **4–111** where conditions of a planning consent are not complied with. The breach of condition notice is served by the local planning authority in much the same way as an enforcement notice, either on the person carrying out the development or (if different) the person having control of the land. The notice requires compliance with conditions and must specify the steps required by the authority to be taken to secure compliance. The period allowed for compliance must be not less than 28 days from service of the notice. Non-compliance is a criminal offence unless the defendant establishes that he took all reasonable measures to secure compliance or that he did not have control of the land at the relevant time. The Act does not provide for any appeal against a breach of condition notice.

However, as with a challenge to a stop notice, it may be appropriate to proceed by way of judicial review (see above); see *Dilieto v Ealing LBC*.[98]

Injunctions

The High Court and county courts have powers to grant injunctions in **4–112** respect of any actual or apprehended breach of planning control, but the right to apply will usually be limited to cases where an injunction is

---

[97] Advice on stop notices is to be found in DoE Circular 10/97, Annex 3.
[98] [1998] 3 W.L.R. 1403.

necessary or expedient. This will almost always refer to flagrant breaches of the law including, perhaps, repeated failures to comply or to pay earlier fines.[99]

---

[99] TCPA 1990, s.187B.

CHAPTER 5

SPECIAL CONTROLS AVAILABLE TO LOCAL PLANNING AUTHORITIES

Local authorities have extensive powers and duties in relation to trees and **5–001** hedges. These fall into three broad categories:

   (a) A general duty under s.197 of TCPA 1990 to ensure, when granting planning permission, that sufficient provision is made by the imposition of conditions for the preservation or planting of trees.
   (b) To make tree preservation orders. Orders may be made in respect of individual trees, groups or woodlands (see TCPA 1990, s.198).
   (c) To enforce the requirements concerning hedgerows in accordance with s.97 of the Environment Act 1995 (see below).

Tree preservation orders

Orders are made by the local authority, which will usually prohibit the **5–002** cutting down, topping, lopping, uprooting, wilful damage or wilful destruction of trees without the authority's consent. The provision of replacement trees may be ordered. A preservation order may not be confirmed without giving owners, occupiers and the public the opportunity to make representations. The procedures are set out in the Town and Country Planning (Trees) Regulations 1999.[1]

Once the order is in force in relation to any given tree or trees then the action prohibited by the order can be taken only with the authority's approval, in respect of which conditions may be imposed. There is a right of appeal to the Secretary of State.

There are penalties for failure to comply with tree preservation orders.[2] Additional powers are available to require replacement of trees felled in the course of permitted forestry operations or illegally uprooted or destroyed.

There are various exemptions from the consent requirements. These include:

---

[1] SI 1999/1892.
[2] TCPA 1990, s.210.

- the cutting down, uprooting, topping or lopping of trees which are dying or dead or have become dangerous (there is normally a requirement to plant replacements);
- in compliance with obligations imposed under an Act of Parliament;
- for the prevention or abatement of a nuisance;
- during open cast operations;
- in accordance with operational forestry plans;
- where the cutting down, etc. is authorised by planning permission;
- in the case of certain cultivated fruit trees;
- in the case of certain trees affected by the operations of statutory undertakers;
- where the tree in question interferes with electricity lines;
- in the case of certain felling authorised by a felling licence under the Forestry Act 1967;
- to enable the EA to undertake certain development under the Town and Country Planning (General Permitted Development) Order 1995; and
- where certain trees interfere with or are likely to interfere with the obligations of a drainage body constituted under the Land Drainage Act 1991.

In certain circumstances compensation may be paid under the 1999 Regulations where an application in relation to a tree has been refused.

Conservation areas

5–003   Special controls for trees are also imposed by s.211 of TCPA 1990 where such trees are located in a conservation area. In simple terms, all trees in conservation areas are the subject of the same controls as if they were protected by a tree preservation order.

Hedges

5–004   The Hedgerow Regulations 1997[3] were made under the provisions of s.97 of the Environment Act 1995 and came into force on June 1, 1997. The Regulations restrict, subject to certain exceptions, the removal of any hedgerow growing in or adjacent to any common land, nature reserves or areas of special scientific interest or land used for agriculture, forestry or the breeding or keeping of horses, ponies or donkeys, provided it has a continuous length of at least 20 metres or, if less than this, intersects or connects with another hedgerow. Most hedgerows associated with dwelling-houses are not controlled.

[3] SI 1997/1160.

Hedgerows the subject of the Regulations may not be removed unless notice has been given by the owner to the local planning authority, which has 42 days in which to approve. Where approval has been signified or there has been no decision within the 42 days, there is a right to remove, provided it is carried out in accordance with the proposal and within two years of the date of service of the notice. If the local planning authority oppose the removal, it may respond with a hedgerow retention notice but may only do this if the hedgerow falls within a category specified as "important". The Regulations identify a hedgerow as important if it or the hedge of which it is a part has existed for 30 years or more and satisfies at least one of the criteria listed in Pt II of Sch.1 to the Regulations. These criteria relate to archaeological, historic, wildlife and landscape factors.

A hedgerow removal is permitted without the need for the above procedure in a range of circumstances identified in reg.6. These include obtaining access to land, for national defence, in accordance with permitted development, for flood defence or land drainage reasons, for pest control, for certain highway functions, for the prevention of interference with electricity lines or for the proper management of the hedgerow.

Failure to comply with the Regulations is an offence, subject to a fine. A hedgerow removed in contravention of a regulation may be the subject of a notice to the owner requiring replanting. Appeals against a hedgerow retention notice may be made to the Secretary of State within 28 days (reg.9). For a case concerning an unsuccessful prosecution for hedgerow removal see *Conwy CBC v Robert Lloyd*.[4]

POWER TO REQUIRE PROPER MAINTENANCE OF LAND

There will be many occasions where land not the subject of appropriate conditions under a planning consent is in such a condition that it affects the amenity of an area adversely. A little known but very useful power is available in s.215 of TCPA 1990, which provides that in these circumstances the local authority may serve a notice on the owner and occupier of the land in question, requiring steps to remedy the condition of the land. It is an offence to fail to comply with the notice, but there is a right of appeal against its requirements to the magistrates' court under s.217 of TCPA 1990. The Town and Country Planning General (Amendment) Regulations 1997[5] allow local authorities to place a charge on land to recover their expenditure on the clean-up of sites under s.215. See also DETR Circular 2/98, "Prevention of Dereliction through the Planning System". **5–005**

ADVERTISEMENTS

In general, advertisements are controlled by s.220 of TCPA 1990, although the detail is contained in the Town and Country Planning (Control of Advertisements) Regulations 1992,[6] as amended. The description is defined widely to include: **5–006**

[4] Unreported, February 3, 2003, Administrative Court.
[5] SI 1997/3006.
[6] SI 1992/666.

"any word, letter, model, sign, placard, board, notice, awning, blind, device or representation, whether illuminated or not, in the nature of and employed wholly or partly for the purposes of, advertisement, announcement or direction, and (without prejudice to the previous provisions of this definition), includes any hoarding or similar structure used or designed or adapted for use and anything else principally used or designed or adapted principally for use for the display of advertisements, and references to the display of advertisements shall be construed accordingly."

A number of advertisements are made exempt, as described in Sch.2 to the Regulations. These exceptions relate mainly to simple advertisements or notices (*e.g.* displayed on enclosed land or in a vehicle, traffic signs and displays inside a building).

A second classification of advertisement carries a deemed consent under the Regulations, but such consent may be removed either by the Secretary of State or by a planning authority. There are various classes of deemed consent advertisements, including those relating to premises on which they are displayed, temporary advertisements, flags, hoardings, highway structures, etc. However, close attention needs to be paid to the detailed descriptions and the conditions and limitations of each consent. These are all set out in the Regulations.

Applications for consent

5–007   No special planning permission is required for an advertisement if it has approval under the Regulations. Otherwise, all advertisements need to be the subject of an application for formal consent by the local planning authority, for which fees are payable.

Areas of special control

5–008   Some areas, both rural and urban, are designated by the Secretary of State as of special control, usually on the grounds of special amenity. In these areas there are no general rights to display commercial advertisements, and other non-commercial advertisements are limited. These are also described in the Regulations.

Enforcement

5–009   Section 224 of TCPA 1990 provides for a local planning authority to require the removal of advertisements which do not comply. A person who displays an advertisement in contravention of the Regulations is committing a criminal offence, although there are some limited defences.

Further information

See DoE Circulars 5/92 and 15/94 and PPG19, "Outdoor Advertisement   **5–010**
Control".

PLANNING (LISTED BUILDINGS AND CONSERVATION AREAS) ACT 1990

When planning legislation was consolidated in 1990 it was apparent that the   **5–011**
branch of the law dealing with control of buildings of special architectural
or historic interest was sufficiently comprehensive as to justify its own
separate act. Until then such controls had been embodied largely in TCPA
1971.

Listed buildings (Part I)

Lists of special buildings

Arrangements for control are based upon the provision by the Secretary of   **5–012**
State of lists of buildings of special architectural or historic interest. In
practice, the compilation of the list is the role of the Historic Buildings and
Monuments Commission (better known as English Heritage). The Commission compiles and publishes lists and amendments thereto and the Secretary of State has the statutory responsibility for approval (s.1).

Definition of "listed building"

The definition of "listed building" is important because it includes "any   **5–013**
object or structure fixed to the building or within the curtilage of the
building which although not fixed to the building forms part of the land and
has done so before 1 July 1948". This usually means that enclosure walls,
outbuildings and other structures within the immediate vicinity of a
building can also be regarded as controlled. The definition of "building" is
also relevant. The Act defines "the building" in the same way as in TCPA
1990, so as to include "any structure or erection and any part of a building
as so defined, but does not include plant or machinery comprised in a
building". However, there is an important caveat in that the TCPA 1990
definition only applies "except insofar as the context otherwise requires".
The difference in approach was highlighted in the House of Lords
judgment in *Shimizu (UK) Limited v Westminster City Council*.[7] In that case,
the court found that the definition in the TCPA 1990 did not apply.

Procedure following listing

The placing of a building on the list has immediate effect. The local   **5–014**
planning authority is notified and it, in turn, is required to ensure that every
owner and occupier is advised (s.2). There is no right of appeal against

---

[7] [1997] 1 All E.R. 481.

listing, but requests for delisting can be made to the Secretary of State.[8] Lists are kept by the local planning authority (usually the unitary or district council in England and Wales) and are open to public inspection.

Advice whether a building will be listed

5–015   An owner or potential purchaser may wish to be assured that a building nwill not be listed. There is a procedure in s.6 of the Act whereby the Secretary of State can be asked to confirm that he will not list a building. Such confirmation guarantees against listing for five years. The application may be made by anyone, but only where an application has been made or granted for planning permission authorising the alteration, extension or demolition of the building in question. The section is useful in that, without the guarantee, both the Secretary of State and the local planning authority have certain powers to list on an emergency basis and otherwise. While the effect may only be temporary, this can sometimes be disruptive from the point of view of any new and unsuspecting owner or developer.

Effect of listing

5–016   The result of placing a building on the list is that no person may execute or cause to be executed any works for the demolition of a listed building or for its alteration or extension in any manner which would affect its character as a building of special architectural or historic interest, unless those works are authorised (s.7). The practical effect is that only works authorised by a listed building consent under s.8 will be lawful. The failure to follow the procedures in s.7 or to comply with the requirements of any authorisation granted under s.8 will usually result in the commission of a criminal offence (s.9).

Listed building consent

5–017   Consent under the Act is required in addition to any planning permission under TCPA 1990. The procedure is similar to that for a planning application and is set down in the Planning (Listed Buildings and Conservation Areas) Regulations 1990.[9] A form of application is obtainable from the local planning authority. The authority has the responsibility to advertise the application. Certain amenity groups are entitled to notification, as well as the Historic Buildings and Monuments Commission (English Heritage). There are rights of appeal against the refusal of consent or against conditions imposed on any approval. Following consent, notification to English Heritage is required by the applicant before any demolition can take place. English Heritage are authorised to have access to the building for at least one month after listed building consent has been granted but before any demolition works may start, unless they have stated in writing that they have completed their recording or do not wish to record it.[10]

[8] See PPG15, "Planning and the Historic Environment", para.6.26.
[9] SI 1990/1519.
[10] For further information see DETR Circular 01/01, "Arrangements for Handling Heritage Applications—Notification and Directions by the Secretary of State".

Enforcement

The local authority has the power to issue enforcement notices if   **5–018**
unauthorised works have been carried out on a listed building where prior
consent was necessary (s.38). Restoration to its former state or the
undertaking of appropriate works to alleviate the effect of the unauthorised
works can be required. There are rights of appeal to the Secretary of State
against the enforcement notice, but once it takes effect there is criminal
liability for failing to comply. There are no time limits for the service of an
enforcement notice (s.39), even where ownership changes have taken place.
In the event that a valid notice is not complied with, the local planning
authority may take the steps required by the notice and recover its expenses
from the landowner (s.42). For the legal basis upon which expenses can be
claimed, see *R. v Secretary of State for Wales Ex p. The City and County of
Swansea.*[11]

Neglect of listed buildings

Owners are not formally obliged to maintain listed buildings in good repair,   **5–019**
at least under the Act. There may be other powers,[12] and local and other
legislation to require unsafe or ruinous buildings to be attended to. The
only effective powers available to local planning authorities under the Act
are:

    (a) to serve a repairs notice under s.48 of the Act;
    (b) to follow up with compulsory acquisition (s.47); and
    (c) to undertake urgent works to preserve an unoccupied listed
        building and require the cost to be paid by the owner (ss.54, 55),
        but this power is subject to notice and other conditions.

Compensation on compulsory acquisition

An owner and other persons with an interest may be entitled to compensa-   **5–020**
tion on the acquisition of a listed building. Normal valuation principles
apply, with one important exception: a listed building deliberately left
derelict attracts only minimum compensation. The effect is that compensation will be restricted to the market value of the building as it stands
without any prospect of development.

General guidance

Guidance on listed buildings is available in PPG15 (see para.5–014 above).   **5–021**
However, note the modifications published by the DETR in Environment
Circular 14/97, "Planning and the Historic Environment—Notification and
Directions by the Secretary of State".

Conservation areas (Part II)

Conservation areas are areas designated of special architectural or historic   **5–022**
interest, the character or appearance of which it is desirable to preserve or
enhance. Further information is available in the Department of the

---

[11] [1999] J.P.L. 5243.
[12] *e.g.* under TCPA 1990, s.215—see para.5–005 above.

Environment and Department of National Heritage guidance note PPG15 (see para.5–014 above). It follows that an area can include not only buildings but other features, including the setting of buildings. The most obvious conservation areas will include historic towns and cities and attractive villages.

The effect of designation

5–023   There are a number of consequences of designation, but the main ones are:

     (a) demolition of most buildings is forbidden without consent;

     (b) the cutting down or interference with trees is prohibited without consent;

     (c) the local planning authority, when considering planning applications etc., must pay special attention to the desirability of preserving or enhancing the area's character or appearance. For guidance on the proper approach to the local planning authority's duties, see the House of Lords' judgment in *South Lakeland DC v Secretary of State for the Environment*[13];

     (d) general development order rights (see para.4–009 above) are restricted, as are rights to display certain advertisements.

Planning policy guidance

5–024   Further information is available from PPG15 (see para.5–014 above), published jointly by the Departments of the Environment and National Heritage.

ANCIENT MONUMENTS AND ARCHAEOLOGICAL AREAS ACT 1979

5–025   Although there is a relationship between this Act and the 1990 legislation relating to listed buildings and conservation areas, no attempt has been made to consolidate the 1979 Act. However, the procedures have some similarities.

Schedule of monuments

5–026   By s.1 of the Act, the Secretary of State is required to maintain a schedule of monuments and keep it up to date. The definition of "monument" is extensive, but can include a building, structure or work, cave or excavation and can comprise the whole or part or remains of any vehicle, vessel, aircraft or other movable structure. The concept is primarily the protection of nationally important features of historic, architectural, traditional, artistic or archaeological interest.

The effect of scheduling

5–027   Section 2 of the Act creates a criminal offence if any person executes, or causes or permits to be executed, any works resulting in the demolition or destruction of or any damage to a scheduled monument, any works for

[13] [1992] 1 All E.R. 573.

removing or repairing it, or any flooding or tipping operations where a scheduled monument exists. However, consent to works to, or affecting, an ancient monument may be granted by the Secretary of State, subject to conditions. The Secretary of State has powers of entry and execution of works for the preservation of a scheduled monument in cases of urgency. Compensation may be payable under s.7 in certain circumstances.

Archaeological areas

Part II of the 1979 Act relates primarily to the carrying out of rescue **5–028** archaeology in circumstances where authorised development may destroy archaeological remains. The Act provides for the designation of areas as of archaeological importance. The effect is that any person requiring to carry out operations to disturb the ground, or involving flooding or tipping within such an area, must give the local authority six weeks' notice, known as an "operations notice". Powers are available to the local authority or other "investigating authorities" (often a local archaeological society) to undertake investigations. This authority may examine the site (including excavation) and may record its findings. It has up to four months and two weeks from the expiry of the operations notice. During this time, on pain of criminal action, none of the operations mentioned above may be carried out by the developer. It will be appreciated that if a rescue excavation identifies an important archaeological site there is a likelihood of its being scheduled as a monument under s.1 of the Act (see above).

Further information

The DoE has published a planning policy guidance note relating to **5–029** archaeology and planning.[14]

PLANNING (HAZARDOUS SUBSTANCES) ACT 1990

This Act, like the Planning (Listed Buildings and Conservation Areas) Act **5–030** 1990, establishes a regime of special control in town and country planning. Its provisions started life by being introduced into TCPA 1971. Now, following the 1990 consolidation, the regime merits a separate measure. It exists primarily because of advancing public concern, in the 1970s particularly, that there were considerable gaps in the control of the storage and use of hazardous substances on land. While, by the Health and Safety at Work etc. Act 1974 and other legislation, certain controls relating to safety had been imposed, these did not go far enough to provide the local planning authority with a sufficiency of control in the interests of its

[14] See PPG16.

community as a whole. Because the town and country planning legislation normally permits, without formal application, a range of changes of use, primarily through the GDPO 1995 (see para.4–009) and the Use Classes Order (see para.4–006), it was possible to secure a change to a use involving hazardous activities without any adequate check on questions of public amenity and safety.

The controls

5–031 The controls were introduced in two main steps. In 1983, amendments were made to the GDPO 1995 and the Use Classes Order, which effectively removed the immunity from planning control where development involved a notifiable quantity of hazardous substances. Since the introduction of such substances to a site might not involve a material change of use, these amendments do not go far enough, and, by the Housing and Planning Act 1986, TCPA 1971 was modified to introduce the new system of control. This is now embodied in the Planning (Hazardous Substances) Act 1990. The provisions came into force on June 1, 1992.

What are hazardous substances?

5–032 The term "hazardous substance" is not defined by the Act, but by s.5 the Secretary of State is given power to make regulations which identify a list and the quantity of each substance which will be liable to control. These are scheduled in the Planning (Hazardous Substances) Regulations 1992,[15] as amended by the Planning (Control of Major Accident Hazards) Regulations 1999.[16] The Act and the Regulations exempt some substances, controlled by other legislation, including explosives,[17] controlled waste[18] and radioactive waste.[19] There are also exceptions from the requirements for consent. These are also set out in the Act and the Regulations.

The system of control

5–033 By the terms of the Act, the presence on, over or under land of any hazardous substance beyond the controlled quantity requires consent from the hazardous substances authority. This authority is usually the local planning authority (*i.e.* mainly the unitary and district councils), but note that, in relation to land used for mineral working or waste disposal, the authority will be the county council (where this exists), as it usually is for

---

[15] SI 1992/656.
[16] SI 1999/981.
[17] Explosives Act 1875.
[18] EPA 1990 (see para.10–031 below).
[19] Radioactive Substances Act 1993.

normal planning control. Applications for consent will be made to the authority, which will consult with the Health and Safety Executive as appropriate and may then grant consent unconditionally or subject to conditions, or may refuse. There are rights of appeal to the Secretary of State and he has other powers of intervention. From June 1, 1992 there was a transitional period of six months where any applicant with hazardous substances present on land 12 months before the commencement date was entitled to a consent as of right. However, an application needed to be made within the six-month period.

Enforcement and other controls

Section 23 of the Act creates various offences. These arise if a person has   **5–034** hazardous substances on land equal to or in excess of the controlled quantity and he has no consent, or the quantity is in excess of what has been consented. An offence also arises where there has been a failure to comply with a condition of the consent. The maximum penalty is a fine of £20,000, where there is a conviction in the magistrates' court, or an unlimited fine where conviction is on indictment. Furthermore, the authority has power to issue a hazardous substances contravention notice, which has similarities to a standard enforcement notice, identifying the alleged contravention and the steps required to remedy. There are certain exemptions from liability to the service of a notice set out in s.23 and there are rights of appeal to the Secretary of State (ss.24 and 25).

The hazardous substances authority may also revoke or modify a consent under s.14. Compensation is payable in certain cases. Such an order is required to be confirmed by the Secretary of State.

It is important to note that on any change in control of the land in question a hazardous substances consent comes to an end automatically. It follows that prior to the date of change of control, a new consent will be required.

Further information

See DETR Circular 04/00, "Planning controls for hazardous substances".   **5–035**

Relationship with health and safety legislation

The Act acknowledges the likelihood that there will be duplicate controls in   **5–036** that the Health and Safety at Work etc. Act 1974 will continue to apply. This is resolved in s.29 of the Act, which makes clear that in the event of any conflict between the two regimes, action taken under the 1974 Act will prevail.

CHAPTER 6

OTHER LEGISLATION RELEVANT TO DEVELOPMENT CONTROL

NATIONAL PARKS AND ACCESS TO THE COUNTRYSIDE ACT 1949

This Act made provision for national parks in England and Wales,   **6–001**
established systems for control and regulation and largely consolidated the
law relating to public rights of way. The Act has been modified on a
number of occasions, notably by the Countryside Act 1968, the Wildlife and
Countryside Act 1981 and the Countryside and Rights of Way Act 2000
(see below). Changes to administrative arrangements were introduced by
the Environmental Protection Act 1990 and the Environment Act 1995.
Administration is largely in the hands of:

(a) the Secretary of State for Environment Food and Rural Affairs
    who has a general overseeing role; however, with effect from July
    6, 1999 almost all functions in relation to Wales were taken over
    by the National Assembly for Wales;

(b) the Countryside Agency and the Countryside Council for Wales
    have responsibility for designation of national parks and areas of
    outstanding natural beauty as confirmed by the Secretary of State;
    there is also a general advisory role;

(c) the Nature Conservancy Councils (one each for England, Scotland
    and Wales) have responsibility for designation and maintenance of
    nature reserves and sites of special scientific interest; the NCC for
    England is more usually known as "English Nature"; and

(d) each of the national parks is now administered by a separate
    authority responsible for the exercise of all functions of a district
    or county council, including town and country planning and
    related legislation; functions in national parks, other than plan-
    ning, will be undertaken normally by central agencies such as the
    Health and Safety Executive and the EA, but otherwise the
    national park authority assumes the functions of all local govern-
    ment responsibilities.

CARAVAN SITES AND CONTROL OF DEVELOPMENT ACT 1960

The use of land for stationing a caravan requires planning permission, but   **6–002**
exemptions are provided in certain circumstances. The Caravan Sites and
Control of Development Act 1960 introduces a second layer of control, in

that once planning permission is obtained a site licence may be required in a range of circumstances. However, Sch.1 to the Act provides a number of exemptions (*e.g.* where use is required for agricultural and forestry workers or on building and engineering sites).

COUNTRYSIDE ACT 1968

6–003 See the National Parks and Access to the Countryside Act 1949, above.

WILDLIFE AND COUNTRYSIDE ACT 1981

6–004 The Wildlife and Countryside Act 1981 is an important Act, containing provisions of some significance to the waste management industry concerning the protection of wildlife (Pt I) and nature conservation and national parks (Pt II). The Act has been amended by the Countryside and Rights of Way Act 2000 (see below).

Sites of special scientific interest (SSSIs)

6–005 Areas of special importance because of flora, fauna, geological or physiographical features are required to be notified to local planning authorities for the area in question, owners and occupiers and the Secretary of State (s.28). Responsibility for notification rests with English Nature, Scottish National Heritage and the Countryside Council for Wales. There is no appeal against a notification, but the opportunity is available to make representations (*e.g.* that the designation is inappropriate). Sometimes, there may be an opportunity to challenge the designation on procedural grounds.[1] The effect of designation is that the existence of an SSSI is required to be taken into account by the planning authority in undertaking particularly its development control responsibilities. The notification will specify why the site is special and will identify any operation regarded by the council as harmful. Some of these operations may not normally require planning permission (*e.g.* ploughing), but under the Act they may not be carried out unless the NCC has first been notified and there is a formal consent or agreement, or a period of four months has expired since the notice was given.

Changes in the Act of 2000

6–006 The Countryside and Rights of Way Act 2000 effected significant changes to the law relating to SSSIs. The effect of the changes is to:

---

[1] See, for example, *R. v Nature Conservancy Council Ex p. Bolton MCB* [1996] J.P.L. 203 and *R. v Nature Conservancy Council Ex p. London Brick Property Ltd* [1996] J.P.L. 227.

(a) secure improvement in the systems for protection and management of SSSIs;

(b) provide increased powers for the conservation agencies;

(c) provide for management schemes aimed at overcoming neglect. A system of management notices is established and there is now power to refuse consent for activities which are likely to be damaging to the SSSI. Appeal procedures are added;

(d) greater powers for English Nature and the other agencies to enter land in pursuance of the provisions of the legislation;

(e) new powers to purchase land compulsorily;

(f) increases in penalties for deliberate damage, including fines of up to £20,000 for conviction in the magistrates' court and unlimited fines in the Crown Court. The power is available for the court to order restoration of any damage;

(g) a new offence relating to any damage to an SSSI.

Guidance has been published in 2003 by DEFRA.[2]

EU Habitats Directive

The requirements for the protection of the natural environment set out in the Habitats Directive[3] are in part implemented by the Conservation (Natural Habitats, etc.) Regulations 1994.[4] The relevant Nature Conservancy body must exercise its functions under the Acts in accordance with the Directive. See also the Conservation (Natural Habitats etc.) (Amendment) (England) Regulations 2000.[5] Guidance appears in Planning Policy Guidance Note PPG9 on Nature Conservation, supplemented by DEFRA Circular 2/2002, "New Guidance for Local Authorities on European Protected Species and Changes in Licensing Procedures".   **6–007**

DERELICT LAND ACT 1982

The Derelict Land Act 1982 gives power to the Secretary of State for the Environment Food and Rural Affairs and the Welsh Development Agency to pay to any person grants to reclaim derelict land or to enable that land to be brought into use. The grant is payable in respect of derelict, neglected or unsightly land, or land which is apprehended by the local authority to be likely to become so in certain circumstances. Grants are payable not only for works, but also for surveys. In the case of apprehended dereliction etc., grant aid is payable only to the local authority, but otherwise it is available to any applicant, up to 100 per cent in respect of development areas, intermediate areas and derelict land clearance areas.   **6–008**

---

[2] "Sites of Special Scientific Interest: Encouraging Positive Partnerships".
[3] 92/43/EEC.
[4] SI 1994/2716.
[5] SI 2000/192.

Highways, bridleways and footpaths

6–009   The obstruction of highways (including bridleways and footpaths) is usually an offence under highways law. Obstructions can include development across the highway and, therefore, waste managers need to be particularly careful to avoid encroachments.

Diversion and closure of highways

6–010   Extinguishment and diversion of public rights of way, whether roads, bridleways, footpaths or others, are controlled mainly by orders made under Pt VIII of the Highways Act 1980 and Pt X of TCPA 1990. In those cases, where development granted by a planning permission is prevented by the existence of a public path, applications may be made under the 1990 Act.[6]

Interference with highways

6–011   Under Pt IV of the Highways Act 1980 there are a number of provisions for the general protection of public rights to use highways. However, there will be occasions when private bodies, including waste managers, may need to make alterations to a highway. This will often arise following the grant of planning permission which imposes conditions requiring improvement of access, sight lines, etc. The work will normally be carried out by arrangement with the highways authority, but the authority may authorise works where they disturb a footpath or bridleway.[7]

Countryside and Rights of Way Act 2000

6–012   This Act makes important changes and introduces new rights in relation to the countryside and access to it—see earlier references above.

Access to the countryside

6–013   Part I of the Act introduces a new right to roam over open land in England and Wales. The provisions are not yet fully in force but it is ultimately intended to provide a right of access on foot for recreational purposes. The right will apply to "access land" as defined in s.2. This definition includes:

> (a) Open country or registered common land—to be illustrated on maps to be prepared by the Countryside Agency and the Countryside Council for Wales. "Open country" is defined as including

---

[6] For further details see Pt X of TCPA 1990 and the Town and Country Planning (Public Path Orders) Regulations 1993 (SI 1993/10); see also DoE Circular 2/93, "Public Rights of Way".
[7] Highways Act 1980, s.135.

mountain, moor, heath or down but excluding improved or semi-improved grassland. Some land, defined as "excepted land", is excluded from that where a right of access is available. This excepted land will include land ploughed or drilled in the previous year, quarries, gardens, land within the curtilage of buildings and livestock areas.

(b) Land over 600 metres above sea level or certain registered common land.

(c) Certain land subject to voluntary access arrangements.

The Countryside Agencies are required to publish (with maps) proposals for designating the land as open country and registered common land. Landowners have a right of appeal to the Secretary of State or to the National Assembly for Wales against the inclusion of their land in provisional maps.

Even if land is designated as open land, access to the public can be excluded or restricted in the following ways:

(i) for a period of up to 28 days in any year;

(ii) (with authority from the Countryside Agencies) for land management purposes, for safety reasons or to avoid the risk of fire, for the protection of nature conservation or historical heritage;

(iii) with approval of the Secretary of State (national security or defence reasons).

The exercise of rights of access can be limited. For example, the lighting of fires, swimming, interfering with livestock, hunting, the disturbance of lawful activities, the feeding of livestock or the use of a metal detector are all forbidden.

See also the Access to the Countryside (Provisional and Conclusive Maps) (England) Regulations 2002.[8]

Other changes

Amendments were made to provisions for the control of highways and other rights of way (see above) as well as nature conservation and areas of outstanding natural beauty.   6–014

DETR Circular 04/2001, "Countryside and Rights of Way Act 2000"

This covers in some detail the new provisions relating to rights of way, common land, nature conservation and wildlife protection and areas of outstanding natural beauty. It deals with a new category of restricted byway   6–015

---

[8] SI 2003/32. DEFRA has published on July 26, 2002 a circular letter which is intended to assist with interpretation of the regulations.

which will have the effect of excluding mechanically propelled vehicles, enhanced powers to regulate traffic in the interests of conserving natural beauty in national parks, AONB's etc, to include unclassified roads and byways outside these special areas and a requirement for an AONB management plan including the setting up of conservation boards with management responsibilities.

PART III

ENVIRONMENTAL LEGISLATION RELATING TO WASTE PRODUCTION AND DISPOSAL

CHAPTER 7

WATER: ABSTRACTION AND POLLUTION

INTRODUCTION

Following the Water Act (WA) 1989, responsibility for control of water **7–001** abstraction was with the National Rivers Authority (NRA). The Water Resources Act 1963 was the first statutory provision to impose a comprehensive control over the abstraction and impounding of water. With the coming into force of this Act, abstraction and impounding were forbidden, except by licence of the various regional river authorities set up at that time. Some exceptions were allowed (*e.g.* in connection with domestic and some agricultural uses). The prohibition was in respect not only of abstraction from a surface supply, such as a river or lake, but also from any well or borehole designed to withdraw water from underground.

There were exceptions which permitted abstraction for the purposes of land drainage or to prevent interference with mining, quarrying, engineering, building or a similar operation.

Responsibility for control of water abstraction and water pollution is now vested primarily in the Environment Agency (EA) under WRA 1991, as amended by the Environment Act 1995.

In respect of most water legislation, consolidating Acts were passed during 1991. Abstraction of water is now the subject of WRA 1991, which came into force on December 1, 1991. Restrictions on abstraction are now controlled by s.24. The right to impound an inland water is restricted by s.25. Impounding is defined as including the provision of a dam, weir or works for diversion. A licence for such works may be granted under s.34 and subsequent sections.

WATER ACT 2003

The main provisions of this Act are not yet in force but it is nonetheless of **7–002** considerable importance to the waste management industry implementing as it does the EU Water Framework Directive.[1] The overall aim of the Act is to implement steps to improve water conservation and management and to create a more stable and transparent regulatory environment. The Act makes provisions for:

---

[1] (2000/60/EC—see para.15–004.

- a requirement for an abstraction licence where at least 20 cu metres of water is extracted per day;
- simplification of the application process for licences and modifications and transfers of licences;
- a new regulatory authority, the Water Service Regulation Authority, and a new independent Consumer Council for Water;
- changes to the definition of contaminated land in relation to water pollution in order that minor cases of water pollution are not subject to inappropriate remediation requirements;

- improved arrangements for the funding for flood defences.

Water Framework Directive Regulations 2003

7–003　Complementing the Water Act 2003, the Water Environment (Water Framework Directive) England and Wales Regulations 2003[2] brought into force on January 2, 2004, certain obligations of the directive. This transposition exercise is only the first step in relation to the directive and the Act; other regulations and controls will follow. Indeed, "daughter" directives will emerge from the EU. In general terms, the regulations require production by December 22, 2004 of an analysis of the characteristics of each river basin district and the impact of human activity on surface and groundwaters along with an economic analysis by the Secretary of State and the Welsh Assembly, by the same date. The Agency is required to identify water used for human consumption and the measures for protection. The Agency must produce proposals for environmental objectives and the measures to achieve these. These are to be provided by December 22, 2009 and shall be made operational three years thereafter. The Agency is also required to submit appropriate river basin management plans no later than December 22, 2009. All plans and proposals will be subject to regular review.

LICENCES TO ABSTRACT WATER

7–004　Under WRA 1991 there are a limited number of people who may apply for a licence to abstract. Occupation is usually required of the land adjacent to the inland water or above the strata from which the water is drawn.

Inland water

7–005　An inland water is defined by s.221 of WRA 1991 and, in general, includes a river, stream or other watercourse, either natural, artificial or tidal. The definition includes any lake or pond, reservoir or dock. It does not matter whether the water resource is natural or artificial. The definition includes so

[2] SI 2003/3242.

much of any channel, creek, bay, estuary or arm of the sea which lies within the administration area. Precise boundaries are identified by the EA. A person who wishes to abstract from an inland water must be the occupier of land on its bank or have right of access. The right merely to insert a pipe into, for example, a river, granted by the riparian landowner, will suffice for this purpose.

Underground strata

Section 221 defines underground strata which has its general everyday meaning. The person who may be authorised to abstract is the occupier of the land where the underground strata is. Where there is an excavation into underground strata, such as a well or adit, the person who has a right of access to the land above the underground strata is the person entitled to apply for the licence.

7–006

Applications for licences to abstract

The Water Resources (Licences) Regulations 1965[3] provide the procedure for applications. An application is made to the EA on the form which is obtainable from them. The application must be accompanied by a map to a scale not less than six inches to one mile or the metric equivalent and must show every point of abstraction proposed and the land occupied by the applicant. Invariably, the application must also show the land on which it is proposed to use the water. Where water is to be used for different purposes, these should be distinguished on the map. Sometimes the applicant is not the occupier and, in these circumstances, evidence must show that access to the relevant land will be available if the licence is granted (*e.g.* by a letter showing landowner's intent etc.). A fee is payable for the application, according to a scheme made under s.41 of the Environment Act 1995.

7–007

Publicity for applications

Section 37 of WRA 1991 provides for publicity in relation to applications in two ways. First, a notice of the application for a licence must be published in the London Gazette, as well as at least once in each of two successive weeks in local newspapers. If the licence is for abstraction from an inland water then, on or before the date on which it was first published in the local newspaper, notice must be given to any navigation authority, harbour authority or conservancy authority responsible for the inland water where the abstraction is proposed. Other interested parties to be served with notice are any internal drainage board and any local water undertaker.

7–008

---

[3] SI 1965/534.

The newspaper notice is to be in the form set out in Sch.2 to the 1965 Regulations.

Documents required for the application

7–009   The following documents must be supplied on application:

- form of application;
- the plans;
- copies of the newspapers containing the appropriate notices and a declaration signed on behalf of the applicant that the notice has been published in the London Gazette (giving the date of publication). This declaration must also identify details of any notices served on any authority.

Application period

7–010   The EA has three months to consider applications. In default of their decision within that period, or such extended period as is agreed with the applicant, there may be an appeal to the Secretary of State on grounds of non-determination. Procedures for appeals are governed by reg.12 of the 1965 Regulations.

Application for impounding

7–011   Procedure is controlled by reg.8 of the 1965 Regulations and is much the same as that for an application for an abstraction licence. The documents to be submitted must include not only an application form, but also a map showing the location of the impounding works and the extent of land to be submerged, together with any points of discharge. Newspaper advertisements and notices to other authorities are required in the same way as a licence to abstract. A fee is chargeable according to a scheme made under s.41 of the Environment Act 1995.

Sometimes a combined abstraction and impounding licence needs to be sought; the requirements are set out in reg.8.

Succession to a licence

7–012   Sections 49 and 50 of WRA 1991 deal with the transfer of a licence from one abstractor to another, usually on the succession of the latter to occupation of the land where the abstraction takes place. The procedure is mainly a formal matter of notification to the EA.[4]

---

[4] See also the Water Resources (Succession to Licences) Regulations 1969, SI 1969/976.

Revocation or variation of a licence

The procedures for revocation or variation are different, depending upon   **7–013**
whether the proposal is made by the licence holder or by the EA. An
application by a holder is a simple procedure under s.51 of WRA 1991 and
reg.9 of the 1965 Regulations. In the case of variation, the procedures for
publicity will apply as they do for the original licence application (see
above), unless the variation relates merely to reducing the quantity of water
authorised to be abstracted.

Where the initiative for revocation or variation is with the EA, there is
an obligation to notify the holder and give publicity similar to that
mentioned above. The holder has a right to object (s.53), at which stage the
proposals are referred to the Secretary of State, who will make the decision.
Where no objection is raised the matter may be resolved by the EA. In
some cases (see s.61), compensation for revocation or variation will follow.

Appeals

There are rights of appeal against decisions of the EA or as a consequence   **7–014**
of its failure to reach a decision within specified time limits. The appeal is
made to the Secretary of State. The appeal is required to be in writing and
a copy must be served on the EA. This must be undertaken within 28 days
from the date when any decision was notified to the appellant.

Charges for water abstraction

The EA has power to make schemes imposing water resources charges both   **7–015**
for licences under WRA 1991 and for the abstraction of water once
licensed.[5] The EA publishes schemes from time to time.

Environment Act 1995

The primary function of the 1995 Act was to establish the EA (for England   **7–016**
and Wales) and the Scottish Environmental Protection Agency. The EA
took over all the functions of the NRA with effect from April 1, 1996.
These functions included water resources management, control of water
pollution, flood defence and land drainage and responsibilities relating to
fisheries. It also assumed certain air pollution and waste management
duties respectively from H.M. Inspectorate of Pollution and the waste
regulation authorities (see below). Section 6 of the Act imposed a duty on
the EA (but within its own discretion) to promote the conservation and
enhancement of natural beauty and amenity of inland and coastal waters

---

[5] Environment Act 1995, s.41.

and of land associated with such waters. It also has a similar duty in regard to the conservation of flora and fauna dependent on the aquatic environment. Finally, the duty extends to the promotion of the use of waters and land for recreational purposes.

The EA is responsible primarily to the Secretary of State for the Environment, Food and Rural Affairs, but there are lines of responsibility also to the Welsh Assembly.

Drought

7–017 WRA 1991 introduced provisions for the control of water supply in times of drought. A supply by a pipeline from a water company is often regulated by a formal agreement which should contain provisions which will apply in the event of drought. Furthermore, operating agreements made between the EA and water undertakers under s.20 of WRA 1991 will usually contain provisions.

Drought orders

7–018 Drought orders (in different form) will usually be made under s.74 of WRA 1991. The Secretary of State (or the Welsh Assembly in Wales) must be satisfied that by reason of an exceptional shortage of rain a serious deficiency of water supplies exists or is threatened in any area. Where it seems likely that the drought will impair the economic or social well-being of persons in any area, emergency drought orders may be made under s.75. The right to recover any fixed or minimum charge still applies during the period of the drought order, even though no supply has been made.

The effect of the order depends upon its terms. It may permit the EA to suspend or modify any restrictions, abstraction licence or water supply agreement. Any order may authorise the taking and transfer of water supplied from one place to another during the emergency period. It may also temporarily restrict certain uses of water including the use of hoses, irrigation, etc.

Compensation

7–019 Usually only limited compensation is available for loss or damage sustained by any party as a result of the drought order. However, activities or restrictions which may be subject to compensation include the use and occupation of land, including any loss or damage as a result of entry. Schedule 9 to WRA 1991 provides for compensation and contains a provision for a claim by persons who sustain loss or damage arising from an ordinary drought order (but not an emergency order). Loss or damage resulting from the order may be the subject of a claim which must be made within six months of the ending of a particular power granted by the order.

Spray irrigation

The EA also has powers to restrict or stop spray irrigation in circumstances   **7–020**
of drought or similar emergency. The EA must be satisfied that the licensed
activity will affect the flow level or volume of an inland water (generally not
including a lake or pond).

WATER POLLUTION

Earlier legislation

While the main statutory controls relating to the prevention of water   **7–021**
pollution in England and Wales now derive from WRA 1991 (replacing,
from December 1, 1991, the Control of Pollution Act (COPA) 1974 and
WA 1989), there are still some surviving earlier provisions of importance.
For example, s.259 of the Public Health Act 1936 continues to identify, as a
statutory nuisance,[6] ponds, ditches etc. which are prejudicial to health or a
nuisance, or silted-up watercourses.

Water Industry Act 1991

Sections 119 *et seq.* of the Water Industry Act (WIA) 1991 provide the legal   **7–022**
basis upon which the occupier of any trade premises may, with the
sewerage undertaker's consent, discharge his trade effluent into the local
sewers. The sewerage undertaker will usually be the water company for the
region in question. These companies were privatised as a result of WA
1989.

It is the responsibility of the occupier of trade premises to give notice to
the undertaker specifying the nature or composition of the effluent, the
maximum quantity to be discharged per day and the highest rate of
discharge. The water company may prohibit or regulate by conditions the
nature, composition or quality of the effluent to be discharged, and other
matters. In the event of dispute, there is an appeal to the Director General
of Water Services.

A sewerage undertaker is entitled, by s.124, to vary the conditions of a
trade effluent discharge consent. Normally, a variation cannot be introduced less than two years from the date of the consent, or from its last
variation, unless the occupier of the trade premises agrees. However,
variation may be imposed under s.125 within the two-year time limit if this
is necessary to provide proper protection for persons likely to be affected
by the discharges. In these circumstances, liability to pay compensation by
the sewerage undertaker will normally follow. The owner or occupier of
trade premises may appeal where he is dissatisfied with any variation. The
appeal is made to the Director General of Water Services.

[6] See para.12–009 below.

Section 129 provides that agreements may be made between the sewerage undertaker and an owner/occupier of trade premises which would provide for the reception and disposal of trade effluent or of substances produced in the course of treating such effluent.

EC Directive 91/271/EEC

7–023   The Urban Waste Water Treatment (England and Wales) Regulations 1994[7] implement EC Directive 91/271/EEC on urban waste water treatment. The regulations impose both a general duty on sewerage undertakers to collect and treat urban waste water and also set the standard of water treatment. There is an obligation on the EA to secure after the end of 2000 that discharges of biodegradable waste water from industrial sectors listed in Annex III to the Directive are subject to appropriate conditions.

Water Resources Act 1991

7–024   While a good deal of effluent and pollution is discharged to sewers there is also a considerable amount received by rivers and other watercourses and bodies. The legislation was developed originally through the Rivers (Prevention of Pollution) Acts 1951 and 1961, embodying a system of licences and consents, but control is now within WRA 1991, which replaced WA 1989 with effect from December 1, 1991. Most discharges of trade effluent to surface or underground waters will now require formal approval of the EA.

Environmental Protection Act 1990, Part I

7–025   The most important exception to the requirement for a licence for the discharge of trade effluent arises from the interaction with Pt I of EPA 1990 and with the Pollution, Prevention and Control Act 1999. Certain processes, perceived as major potential polluters, are the subject of integrated pollution control provisions of Pt I (see para.8–002 below) or of the 1999 Act (see para.9–001). In circumstances where such provisions apply, pollution control in relation to a process is considered comprehensively, having regard to all impacts and discharges. Administration is the EA's responsibility.

Pollution Prevention and Control Act 1999

7–026   At the time of writing, this Act is not fully in force, but the intention is that it will progressively replace EPA 1990. Progressive replacement will be undertaken over a period of a number of years. Existing processes the

---

[7] SI 1994/2841.

subject of EPA 1990 will become, instead, the subject of the 1999 Act under the terms of a programme of gradual transition (see para.9–001 below).

Definitions

The concept of control under WRA 1991 relies on three significant **7–027** elements: "controlled waters", "water quality objectives" and the attainment of those objectives.

"Controlled waters" are defined in s.104 as including lakes and ponds, rivers, estuaries, water in underground strata and certain coastal waters. "Water quality objectives" are defined by s.83. The Secretary of State must set these objectives and must review them, usually every five years. These objectives (as their name implies) establish standards which are required to be met by the EA in carrying out its functions for pollution control, as well as the protection of water resources generally. Thus, the EA must attain those objectives in undertaking its responsibilities under the Act.

The system for classifying the quality of inland waters is set out in the Surface Waters (Abstraction for Drinking Water) (Classification) Regulations 1996,[8] the Surface Waters (Fish Life) (Classification) Regulations 1997[9] and the Surface Waters (Shell Fish) (Classification) Regulations 1997.[10] Regulations partly implementing EC Directive 76/464/EEC on pollution caused by certain dangerous substances discharged into the aquatic environment came into force on November 26, 1997. The Surface Waters (Dangerous Substances) (Classification) Regulations 1997[11] and the Surface Waters (Dangerous Substances) (Classification) Regulations 1998[12] classify certain inland fresh waters, coastal waters and relevant territorial waters in accordance with the Directive's requirements.

The control of pollution

What the above definitions and requirements mean to the waste manage- **7–028** ment industry is that, by s.85 of WRA 1991, offences are committed in circumstances where:

(a) any poisonous, noxious or polluting matter or solid waste matter is caused or knowingly permitted to enter controlled waters;

(b) any matter, other than trade effluent or sewage effluent, is caused or knowingly permitted to enter controlled waters by being discharged from a drain or sewer in contravention of a prohibition imposed under s.86;

[8] SI 1996/3001.
[9] SI 1997/1331.
[10] SI 1997/1332.
[11] SI 1997/2560.
[12] SI 1998/389.

(c) any trade effluent or sewage effluent is caused or knowingly permitted to be discharged into any controlled waters or from land through a pipe into the sea outside the seaward limits of controlled waters;

(d) any trade effluent or sewage effluent is caused or knowingly permitted to be discharged in contravention of any prohibition imposed under s.86, from a building or from any fixed plant onto or into any waters of a lake or pond which are not inland fresh waters; and

(e) any matter whatever is caused or permitted to enter any inland fresh waters so as to tend (either directly or in combination with other matter which has been caused or permitted to enter the waters) to impede the proper flow of the waters in a manner leading or likely to lead to a substantial aggravation of pollution owing to other causes or the consequences of such pollution.

The offence of polluting controlled waters will extend in appropriate circumstances to dried-up watercourses and those which have overflowed (see *R. v Dovermoss Ltd*).[13] In *National Rivers Authority v Biffa Waste Services Ltd*,[14] the High Court held that the riverbed was part of controlled waters.

"Caused or knowingly permitted"

7–029   The phrase "caused or knowingly permitted", repeated as it is in s.85, has caused considerable difficulties in interpretation, but the courts have provided some clarification. "Causing" appears to require some positive action and the courts have found that passive inaction is usually not sufficient.[15] A company can be guilty of "causing" even if the offence arises as a result of acts of its employees.[16] Even pollution arising as a result of acts of vandalism can result in a conviction. See further *Empress Car Co (Abertillery) Ltd v National Rivers Authority*,[17] where the House of Lords provided an up-to-date assessment of the definition of "causing".

"Knowingly permitting" does not require a positive act by the defendant, but requires only a failure to prevent the entry causing pollution of the controlled waters.[18] Guidance on what is "polluting matter" has been provided in *National Rivers Authority v Egger* (UK).[19]

---

[13] (1995) *The Times*, February 8.
[14] (1995) *The Times*, November 21.
[15] See *AlphaCell Ltd v Woodward* [1972] A.C. 824; *Wychavon DC v National Rivers Authority* [1993] 2 All E.R. 440.
[16] See *National Rivers Authority v Alfred McAlpine Homes East Ltd* (1994) *The Times*, February 3.
[17] [1998] 2 W.L.R. 350.
[18] See *Schulmans v National Rivers Authority* [1992] 4 L.M.E.L.R. 130.
[19] [1992] 4 L.M.E.L.R. 130.

Other definitions

A "prohibition" is usually effected by an EA notice under s.86 prohibiting **7–030** any discharge or imposing any conditions for discharge. Where the discharge contains substances or concentrations, the prohibition may be achieved directly by s.86. "Inland freshwaters" are defined in s.104 to include mainly lakes or ponds or so much of a river or watercourse above the freshwater limit.

Penalties

Penalties for contravention of s.85 are severe. The convicted person is **7–031** liable, on summary conviction, to imprisonment not exceeding three months, or to a fine not exceeding £20,000, or to both. On conviction on indictment, imprisonment may be for a term not exceeding two years, or an unlimited fine, or both.

Defences

A business or individual avoids an offence under s.85 if a consent has been **7–032** granted under s.88. This consent may be by various means, but includes approvals under WRA 1991, COPA 1974, Pt I of EPA 1990 (see para.8–007 above), Pt II of that Act (waste management or disposal licence), (para.10–046) or PPCA 1999 (see para.9–006).

There is no offence against s.65 in respect of the entry of any matter into any waters or any discharge if:

(a) the entry is caused or permitted or the discharge is made in an emergency in order to avoid danger to life or health;

(b) the person who might otherwise be guilty of the offence takes all such steps as are reasonably practicable in the circumstances for minimising the extent of the entry or discharge and of its polluting effects; and

(c) particulars of the entry or discharge are given to the Environment Agency as soon as reasonably practicable.

In certain restricted circumstances the deposit of the solid refuse of a mine or quarry onto any land so that it falls or is carried into an inland fresh water is not an offence if the deposit has the consent of the Agency, there was no other reasonably practicable site and the potential offender has taken all reasonably practical steps to prevent the entry of the material into the inland fresh water. For the definition of "inland fresh water", see above.

Powers to remedy pollution

While it is normally for the EA to prosecute for breaches of WRA 1991 **7–033** and for the polluter to undertake the necessary clean-up, there are further powers under ss.161–161D of the Act. Most of these powers were inserted into the Act by the Environment Act 1995. They provide the EA with powers to undertake necessary clean-up themselves. They apply where it appears that any poisonous, noxious or polluting matter or any solid waste matter is likely to enter any controlled waters or is, or may have been, present there at some time. The EA normally serves a works notice under s.161A on the person who caused or knowingly permitted the pollution. That person will be required to carry out works or operations to remove or alleviate the pollution. There is a right of appeal available to the person served with the notice, which must be made within 21 days to the Secretary of State or the Welsh Assembly, as appropriate. See also the Anti-pollution Works Regulations 1999,[20] below.

Enforcement notices

7–034 Where a consent holder is not complying with any conditions of a consent, a prosecution may ensue. However, by virtue of s.90B of WRA 1991, inserted by the Environment Act 1995, the EA may serve an enforcement notice on the consent holder specifying the nature of the failure to comply, the steps necessary to remedy and the time for compliance. Failure to comply is an offence. On summary conviction, there may be a fine not exceeding £20,000 or up to three months' imprisonment or both. On indictment the fine may be unlimited and/or imprisonment can be up to two years. The EA is also empowered to seek an injunction to secure compliance with its notice.

A consent holder may appeal against an enforcement notice. The procedure is similar to that for discharge consent appeals (see para.7–046). Notice of appeal must be given within 21 days of receipt of the enforcement notice and the EA is obliged to respond within 14 days. The appeal is made to the Secretary of State or Welsh Assembly. The notice may be quashed, affirmed or modified, but it is not suspended during the period of appeal. For appeal procedures see the Anti-pollution Works Regulations 1999.[21]

Groundwater Regulations 1998

7–035 The Groundwater Regulations 1998[22] fill certain loopholes in the UK's compliance with the 1980 EC Directive on groundwater protection. The Regulations largely concern the prevention of pollution of groundwater by the most hazardous "List I" substances and by the less hazardous "List II" substances. Both lists are in the Schedule to the Regulations and are annexed to the 1976 Dangerous Substances Directive. For the most part, control is by means of existing systems such as discharge consents and IPPC/IPC authorisations under either PPCA 1999 or Pt I of EPA 1990.

[20] SI 1999/1006.
[21] SI 1999/1006.
[22] SI 1998/2746.

Waste management activities are not controlled under the 1998 Regulations since these are perceived to be dealt with under Pt II of EPA 1990, as it has been adapted by PPCA 1999.

However, there are a number of activities not regulated by the above means and a majority of these are concerned with agricultural activities. Such activities require authorisation under the Regulations for disposal by tipping of any list I or II substances. The EA has power to serve notice where it anticipates that an activity may lead to an indirect discharge of such substances. Such notices may prohibit an activity or permit it subject to conditions.[23]

Water protection zones and nitrate sensitive areas

Powers contained within WRA 1991 are in ss.93 (water protection zones) and 94 (nitrate sensitive areas). **7–036**

Section 93 enables the Secretary of State for the Environment Food and Rural Affairs to prohibit or restrict the carrying on in any particular area of activities likely to result in the pollution of controlled waters. These special powers may be used to prevent or control the entry of any poisonous, noxious or polluting matter. Section 94 is more specific in that the Secretary of State in England is given the obligation to prevent or control the entry of nitrates into controlled waters, resulting from their use for agricultural purposes. Codes of good agricultural practice have been established under s.97. Bearing in mind the frequency with which a landfill operator will wish to restore the site, at least initially, to agricultural purposes, the exercise of the s.93 power is of some importance, particularly if significant fertilising of the land is required to secure its rehabilitation. It will, therefore, be advisable to have a clear understanding of DEFRA intentions before committing to a restoration and aftercare scheme. See the Nitrate Sensitive Areas Regulations 1994,[24] as amended, the Protection of Water Against Agricultural Nitrate Pollution (England and Wales) Regulations 1996,[25] and the Action Programme for Nitrate Vulnerable Zones (England and Wales) Regulations 1998[26]: these Regulations prescribe an action programme to protect waters against nitrates pollution. Under the Nitrate Sensitive Areas (Amendment) Regulations 2002,[27] payments for grants to farmers under the 1994 Regulations where there were restrictions on nitrate use have been reduced. Major additions to the list of nitrate vulnerable zones were brought into force by the Nitrate Vulnerable Zone (Additional Designations) (England) (No. 2) Regulations 2002.[28] Possible grants, to meet the

---

[23] See DEFRA, "Guidance on the Groundwater Regulations 1998". See also DEFRA code of practice, "Petrol stations and other fuel dispensing facilities involving underground storage tanks", which provides a basis for compliance with the regulations.
[24] SI 1994/1729.
[25] SI 1996/888.
[26] SI 1998/1202.
[27] SI 2002/744.
[28] SI 2002/2614.

obligations, are set out in the Farm Waste Grant (Nitrate Vulnerable Zones) (England) Scheme 2003.[29]

APPLICATIONS FOR CONSENT TO DISCHARGE TO SEWERS AND WATERCOURSES

Water Industry Act 1991

7–037 Subject to WIA 1991 provisions and other matters, a waste operator will have the right to discharge trade effluents into public sewers. A "trade effluent" is defined by s.141 of the Act to mean any liquid, either with or without particles of matter in suspension therein, which is wholly or in part produced in the course of any trade or industry carried on at trade premises and, in relation to any trade premises, means any such liquid produced in the course of any trade or industry carried on at those premises; it does not include domestic sewage.

"Trade premises", with some exceptions relating to agriculture, means any premises used or intended to be used for carrying on any trade or industry. It follows that installations such as incinerators, as well as landfill operations, fall within the definition of trade premises. The water company may also impose conditions to satisfy the requirements of the Urban Waste Water Directive (see para.15–004) and the Urban Waste Water Treatment (England and Wales) Regulations 1994.[30]

On occasions, the application for consent will relate to what is known as "special category effluent", generally containing specially polluting substances. That term is defined in s.141 and is prescribed by the Secretary of State under the Trade Effluents (Prescribed Processes and Substances) Regulations 1989.[31] Such application is required to be referred to the Secretary of State under the procedures set out in s.120.

Procedure

7–038 For trade effluent to be discharged from any trade premises, a written notice must be served on the appropriate water company for the area (as the sewerage undertaker). There is no prescribed form, but s.119 of WIA 1991 specifies that the notice must contain details of the effluent, the maximum quantity proposed to be discharged per day, and the highest rate at which the discharge will take place. The notice is required to be served on the undertaker by the owner or occupier of the premises in question, at least two months before the discharge actually starts (unless a lesser period has been agreed).

Upon the receipt of the notice it is for the undertaker to decide whether to prohibit the discharge or issue a consent with or without conditions (s.121).

[29] SI 2003/562.
[30] SI 1994/2841.
[31] SI 1989/1156.

Appeals

If an owner or occupier is dissatisfied with the response of the undertaking   **7–039**
he may appeal to the Director General of Water Services (s.122).

Trade effluent agreement

Section 129 provides for agreements to be made with the appropriate water   **7–040**
company for the area, which can relate to the reception and disposal of any
trade effluent produced. The agreement can deal with the construction by
the water company of any works required for reception or disposal and
payment of expenses by the owner or occupier. It is important to note that
the agreement binds only the owner or occupier at the time when it was
made. It follows that a fresh agreement would be required on any change of
ownership or occupation.

Powers to vary conditions

The undertaker has the power to vary conditions of any previously   **7–041**
consented discharge into a public sewer. These powers are to be found in
ss.124 and 125.

Water Resources Act 1991: authority for discharges

The above provisions relate only to discharge to sewers. Different legisla-   **7–042**
tion applies to discharges to "controlled waters" (for definition, see para.7–
027 above).

Consents for effluent and similar discharges

A person avoids an offence under s.85 of WRA 1991 by obtaining and   **7–043**
compliance with consents or licences under:

- WRA 1991;
- the Food and Environment Protection Act 1985 (discharge of
  substances into the sea);
- EPA 1990 (IPC authorisations), or
- PPCA 1999.

Here, only the application for consent under WRA 1991 is discussed, which
is likely to be the more usual route for the waste operator until PPCA 1999
applies to landfill operations (see para.9–002).

Applications for consent

Applications for consent to discharge effluent to controlled waters are   **7–044**
required under s.88 of WRA 1991 and a new Sch.10 to that Act which was
substituted by the Environment Act 1995. Procedures are also governed by

the Control of Pollution (Applications Appeals and Registers) Regulations 1996,[32] as amended by the Anti-Pollution Works Regulations 1999.[33] An application must be made on the form provided by the EA, supported by all information required by the EA or as prescribed in the Regulations. Notice of the application must be published in one or more newspapers circulating in the locality and in the London Gazette, although sometimes these requirements are dispensed with where the Secretary of State (or in Wales, the Welsh Assembly) is satisfied that the information is commercially confidential. It is also within the EA's power to conclude that an application need not be advertised if the information affects national security or because the activities concerned are unlikely to have an appreciable effect on the controlled waters in the area.

The EA is required to consult a range of consultees about the application, but not usually where the application does not need to be advertised. If the EA is satisfied that it may properly do so, it may issue a consent subject to such conditions as it thinks fit. These may specify the place and outlet for the discharge and require certain standards of quality and quantity. A fee is payable for an application and a further fee is payable annually during the currency of any consent.[34] Failure to pay fees and charges can result in the suspension and ultimately the revocation of any consent.[35]

Application period

7–045   The EA has three months to consider applications. In default of a decision within that period or such extended period as agreed with the applicant there may be an appeal to the Secretary of State or Welsh Assembly on grounds of non-determination.

Appeals

7–046   An appeal against the EA's decision (or its failure to reach a decision) is made to the Secretary of State or the Welsh Assembly.[36] Notice of appeal must set out the grounds and is required to be accompanied by copies of any relevant application, consent and other document. The EA must be notified of the appeal and it normally needs to be made within three months of the decision complained of or, if no decision has been made, of the date when the period for making that decision has expired. The appeal is normally dealt with by written representations or hearing, at the appellant's discretion.

---

[32] SI 1996/2971.
[33] SI 1999/1006.
[34] Environment Act 1995, s.41.
[35] Environmental Licences (Suspension and Revocation) Regulations 1996, SI 1996/508.
[36] Control of Pollution (Applications Appeals and Registers) Regulations 1996, SI 1996/2971.

Review and transfer of consents

The EA may review all consents granted and has power to revoke, modify   **7–047**
or specify additional conditions. The consent holder may apply to the EA
for variation. The procedures are similar to those for granting consent and
appeal provisions apply. On change of ownership or for other reasons,
consents can be transferred from the existing holder to the new one. The
procedure for transfer is by simple application. For the processes of review
and transfer, see Sch.10 to WRA 1991, as substituted by the Environment
Act 1995.

CHAPTER 8

POLLUTION CONTROL POWERS, ENFORCEMENT AND OFFENCES

INTRODUCTION

Many of the processes of the waste management industry are the subject of comprehensive controls provided in Pt I of EPA 1990. The extent to which processes are caught is described below. The provisions of Pt I are currently wholly in force, having been applied progressively over a period of years. Note that Pt I will be replaced progressively by the Pollution, Prevention and Control Act (PPCA) 1999 (see Ch.9). **8–001**

ENVIRONMENTAL PROTECTION ACT 1990

EPA 1990 was passed in November 1990. Industrial processes which have a major potential for pollution were made the subject of new systems of control, known as integrated pollution control. Processes having less significance to pollute are under the control of the local authorities (Part B), whereas the major industries are regulated by the EA (Part A). Processes and substances the subject of Pt I of EPA 1990 are set out in the Environmental Protection (Prescribed Processes and Substances) Regulations 1991,[1] as amended. A summary of the controlled processes likely to affect the waste management industry is set out in the table below. **8–002**

The meaning of "integrated pollution control"

The control system is established through a scheme of authorisation, control and enforcement of processes capable of causing pollution to the environment. A process is categorised if it releases to air, water or land substances which are capable of causing harm to man or to any other living organism supported by the environment.[2] The definition is very wide, but a process is not caught by the IPC requirements unless prescribed by the Secretary of State (see the 1991 Regulations above). **8–003**

The table below sets out the processes and substances subject to Pt I of EPA 1990, and indicates whether they fall within EA (Part A) or local authority (Part B) control.

[1] SI 1991/472.
[2] EPA 1990, s.1.

Process	Part
Acid recovery processes	A
Combustion processes over 3 MW powered by waste, recovered oil or other waste-derived fuel	A
Combustion of waste, recovered oil or heat treated waste, under 3 MW	B
Combustion of waste fuel, below 3 MW but at least 0.4 MW	B
Waste-derived fuel production	A
Waste incineration (most)	A
Waste incineration (cremation of animal remains 1 tonne per hour or more)	A
Other incineration of animal remains, 50 kg per hour or more	B
Cremation of human remains	B
Waste recovery	A

The table is simplified. For full details, the 1991 Regulations (see above) should be consulted. Section 2 of EPA 1990 provides the power for the Secretary of State to prescribe processes and he may add to the 1991 Regulations (or modify them in some other way) as he deems necessary. Such processes which are designated require an authorisation under s.6 (see below).

The 1991 Regulations provide power for the Secretary of State to prescribe processes by reference to characteristics, or the area, or other circumstances in which the process is carried on, or the description of the person undertaking it. The more technical processes have been assigned by the Regulations for control by the EA, but a wide range of processes are designated for control by local public health authorities in England and Wales.

Quality targets

8–004   The EPA 1990 sets out a requirement for the Secretary of State to establish standards and objectives in relation to prescribed processes or particular substances. The aim, as embodied in s.3(5), is to secure a progressive improvement in the quality objectives and standards. The Secretary of State's plans may be revised from time to time for this purpose.

Division of powers between the EA and local authorities

8–005   It has already been seen that the responsibilities for regulation under EPA 1990 are split between the EA and the local public health authorities.[3] There are no geographical limits within England and Wales for EA inspectors, but the local public health authorities are responsible only for

[3] EPA 1990, s.4.

the processes carried on within their area. Furthermore, their functions are applicable to such processes only in respect of air pollution and not to other discharges to other environmental media such as land or water (although they may have other powers.[4] The EA powers in relation to IPC relate to discharges from prescribed processes to any environmental medium, although there are some restrictions on the extent to which these powers may be exercised. Special arrangements have been made in s.4 in the case of mobile plant. Such plant requires authorisation by the public health authority in whose area the person carrying on the mobile process has its principal place of business.

Section 4 gives the Secretary of State power to transfer responsibilities for a process from a local authority to the EA but, under these circumstances, the limits of control in respect of air pollution only do not change.

The local authority

The appropriate authorities are defined in s.4(11) of EPA 1990 to mean:　**8–006**

- (a) in Greater London, the London borough council, the Common Council of the City of London, the Sub-treasurer of the Inner Temple and the Under-treasurer of the Middle Temple;
- (b) outside Greater London, the unitary or district council and the council of the Isles of Scilly. In some circumstances a port health authority will take over the responsibilities of Pt I of EPA 1990 from the local authority.

Authorisations

By the terms of s.6 of EPA 1990, no person may carry on a prescribed **8–007** process (after the prescribed date) except by virtue of an authorisation granted either by the EA or the local authority and in accordance with the conditions of that authorisation. The enforcing authority has the responsibility under s.6 either to grant the authorisation on the application made, subject to conditions, or to refuse it. The enforcing authority is expressly forbidden to grant an authorisation if it considers that the applicant cannot carry on the process so as to comply with the conditions which it would normally include.[5]

Reviews of authorisations

The enforcing authority is responsible, from time to time but at least once **8–008** in every four years, to carry out a review of the conditions of the authorisation.

---

[4] *ibid.*, Pt III (statutory nuisance.
[5] See *R. v Secretary of State and Compton Ex p. West Wiltshire DC* [1997] J.P.L. 210.

Applications for authorisations

8–009   Schedule 1 to EPA 1990 requires applications for authorisations to be made in accordance with the Environmental Protection (Applications Appeals and Registers) Regulations 1991,[6] as amended. A fee must accompany the application and it will usually be necessary to advertise in accordance with the requirements of the Regulations. The authority is entitled to all relevant information which must be supplied within a specified timetable and, in the event of the absence of information, the application may not proceed. The prescribed application form is a complex one. A considerable amount of care is required in its completion and in the provision of supplementary information. A fee is payable.

Consultations

8–010   The enforcing authority is required to consult with a number of persons prescribed by the 1991 Regulations, and any representations from those consultees (together with any made by other parties) must be considered by the authority in making a decision. There is a 28-day period within which consultees must make representations, starting respectively from the date on which the notice of application was given or the advertisement of it was made.

In normal circumstances the enforcing authority has four months to make a decision on the application, or such longer period as may be agreed with the applicant. In the absence of a decision within the relevant period there are rights to appeal to the Secretary of State on the basis of a deemed refusal.

The Secretary of State has power to call in any application for his own decision and a local inquiry is likely to be held subsequently, at which the applicant and the authority have a right of audience. EPA 1990 requires that the Secretary of State will not make the final decision himself in call-in cases, but will be required to give directions to the enforcing authority as to whether to grant the application and as to the conditions to be attached to any authorisation.

Conditions of authorisations

8–011   Section 7 of EPA 1990 sets out the basis upon which conditions are imposed. This is an important section since it lays the ground for the system both of IPC and local authority control. However, since the approach is different in each case, they should be considered separately.

Objectives of IPC

8–012   Section 7(2) of EPA 1990 sets out the objectives of control as follows:

[6] SI 1991/507.

(a) that in carrying on the prescribed process the best available techniques not entailing excessive cost (BATNEEC) will be used (see below);

(b) that compliance is necessary with:

    (i) any directions by the Secretary of State in pursuance of any UK obligations under EU or international law relating to environmental protection;

    (ii) any limits or requirements and achievement of quality standards or objectives prescribed by the Secretary of State; and

    (iii) any requirements of a plan for general improvement made under the provisions of s.3(5), which relates to total release limits, quotas etc.; and

(c) where IPC applies and where it is likely that the process will involve the release of substances into more than one environmental medium, the BATNEEC obligation extends to minimising pollution caused to the environment taken as a whole by the releases, having regard to the best practicable environmental option (BPEO — see below).

BATNEEC

Section 7 of EPA 1990 defines the necessary components of BATNEEC. In **8–013** relation to a process these include (in addition to references to any technical means and technology) reference to the number, qualifications, training and supervision of persons employed in the process and the design, construction, layout and maintenance of buildings in which it is to be carried on. The enforcing authority has a duty by s.7(1) to have regard to any guidance issued by the Secretary of State for the purposes of s.7, with particular reference to the techniques and environmental options that are appropriate for any description of the prescribed process (see "Process guidance notes" at para.8–019 below and Appendix 2).

Under s.7(2), in carrying on a prescribed process BATNEEC is used for preventing the release of substances prescribed for any environmental medium into that medium. Where that is not practicable, it is used to reduce the release to a minimum, and to render harmless any such substances which are so released and any other substances which might cause harm if released.

BPEO

In connection with IPC processes, the responsibility will be on the EA to **8–014** authorise only such processes which use the optimum pollution control system (*i.e.* BPEO). For example, discharges from a given process ultimately to land may be preferred as the least damaging environmentally when compared with other discharges to air or water. Thus, a form of environmental assessment is necessary to consider the pollution control and waste disposal options. Since authorisations are required in respect of established plant, hitherto accepted methods of such control and disposal may well have to be changed if they do not comply with the BPEO requirements. However, it will be a relevant consideration in deciding what is "practical" that an existing pollution control system is already installed, and to make changes would be impractical having regard to such factors as cost of reinvestment, disruption to processes etc.[7]

Recycling and waste minimisation

8–015 Note that the concepts of BATNEEC and BPEO require to take into account the potential for the process in question to be installed or modified to maximise the prevention of waste and the opportunities for recycling of elements of both process and product.

Fees

8–016 Under the provisions of s.41 of the Environment Act 1995, the Secretary of State has powers to impose charging schemes for the regulation of processes and activities under EPA 1990. The failure to pay fees and charges can result in the suspension and ultimately the revocation of any authorisation.[8]

Avoidance of duplication of controls

8–017 Section 28 of EPA 1990 provides for the avoidance of conflict between different types of statutory control, as follows:

(a) no condition may be attached to an authorisation to regulate the final disposal by deposit in or on land of controlled waste (this is now dealt with under Pt II of EPA 1990 or PPCA 1999); and

(b) in circumstances where an authorisation is required under Pt I and also under the Radioactive Substances Act 1993, and different obligations are imposed, the Pt I provision will not be binding on the person carrying on the process.

Note also that an IPC authorisation will control discharges to air, water and land, so that any further licence (*e.g.* a licence under Pt II of EPA 1990) is

---

[7] The EA has published Technical Guidance Note (environmental) E1, "Guidance for Operators and Inspectors of IPC Processes. Best Practicable Environmental Option Assessments for Integrated Pollution Control".

[8] See the Environmental Licences (Suspension and Revocation) Regulations 1996, SI 1996/508.

not usually needed. Thus, an incinerator will not require a licence once an IPC authorisation is granted. However, IPC does not extend to the final disposal of waste by deposit on land; here, a licence under EPA 1990 will still be required (*e.g.* for landfill sites). See also PPCA 1999 (Ch.9 below).

Local authority air pollution control

The local authority regulates air pollution for the smaller impact premises. **8–018** The objectives as described in s.7(2) of EPA 1990 are largely the same for local authority control and the imposition of conditions, except that the obligation to achieve BPEO does not apply.

Process guidance notes

A substantial number of individual process and other guidance notes have **8–019** been produced by the DoE, DETR and the Welsh Office. These guidance notes provide the policy basis upon which authorisations will be considered and administered. Appendix 2 sets out the important guidance notes, relative to the waste management industry.

Transfer, variation and revocation of authorisations

Transfer of EPA 1990, Pt I authorisations

On the change of any authorised holder the responsibility for notifying the **8–020** enforcing authority is on the transferee. Notice must be given within 21 days and, from the date of transfer, the transferee takes on all the obligations of the authorisation and the conditions.[9]

Variation by enforcing authority

Where the enforcing authority wishes to vary an authorisation, it must serve a notice under s.10 of EPA 1990. The notice must be served on the holder of the authorisation and must specify the variations and the dates on which these are to take effect. The notice also requires the holder, within a specified period, to notify the authority of what action, if any, he proposes to take in response to the variation. If the response indicates to the enforcing authority that the variation proposed will involve a substantial change in the process, the authority must notify that opinion to the holder and the latter will be required to advertise the change.

"Substantial change" is defined in s.10(7) as "a substantial change in the substances released from the process or in the amount or any other

[9] EPA 1990, s.9.

characteristic of any substance so released". The Secretary of State has taken power in the Act to give directions to what constitutes a substantial change.[10]

Variation by holder of authorisation

Where the holder needs to make a "relevant change" in the prescribed process, the procedures set out in s.11 of EPA 1990, as amended by Environment Act 1995 are triggered. "Relevant change" is defined as "a change in the manner of carrying on the process which is capable of altering the substances released from the process or of affecting the amount or any other characteristic of any substance so released". Where there is a relevant change the holder must notify the enforcing authority and ask for a determination:

(a) whether the proposed change would involve a breach of any condition of the authorisation;
(b) if there is no breach, whether the authority would be likely to vary the conditions of the authorisation as a result of the change;
(c) if it would involve a breach, whether the authority would consider varying the conditions of the authorisation to enable the change to be made; and
(d) whether the change would involve a substantial change (see definition above) in the manner in which the process is being carried on.

If the authority decides there is no substantial change but that there should be a variation of the authorisation, the holder must be notified of the variations to be considered and must then apply for such variation to enable him to make the proposed change. In the event that the authority decides that the change proposed would be substantial, then the same procedure is to be followed but, in addition, the holder must advertise the change in the prescribed manner.

Once the application for variation is received, the authority may refuse it or vary the conditions as it sees fit and, as appropriate, must serve a variation notice on the holder. A fee is required for this procedure.

Revocation

An enforcing authority is entitled to revoke an authorisation under s.12 of EPA 1990 where it has reason to believe that an authorised process has not been carried on for at least a period of 12 months. Twenty-eight days' notice of revocation is required.

---

[10] Some guidance is available in "Integrated Pollution Control—A Practical Guide" (2nd ed., 2000), issued by the DETR and in individual progress guidance notes.

ENFORCEMENT AND OFFENCES

Enforcement notice

Where there is any contravention of a condition of an authorisation, or **8–021** such contravention is anticipated, an enforcement notice may be served by the enforcing authority. The notice must specify the contravention and steps required to remedy the position, as well as the period within which the required action is to be taken.[11]

Prohibition notice

In more serious cases the enforcing authority may believe that an author- **8–022** ised process involves an imminent risk of serious pollution of the environment. It is not necessary to establish that a condition of the authorisation is being contravened. The prohibition notice states the authority's position, specifies the risk and the steps to be taken to remove it, as well as the period within which action is to be taken. The notice must also direct that the process must stop, either wholly or in part. If part of the process is to be stopped, conditions may be imposed for carrying on the remaining part. The notice remains in force until withdrawn by the authority.[12]

Appeals

There are extensive rights of appeal in Pt I of EPA 1990, as follows: **8–023**

(a) on refusal of the grant of an authorisation, or failure by the EA or the authority to reach a decision within the prescribed period;
(b) on receipt of an authorisation with unsatisfactory conditions;
(c) on refusal of a variation;
(d) on revocation of an authorisation;
(e) on receipt of a variation notice;
(f) on receipt of an enforcement notice;
(g) on receipt of a prohibition notice.

In all cases the appeal is to the Secretary of State.

The Secretary of State has various powers in determining an appeal. For appeals under (a)–(d) above he may:

(a) affirm the decision;
(b) direct the enforcing authority to grant the authorisation or to vary;
(c) quash unsatisfactory conditions; or
(d) quash any revocation.

---

[11] EPA 1990, s.13.
[12] *ibid.*, s.14.

Except in the circumstances of (a) above, directions may be given as to appropriate conditions.

Where the appeal is against a variation, enforcement or prohibition notice the Secretary of State may either quash or affirm the notice in a modified form or otherwise. In some cases an appeal will have the effect of suspending any revocation of an authorisation, but this will not apply where a variation, enforcement or prohibition notice has been served.

Appeal procedures

8–024   The Secretary of State has power to reach a decision on an appeal himself or he may delegate that decision to an inspector appointed for the purposes of the appeal. In practice, responsibility for deciding most appeals concerning both IPC and local air pollution control is transferred to an inspector. Publicity is required to be given to the appeal procedures and, if either the appellant or the enforcing authority request or the Secretary of State so decides, there will be a hearing; otherwise, the matter is dealt with by written representations. The Secretary of State has power to provide that the hearing will take place in private.[13]

Powers of inspectors

8–025   Powers of inspectors appointed either by the Secretary of State or the local authority are set out, for the EA, in general terms in ss.5–8 of the Environment Act 1995 and, for both the EA and authority, in considerable detail in s.108. Powers extend to entry, examination and investigation, to take measurements and other records and samples, to direct that premises should be left undisturbed, to dismantle or test any article or substance found on any premises and to take possession of these. The inspector may demand information and records and require any person to give assistance within that person's control or extent of responsibility. Boreholes may be installed and maintained. There are certain protective powers in s.108 in the interests of process operators and others. Entry may be effected only after seven days' notice (except where there is an emergency) and the occupier's consent or a warrant to enter must be obtained. The exercise of any power to dismantle and/or test an article or substance can only be pursued in the presence of a responsible person who requests that presence. The inspector has responsibilities to consult as to the risks of dismantling and testing. Answers given by any person in response to an inspector's questioning in accordance with s.108 are not admissible in evidence against that person in any proceedings. Otherwise any information obtained as a consequence of entry and exercise of the above powers will be admissible, by virtue of Sch.18 to the 1995 Act.

---

[13] For further details about procedures, see the Environmental Protection (Applications, Appeals and Registers) Regulations 1991, SI 1991/507, as amended.

Compensation

Subject to certain conditions set out in para.6 of Sch.18 to the Environment **8–026**
Act 1995, compensation is payable by the enforcing authority where loss or
damage has been experienced as a result of the exercise of an inspector's
powers or the failure to ensure that premises are left as secure as they were
discovered.

Emergencies

Section 109 of the Environment Act 1995 provides an inspector with special **8–027**
powers where he has reasonable cause to believe that there is an imminent
danger of serious harm caused by an article or substance which he finds on
any premises. There is a power to seize the article or substance and cause it
to be rendered harmless.

Offences

Section 23 of EPA 1990 and s.110 of the Environment Act 1995 provide for **8–028**
a range of offences, including:

(a) failure to comply with the requirements of authorisations under
s.6;
(b) failure to give notice under s.9 on transfer of authorisation;
(c) failure to comply with an enforcement or prohibition notice;
(d) failure, without reasonable excuse, to comply with the requirements of an inspector;
(e) obstruction of an inspector;
(f) failure to comply, without reasonable excuse, with a notice requiring information;
(g) making a false or misleading statement;
(h) making a false entry in any record required to be kept as a
condition of an authorisation;
(i) forgery or use of an authorisation with intent to deceive;
(j) impersonation of an inspector; and
(k) failure to comply with a court order made under s.26 of EPA 1990
(see below).

Penalties

Penalties are substantial. Fines of up to £20,000 and/or imprisonment for **8–029**
up to three months may be imposed on summary conviction and, where an
indictment is preferred, there may be an unlimited fine and/or imprisonment for up to two years or both. The enforcing authority has a right to go

to the Crown Court if the lower court is regarded as inadequate having regard to the seriousness of the offence. Where there is a conviction for failure to obtain an authorisation, failure to comply with conditions or failure to comply with an enforcement or prohibition notice, the court also has power under s.26 of EPA 1990 to order steps to be taken to remedy the offence, if those steps are within the offender's power to so remedy. Additionally, the EA has powers under s.27 to obtain the Secretary of State's authorisation to take steps to remedy harm and to recover the cost from the offender. Directors and senior managers may be personally liable in certain circumstances.[14]

Standards of proof

8–030   Section 25 of EPA 1990 modifies the normal standards of onus of proof. Where proceedings are taken against a person for failure to use BAT-NEEC, it is for the accused to prove that no better available technique not entailing excessive cost was appropriate. Further, the absence of an entry in a record required to be kept is admissible as evidence that the condition relevant to the record has not been observed.

PUBLICITY

8–031   Section 20 of EPA 1990 requires that public registers of information must be kept (usually by local authorities). Such information includes applications for authorisations and the authorisations themselves, variation, enforcement and other notices, details of appeals and convictions, and information obtained in pursuance of conditions (*e.g.* monitoring). IPC process details are kept by the EA in a separate register, but a copy of the information is also to be contained in the local authority register where it relates to any prescribed processes in that area.

Some information may be excluded from the register where the Secretary of State is satisfied that the information would either affect national security or where it is commercially confidential. Information will be regarded as commercially confidential only if the enforcing authority so determines or if the Secretary of State decides after an appeal. However, the Secretary of State may override commercial confidentiality if, in his view, the public interest requires that information be included in the register. If such confidentiality is accepted, it lasts only for four years, whereupon it is up to the supplier of the information to request a further exclusion. Commercial confidentiality would arise if publication would prejudice, to an unreasonable degree, the commercial interests of the individual or person. Appeals are dealt with under the rules set out in the Environmental Protection (Applications, Appeals and Registers) Regulations 1991.[15]

---

[14] See paras 16–019 and 16–023 below.
[15] SI 1991/507.

OTHER LEGISLATION

Clean Air Act 1993

This Act is a consolidation and replacement of the Clean Air Acts 1956– **8–032**
1968, as well as Pt IV of COPA 1974. The Act imposes an offence where an
occupier of buildings causes dark smoke to be emitted. The term "dark
smoke" is defined in s.3 by reference to the Ringelmann Chart (*i.e.* more
than 40 per cent obscuration). However, the court is given a discretion to
decide that smoke is or is not dark smoke, even if there has been no
comparison with the Chart. Note that the offence may be committed from
open sites: fires on landfill operations are now rare, but may still be caught
by these provisions.

The Act requires that certain new furnaces shall be, so far as is
practicable, smokeless and that most larger furnaces should be fitted with
arrestment plant to prevent the escape of grit and dust. It is an offence to
allow the escape of such materials. Furthermore, the installation of plant
without formal approval by the local authority can be an offence.

A provision of the Act, formerly found in COPA 1974, imposes powers
to prevent cable burning except under proper conditions (s.33). The Act
also regulates the sulphur content of furnace or engine oil (s.31).

Air Quality (England) Regulations 2000

Under Pt IV of the Environment Act 1995, local authorities must review **8–033**
the air quality in their area. They are guided in this by the government
publication "The Air Quality Strategy for England, Scotland, Wales and
Northern Ireland; Working Together for Clean Air".[16] The centrepiece of
the strategy remains the list of objectives, now included in the Air Quality
(England) Regulations 2000[17] which came into force on April 6, 2000.[18] The
regulations and the strategy list the main pollutants, the limits of concentra-
tion and the dates by which targets are to be achieved, starting at the end of
2003 and mainly extending to the end of 2005. However, in the case of
benzine, the objectives are required to be achieved by the end of 2010 and
in the case of lead, by the end of 2008. The strategy describes underlying
and EU government policy, the legislative basis of control, standards and
objectives. Various technical annexes deal with a range of pollutants
including benzine, carbon monoxide, nitrogen dioxide, ozone, sulphur
dioxide and particles.[19]

---

[16] Cm. 4548).
[17] SI 2000/928.
[18] For similar regulations for Wales see the Air Quality (Wales) Regulations 2000. SI
2000/1940 (W138).
[19] See also the Air Quality Limit Values (Amendment) Regulations 2002, SI 2002/3117 and
the Air Quality (England) (Amendment) Regulations 2002, SI 2002/3043. There are
corresponding regulations for Wales—see SI 2002/3182 and SI 2002/3183.

CLIMATE CHANGE

The Kyoto Protocol

8–034   The United Nations Framework Convention on Climate Change was agreed at the Earth Summit at Rio de Janeiro in 1992 following growing awareness of the harmful effect of greenhouse gas emissions on the earth's climate. One hundred and eighty-four developed countries signed the Convention with the aim of returning their greenhouse gas emissions to 1990 levels by the year 2000. A further international response was agreed in December 1997 in the form of the Kyoto Protocol. Under the Protocol, developed countries agreed to reduce their overall emissions of carbon dioxide, methane, nitrous oxide, hydrofluorocarbons, perfluorocarbons and sulphur hexafluoride. In 1998 the UK agreed to reduce its emissions by 12.5 per cent and this figure is the UK's legally binding target under the Protocol.

The UK climate change programme

8–035   The UK published its own climate change programme in November 2000. This includes a variety of policies and measures which seek to deliver the UK's Kyoto target. These policies include steps to improve business use of energy, measures to encourage new and more efficient sources of power generation by way of investment in research and reduced costs and the promotion of better energy efficiency in the domestic sector.

A climate change perspective has been incorporated into various areas of government policy including building regulations, flood and coastal defence, water resources, and health. Private and public sector organisations are encouraged to take responsibility for adapting to climate change and the UK Climate Impacts Programme (UKCIP) set up in 1997 provides guidance for organisations wishing to assess their vulnerability to climate change.

The climate change levy

8–036   As part of the UK climate change programme, the government introduced a tax on business energy use, known as the climate change levy. This is a tax on the use of energy in industry, commerce and the public sector. The government claims that the levy entails no increase in the tax burden on industry and provides no net gain for the public finances. The revenues from the levy are "returned" to industry in the form of a cut in the rate of employers' National Insurance contributions and the benefit of various schemes which promote energy efficiency and renewable sources of energy.

Provision for the levy is contained in s.30 of the Finance Act 2000 together with various pieces of subordinate legislation including the Climate Change Levy (Registration and Miscellaneous Provisions) Regulations 2001.[20] The levy was introduced on April 1, 2001 at the following rates: 0.15p/kWh for gas, 1.17p/kg (equivalent to 0.15 p/kWh) for coal, 0.96p/kg (equivalent to 0.07p/kWh) for liquefied petroleum gas (lpg) and 0.43p/kWh for electricity.

The use of fuels by the domestic and transport sectors is unaffected by the levy, as is the use of fuel for non-energy purposes. The levy does not apply to energy used by registered charities for non-business uses, nor that which is used by small firms. Oils, which are already subject to excise duty, are not subject to the levy.

Exemptions from the levy are listed in Sch.6 of the Finance Act 2000. These include electricity generated from new renewable energy, fuel used by good quality combined heat and power (CHP) schemes and fuels used as a feedstock. CHP technology is seen as a key element of the UK climate change strategy and the government is keen to promote the advantages of it, both for business and the environment. The exemption for CHP is detailed in the Climate Change Levy (General) (Amendment) Regulations 2003[21] and the Climate Change Levy (Combined Heat and Power Stations) Prescribed Conditions and Efficiency Percentages (Amendment) Regulations 2003.[22] From November 1, 2003, coal mine methane has been added to the list of levy exemptions by the Climate Change Levy (General) (Amendment) (No. 2) Regulations 2003.[23]

Good quality is verified by CHPQA (quality assurance); a voluntary programme designed to assess, monitor and certify the quality of CHP schemes. If a CHP scheme is judged to be eligible all electricity used on site or sold direct to other users will be exempt from the levy.

Climate change agreements

Energy intensive industries were able to enter into climate change agreements with the government. These agreements set out energy efficiency targets which must be achieved by individual companies if they are to be entitled to an 80 per cent discount from the climate change levy. Those industry sectors which have been designated as "energy intensive" are those which carry out activities listed as either Part A1 or Part A2 processes in Pt 1 of Sch.1 to the Pollution Prevention and Control (England and Wales) Regulations 2000.[24] These include 10 major sectors; aluminium, cement, ceramics, chemicals, food and drink, foundries, glass, non-ferrous metals, paper and steel, together with 30 smaller sectors—see Ch.9.

There are two forms of climate change agreement. The first arrangement is where the government will enter into an umbrella agreement with the

8–037

---

[20] SI 2001/7.
[21] SI 2003/604.
[22] SI 2003/861.
[23] SI 2003/2633.
[24] SI 2000/1973 (as amended by the Pollution Prevention and Control (England and Wales) (Amendment) Regulations 2001, SI 2001/503.

trade association for the relevant industry, together with an underlying agreement between the government and the individual company. The second option is very similar, although the underlying agreement is entered into between the trade association and the company. Should the sector as a whole fail to meet their target under the umbrella agreement, companies' performance will be assessed individually under the underlying agreements. The agreements do not create contractual obligations. However, if a company fails to meet its target within a two year period, the discount for the following two years may be lost.

United Kingdom emissions trading scheme

8–038   An element of the government's climate change policy is the greenhouse gas emissions trading scheme.

The scheme is presently voluntary and started in April 2002. However, a statutory basis has now been provided by the Waste and Emissions Trading Act 2003. At the time of writing, the Act is not yet fully in force. The scheme will enable participants to either meet statutory targets by straightforward reduction, alternatively beat their target and sell or bank the excess allowance or buy allowances from other participants so as to enable the emissions to remain above the target. Explanatory notes have been published by DEFRA to assist in the interpretation of the Act.[25] A range of organisations, mainly trade associations, and individual companies comprising those with major emissions of greenhouse gases have entered into agreements with the government to reduce emissions of carbon dioxide equivalent. For this they receive an agreed amount of incentive payment from the government. In circumstances where a participating organisation has succeeded in reducing emissions below the agreed target, an emissions credit is generated which is capable of being traded under the emissions traded under the emissions trading scheme. In these circumstances, any organisations that has failed to meet its target made by the emissions credit from a more successful participant.[26]

The Greenhouse Gas Emissions Trading Scheme Regulations 2003 came into force on December 31, 2003. The regulations are in four parts: Pt 1 sets out general provisions and identifies the activities emitting carbon dioxide, which are the subject of the scheme. Part 2 sets out the procedures for obtaining any necessary permit for these processes and for the permit's variation, transfer, surrender and revocation. Part 3 provides for the allocation of allowances on the basis of a national plan. Part 4 provides for certain administrative requirements including enforcement, appeals, offences and the like.

---

[25] See Explanatory Notes to the Waste and Emissions Trading Act 2003 (DEFRA, February 2004).

[26] For more information, see "The Rules for UK Greenhouse Gas Emissions Trading Scheme 2002", "Guidelines for the Measurement and Reporting of Emissions in the UK Emissions Trading Scheme" and "DEFRA Guidance on Group Participation in the UK Emissions Trading Scheme, 2001". These documents are all obtainable from DEFRA. See also the Air Quality Limit Values Regulations 2001, SI 2001/2315.

European trading scheme

An EU emissions trading scheme was approved by the European Parlia-   **8–039**
ment in July 2003. The scheme is presently limited to energy intensive
sectors but may be extended at a later date to include others including
chemical, aluminium and transport companies. All installations caught by
the scheme will need to apply for a permit for 2004. There is an option not
to take part in the first phase if that would involve losing the 80 per cent
exemption from the climate change levy.

DANGEROUS SUBSTANCES CONTROL

The European Council Directive 96/59/EC concerning the disposal of   **8–040**
polychlorinated biphenyls and polychlorinated terphenyls (PCBs) has led to
the provision of UK Government regulations. The effect of the Environmental Protection (Disposal of Polychlorinated Biphenyls and Other Dangerous Substances) (England and Wales) Regulations 2000[27] is to deal
primarily with the holding labelling decontamination and disposal of PCBs.
They build on the existing licensing requirements contained within the EPA
1990. The following matters are dealt with:

- a system of registration with the Environment Agency for all
  holders of equipment contaminated by PCBs;
- the banning, after 2000, of the holding of PCBs and equipment
  containing them;
- a requirement for labelling of contaminated and decontaminated
  equipment in a specified form;
- the imposition on the Environment Agency of a range of monitoring, recording and inspection obligations;
- the creation of a number of criminal offences for failure to comply
  with the regulations.

[27] SI 2000/104.

CHAPTER 9

POLLUTION PREVENTION AND CONTROL ACT 1999

INTRODUCTION

This Act and the Pollution Prevention and Control (England) Regulations **9–001** 2000[1] effect the implementation of EC Directive 96/61/EC on integrated pollution, prevention and control (the IPCC Directive). Because a range of waste management operations is required by the terms of the Directive to be controlled, the existing provisions in Pts I and II of EPA 1990 are significantly adjusted. Indeed, Pt I is to be repealed. Those activities currently regulated under the waste management licence system in Pt II but falling within para.5 of Annex 1 to the Directive will, in future, be regulated under the 1999 Act and Regulations. For landfills and similar operations the 2000 Regulations will apply.

The 1999 Act and the 2000 Regulations were brought into force on August 1, 2000. All new operations caught by the provisions will need to be the subject of a permit under these provisions. Most existing operations which are the subject of a substantial change (see para.9–007) will also need a new permit before the change can be effected. All other operations may continue under the terms of their existing approvals. Requirements for permits under the new Act for existing operations will be phased in over a period up to 2007. The government's published intentions were that most waste operations would be phased in between 2003 and 2004.

The implications of the IPPC Directive

By and large the IPPC Directive follows the powers set out in Pt I of EPA **9–002** 1990, which PPCA 1999 will replace. The main differences between the EPA 1990 Act regime and PPCA 1999 are:

(a) control is of "installations" compared with "processes" as in the 1990 Act;

(b) the range of processes now caught by the legislation is significantly increased—in particular, landfills are the subject of the Directive, hence modifications to Pt II of EPA 1990;

(c) the scope of control is wider in the 1999 Act, in that assessment of energy efficiency, consumption of raw materials and noise emissions must be considered before authorisations are granted and

[1] SI 2000/1973.

these matters will need to be the subject of conditions where appropriate; and

(d) a standard of BAT (best available techniques) for avoiding pollution replaces BATNEEC used in the 1990 Act; however, it is envisaged that there will be only minimal difference in practice between the two standards, "available techniques" in BAT being assumed to include consideration of cost.

PPCA 1999 is short, containing only seven sections and three schedules, mainly granting powers to the Secretary of State to make regulations which themselves impose the day-to-day requirements of the legislation. Sch.1 to the Act specifies the purposes for which provision may be made by regulations under s.2. The list of purposes includes:

- establishing standards, objectives or requirements in relation to emissions;
- authorising the making of plans for overall limits for emissions, allocation of quotas or progressive improvement of standards or objectives;
- providing for the making of schemes for trading or other transfer of quotas;
- allocating responsibility for the issue and enforcement of permits and controls;
- giving powers to the Secretary of State to make directions;
- providing for a scheme whereby permits are issued and conditions imposed, prescribing the contents of permits and their review, variation and other changes;
- regulating the transfer or surrender of permits and their revocation together with requirements for preventive or remedial action;
- authorising charging schemes;
- enabling the compilation and issuing of information;
- securing publicity by way of registers and otherwise;
- conferring enforcement obligations and the creation of offences;
- conferring rights of appeal;
- dealing with supplementary provisions concerning particulartypes of pollution.

Pollution Prevention and Control (England and Wales) Regulations 2000 (SI 2000/1973)[2]

9–003 These Regulations came into force on August 1, 2000 and represent the effective substitution for Pt I of EPA 1990. However, it should be appreciated that there will be a transitional period when both Pt I and the

---

[2] This section should be read in conjunction with the requirements of the Landfill (England and Wales) Regulations 2002 (SI 2002/1559)—see para.10–073.

new Regulations will operate side by side. The Regulations have been amended from time. Where appropriate, the changes have been noted in this chapter.

As to waste incineration, see also the Waste Incineration (England and Wales) Regulations 2002.[3]

ADMINISTRATION OF PPCA 1999 AND THE NEW REGULATIONS

Administration of the PPCA 1999 regime is divided generally along the lines applicable to EPA 1990. However, whereas under the latter there were two types of processes, Part A usually administered by the Environment Agency, and Part B, by local authorities (see para.8–002 above), the 2000 Regulations identify three different types of installation. Regulation 8 deals with these matters. **9–004**

Part A(1) installations (including certain mobile plant) will be the responsibility of the EA: such installations will be those which have the most significant potential for pollution. Part A(2) installations and mobile plant will be the function of the local authority in whose area the installation is situated or where the mobile plant is operated. These installations, while not perceived as having the same pollution potential as A(1) installations, are nonetheless being treated as those where an integrated system of control is necessary. The regulators' function will be generally to ensure the reduction of emissions into air, water and land and to consider these matters in an integrated manner. Finally, Part B installations will be the responsibility of the local authority in whose area the installation is situated.

As to mobile plant, the regulator will be the local authority for the place where the operator of the mobile plant has his principal place of business, provided that is in England and Wales. Where the principal place of business is outside England and Wales, the normal rule will be that the permit will be granted by the local authority for the area where the plant is first intended to be operated.

Note that the Secretary of State has power to transfer regulatory responsibilities between the EA and the local authority or vice versa.

Part B installations, whether regulated by the EA or local authorities (as transferred by the Secretary of State), are only the subject of control under PPCA 1999 for the purpose of preventing or reducing emissions into the air. Other emissions are controlled under existing legislation.[4]

The identification of the appropriate local authority is set out in reg.8(15) of the 2000 Regulations and follows the provisions of Pt I of EPA 1990:

(a) in Greater London, a London borough council, the Common Council of the City of London, the Sub-treasurer of the Inner Temple and the Under Treasurer of the Middle Temple;

---

[3] SI 2002/2980—see para.10–073.
[4] *e.g.* WRA 1991—see para.7–027.

(b) in England outside Greater London, a unitary or district council, or where there is no district council, a county council, and the council of the Isles of Scilly; and

(c) in Wales, a county council or county borough council.

Guidance

9–005   PPCA 1999 and the 2000 Regulations authorise the Secretary of State (and the EA) to issue guidance on the legislation generally and on specific installations and processes. General guidance has been issued upon the coming into force of the Regulations.[5] Specific guidance will be published from time to time. Meanwhile, any relevant guidance under Pt I of EPA 1990 will continue to be applied where appropriate, until superseded (see para.8–019 above).

In respect of local government control under the 1999 Act, see the DEFRA Guide, "LA-IPPC and LAPPC Policy and Permitting Procedures". The guidance is statutory and as a consequence local authorities are bound to have regard to it. Guidance for the purposes of compliance with the 1999 Act falls into two categories, so called "horizontal" guidance which will apply, as appropriate, across the whole range of authorised installations, and industry specific guidance. An example of a horizontal guidance note is IPPC H3 Part 1 and Part 2, published by the Environment Agency and dealing with the permitting of emissions of noise and vibration.

PERMIT TO OPERATE

Requirement for permit to operate

9–006   Under the terms of reg.9 of the 2000 Regulations, it will be an offence to operate an installation or mobile plant after the prescribed date. That date is determined under the provisions of Sch.3 to the Regulations and will depend upon a range of circumstances. It will also depend upon whether the installation or plant is the subject of Pt A or Pt B of Sch.1 (see Appendix 4 below).

Prescribed dates for Part A installations or plant (Sch.3, Pt 1)

9–007   In the case of a new Part A installation or plant where an application for a permit to operate has been made before the transitional date (*i.e.* January 1, 2001), the prescribed date is the date when the application is determined. Otherwise, where no application has been made, the date is January 1, 2001. In the case of existing Part A installation or plant the prescribed date

---

[5] See *Integrated Pollution Prevention and Control: A Practical Guide* (2nd ed.), DEFRA, 2002.

will be the date when the application is determined, provided this is made before or during the relevant period. Where no such application is made the permit is required after the relevant period expires. The relevant periods are defined by reference to a table appearing in Pt 1 of Sch.3 and are set out, where appropriate, in Appendix 4.

Sometimes installations will fall within different descriptions in Sch.1 and special rules are provided to determine requirements for the date for application.

The rules about dates of application in respect of new Part A installations or plant also apply where an existing facility is the subject of substantial change.[6]

Thus, it follows that in respect of Part A installations, the onus will be mainly on the operator to ensure that at the appropriate time an application for a permit is made. This is mainly because the requirements of PPCA 1999 are more comprehensive than those in Pt I of EPA 1990. It follows that, for existing installations and plant, a more detailed investigation of the proposed activities and systems of control will need to be made by the regulator before a permit can be granted. Indeed, the conditions of any permit will need to be more comprehensive than those normally found in a Pt I authorisation.

Permits for Part B installations or plant

In the case of most existing Part B installations and plant, the changes effected by PPCA 1999 are more modest. The Government has decided that only in special circumstances will the operator need to take the initiative to secure a PPCA 1999 permit in respect of the installation or plant. Requirements for permits in respect of Part B facilities are intended to be phased in accordance with provisions set out in Pt 2 of Sch.3; the relevant dates are noted in Appendix 4. Note that only in respect of a new or an authorised substantially changed Part B facility will an application be required to be made. When the relevant date arrives, the regulator, usually the local authority, will be required to initiate the necessary procedures for issuing the new PPCA 1999 permit and complete these procedures within 12 months of a deemed application. Neither new nor substantially changed Part B installations will be required to be subject to an application for a PPCA 1999 permit before the phase-in date for their sector.

9–008

Applications for permits (reg.10)

An application for a permit must be made in accordance with Pt 1 of Sch.4 to the 2000 Regulations and be accompanied by a fee prescribed under s.41 of the Environment Act 1995 or reg.22 of the Regulations. The application

9–009

---

[6] For guidance on what constitutes "substantial change", see *Integrated Pollution Prevention and Control: A Practical Guide*, Annex II (DEFRA).

will be made on the form to be supplied by the regulator and will be required to contain significant amounts of information as set out in paras 1—3 of Sch.4. The regulator may require further information to determine the application. It is the applicant's responsibility to advertise his application. The period for this must start 14 days after the application and will end 28 days thereafter. The advertisement must appear in one or more newspapers circulating in the locality and, in the case of Part A facilities, in the London Gazette. The contents of the advertisement are specified in para.6 of Sch.4. Note that a requirement to advertise does not apply in the case of a permit to operate an installation involving only the burning of waste oil in an appliance with a rated thermal capacity of less than 0.4 MW.

A guide to assist with applications for waste management operations, or their modifications, has been published by the Environment Agency. "A practical guide to environmental risk assessment for waste management facilities, version 2" provides:

- "Shell licensing kits", designed to guide proposals in relation to particular types of site. This includes a risk assessment pack, specification of information required for the working plan and details of typical licence conditions.
- Detailed guidance on the requirements for a risk assessment, now required for all applications for waste management licences.
- Detailed guidance on the preparation and maintenance of working plans.

Further guidance in relation to landfills is also available (see para.10–073).

Consultations by the regulator

9–010   Generally the regulator must, within 14 days of receiving an application, send a copy of it to various consultees. These are generally specified in Pt 2 of Sch.4 to the 2000 Regulations and will vary depending upon the type of facility in question, in particular whether it is a Part A or Part B facility. Note that there should be consultation with any person likely to be the subject of an off-site condition. Before any permit is granted, the regulator is required to serve notice on that person, describing the off-site condition in question and the implications of that condition and he must specify the period allowed for representations. The notice will normally be served upon the owner, lessee or occupier of land to be the subject of an off-site condition. Any representations made by such a person must be taken into account.

Off-site conditions are likely to provide for the installation of monitoring and similar matters. Any person who is materially affected by the imposition of such a condition will usually be entitled to compensation, which is determined under the terms of Sch.6 to the Regulations.

The Secretary of State has power to require that any particular application should be referred to him for determination (Sch.4, para.14).

National security and confidential information

Special rules will apply where an application relates to activities or   **9–011**
information affecting national security or where such information is
required to remain confidential. The circumstances are set out in regs 30
and 31. These provisions facilitate the exclusion of certain information from
registers (see para.9–030 below). It is for the Secretary of State to identify
information which affects national security but, in regard to commercially
confidential information, it is generally for the applicant to satisfy the
regulator that the information should be excluded. The procedure for this is
set out in reg.31 and in paras 20–24 of Sch.4. In the event of the
applicability of reg.30 or 31, there are modified rules and regulations for
advertisements of applications.[7]

Determination of applications

The regulator has a range of responsibilities in the determination of   **9–012**
applications, mainly set out in Pt 2 of Sch.4 to the 2000 Regulations.
However, some general principles are set out in reg.10, including the
following:

(a) No permit should be granted if the regulator considers that the
    applicant will not be the person who will have control over the
    operation of the facility or will not ensure that it is operated so as
    to comply with the conditions which would be included in the
    permit.

(b) Where the application for the permit would authorise the carrying
    on of a specified waste management activity (mainly landfills,
    waste processing plants not involving incineration, and recovery
    plants), the regulator must be satisfied that the applicant is a "fit
    and proper person" to carry out the activity. "Fit and proper
    person" provisions are set out in reg.4 and largely follow the rules
    which hitherto have applied under s.74 of EPA 1990 (see para.10–
    063).

(c) In the case of a specified waste management activity, the appli-
    cation site must the subject of a prior planning permission or there
    must be proof that no planning permission is required.

The relaxation of obligations in the case of specified waste management
activities has been achieved by the Pollution Prevention and Control
(England and Wales) (Amendment) (No. 2) Regulations 2003.[8] The
provisions came into force on January 7, 2004. The main effect is to delete
from the definition of specified waste management activity those which are

---

[7] Guidance on the procedures and contents of applications is included in *Integrated Pollution
and Prevention Control: A Practical Guide* (2nd ed., DEFRA 2002).
[8] SI 2003/3296.

carried on at the same installation and are ancillary to any activity which already itself falls within the main polluting processes set out in Pt A(1) of Pt 1 of Sch.1 to the main regulations—see para.9–004 above. Some obligations are also relaxed where the specified waste management activity does not consist of a landfill operation as defined in para.5.2 of Sch.1 to the main regulations—see Appendix 4.

In most cases, the regulator is required to give notice of determination within a period of four months of receipt, but a longer period may be agreed with the applicant. Where the period has expired without a decision, the applicant may treat the application as a refusal but must give notice to the regulator that he is intending to treat the failure as such.

Conditions of permits

9–013   Assuming that the regulator has decided to issue a permit, he must formulate the conditions which should be imposed. Regulation 11 sets out some general principles which must be obeyed. In the case of a Part A facility, these include requirements that it should be operated so that all appropriate preventative measures are taken against pollution (in particular through application of the BAT); that no significant pollution is caused; that waste production is avoided, recovered or, where that is technically or economically impossible, disposed of so as to avoid or reduce the impact on the environment; that energy is used efficiently; and that the necessary measures are taken to prevent accidents and limit their consequences. Furthermore, upon the cessation of activities, measures shall be taken to avoid any pollution risk and to return the site to a satisfactory state. The criteria for this are set out in guidance issued by the Secretary of State.

Otherwise, by reg.12, the regulator is required to impose conditions as are appropriate and which ensure a high level of protection for the environment as a whole. However, in the case of a Part B facility, where the system of control concerns air pollution alone, only the prevention or reduction of emissions into the air is taken into account.

Special arrangements need to apply in relation to Part A(2) facilities and reg.13 deals with these. These arrangements are required because normally a Part A(2) facility will be the subject of regulation by the local authority, but it will need to consider the grant of a permit by reference to the protection of the environment as a whole. Some elements of environmental control will be the responsibility of the EA. Regulation 13 therefore requires that the EA may at any time specify conditions and other limits with particular reference to discharges to water.

Best available techniques

9–014   By the terms of PPCA 1999 and the subsidiary regulations, the regulator and the operator must ensure that BAT is employed throughout the permitted operation. Regulation 3 extensively defines the term as meaning the most effective and advanced stage in the development of activities and their methods of operation which indicates the practical suitability of particular techniques for providing in principle the basis for emission limit values designed to prevent and, where that it is not practicable, generally to reduce emissions and the impact on the environment as a whole. For the purposes of this definition:

    (a) "available techniques" means those techniques which have been developed on a scale which allows implementation in the relevant industrial sector under economically and technically viable conditions, taking into consideration the cost and advantages, whether or not the techniques are used or produced inside the United Kingdom, as long as they are reasonably accessible to the operator;

    (b) "best" means, in relation to techniques, the most effective in achieving a high general level of protection of the environment as a whole; and

    (c) "techniques" includes both the technology used and the way in which the installation is designed, built, maintained, operated and decommissioned.

Schedule 2 to the 2000 Regulations provides greater specification as to the matters to be taken into account in arriving at a determination for what are best available techniques.

Although there is a difference between the BAT criteria under PPCA 1999 and BATNEEC under EPA 1990 (see para.8–013 above), it is thought that the difference will be largely unimportant in itself. This is particularly so having regard to the acceptance in the definition of BAT that economic and technical viability must be taken into account. In these circumstances the absence from the definition of BAT of the addition "not entailing excessive costs" would not appear to be significant.

General binding rules

The IPPC Directive recognises that there may be certain facilities which **9–015** have standard characteristics and/or where environmental impacts are minimal and where the full range of controls and conditions is not justified. Accordingly there is provision for a simplified procedure, implemented in reg.14 of the 2000 Regulations, relating to general binding rules. It is unlikely that other than very few small waste facilities will have such limited pollution potential that the general binding rules will apply. However, reg.14 enables the Secretary of State to make these rules. These will consist of requirements that apply to certain types of facility which can be used instead of specific permit conditions (although the rules will apply in precisely the same way as conditions do and be binding accordingly). General binding rules will be suitable for industry sectors where installations share similar characteristics. The procedures envisage that the applicant will seek a "general binding rules condition" and it will be for the regulator to consider this proposal. Powers are available to the Secretary of State to withdraw the general binding rules condition in respect of any sector or specific facility.

Reviews of conditions of permits (regs 16 and 17)

9–016   The regime of control envisages that regulators will review periodically the conditions of permits. Review can be carried out at any time, but will normally arise where:

> (a) significant pollution is emitted from a facility and the controls need to be changed;
> (b) substantial changes in BAT enable tighter controls to be imposed without excessive costs resulting; or
> (c) the operational safety of the activities requires other techniques to be used.

Changes in the operation of an installation

9–017   Where the operator of an installation decides to make changes, he is required to give 14 days' notice to the regulator, but notice is not required if a variation application is being made under reg.17. Under reg.17, the regulator may at any time vary the conditions of a permit but an operator may seek variation under reg.17(2). This is facilitated by an application made in accordance with Pt 1 of Sch.7 to the Regulations and the application must be accompanied by a fee. The application is considered by the regulator along the same lines as would be employed with an application for a new facility, with some modification as indicated in Sch.7.

Action on review or change

9–018   Where on the initiative of the regulator or the operator, the former decides that the conditions of a permit should be varied, notice is required to be served on the operator (a variation notice) specifying the variations of the conditions of the permit and the date or dates on which the variations are to take effect. If the regulator decides, following an application by the operator to vary, that no variation is appropriate then notice of that decision must be given to the operator. The procedures are set out in Pt 2 of Sch.7. For the rights of appeal see para.9–026 below.

Transfer of permits (reg.18)

9–019   An application for a transfer of a permit is made jointly by the existing operator and the proposed transferee. Details of the requirements of the application are set out in reg.18 and the application must be granted unless the regulator believes that the transferee will not have control over the operation and will not ensure compliance with the conditions. In the case of a specified waste management activity (see para.9–012), the regulator must also be satisfied that the transferee is a fit and proper person to carry out the activity (see para.10–063 below). In the event that the regulator fails to make a decision on the application for a transfer within two months, or such longer period as may be agreed, the applicants are entitled to notify the regulator that the application should be deemed refused and a right of appeal is available (see para.9–026 below).

Surrender of a permit

Provisions relating to the surrender of a permit are set out in regs 19 and **9–020** 20 of the 2000 Regulations. The procedures are different depending on whether the permit is for a Part A or Part B facility. In the case of the former, the procedures involve notice to the regulator of the intention to surrender part or all of the permit. A fee is payable. Regulation 19 specifies certain information which needs to be given to the regulator and this includes a site report, identifying the site's condition. This must be accompanied by a description of any steps which have been taken to avoid any pollution risk and to return it to a satisfactory state. The regulator must be satisfied that the pollution risks associated with the site have been satisfactorily dealt with and only then may he accept surrender, by notice to the operator. If he is not so satisfied then he must issue a refusal notice. This must all be dealt with within three months or such longer period as may be agreed. Again, failure to give notice of determination may be treated as a refusal and appeal provisions apply (see para.9–026 below).

In the case of a permit for a Part B installation, the procedures are much simpler and all that is required is notice from the operator to the regulator, giving limited information and the date on which the surrender is to take effect. There is no requirement for a site report, nor does the regulator have to consider whether the site is in a satisfactory condition. However, in the case of many waste management facilities, it will be appreciated that powers to deal with their condition are also contained in Pt II of EPA 1990 (see para.10–022 below).

Revocation of permits

Permits may be revoked by the regulator, either wholly or in part under **9–021** reg.21 of the 2000 Regulations. Indeed, revocation is possible in the case of a waste management facility if the operator has ceased to be a fit and proper person within the meaning of reg.4. The regulator has powers under reg.21 to revoke the whole or a part of a permit. The notice of revocation must identify the date on which this takes effect, which may not be less than 28 days from the date of service. In the case of Part A facilities, a notice of revocation may require the operator to take steps to avoid pollution risks or to return the site to a satisfactory state. For appeals, see para.9–026 below.

ENFORCEMENT

9–022   There is an obligation under reg.23 of the 2000 Regulations for the regulator to ensure that the conditions of any permit are complied with. He has a number of powers of enforcement, beyond the formal revocation as mentioned above.

Enforcement notices

9–023   The actual or anticipated contravention of any condition of a permit entitles the regulator to serve an enforcement notice under reg.24. The notice is required to state the regulator's opinion about the contravention and the circumstances leading to that opinion, and must specify the steps to be taken by way of remediation and the period within which those steps must be taken. For appeals, see para.9–026; for offences, see para.9–031.

Suspension notices

9–024   The regulator will use a suspension notice invariably when the operation of the facility involves an imminent risk of serious pollution.[9] A suspension notice cannot be used contemporaneously with action under reg.26 (see below). Notice is required to be served on the operator of the facility and can be served whether or not the facility is regulated by or contravenes a condition of the permit. In respect of a waste management facility, the notice can be used in circumstances where the operator has ceased to be a fit and proper person (see para.10–063 above) because the management has ceased to be in the hands of a technically competent person.

The suspension notice is required to state the regulator's opinion about the condition of the plant or of the management, specify the imminent risk and the steps that must be taken to remove that risk. The notice must make clear that until it is withdrawn the authorisation to operate the facility is suspended, either wholly or in part. For appeals, see para.9–026; for offences, see para.9–031.

Prevention or remedying of pollution

9–025   Regulation 26 provides a more proactive power to the regulator to take action where a facility or the operation of it involves an imminent risk of serious pollution. The regulator has power to take steps to remove the risks

---

[9] 2000 Regulations, reg.25.

and to recover from the operator the cost of taking those steps. Notice must be served on the operator relating to the exercise of powers. Costs are not recoverable by the regulator if the operator shows that there was no imminent risk of serious pollution requiring steps to be taken. Regulation 26 powers are most likely to be used contemporaneously with proceedings in respect of offences.[10]

APPEALS

A wide range of appeals to the Secretary of State is available under reg.27 **9–026** of the 2000 Regulations.

Who may appeal?

An appeal may be lodged, depending on the particular circumstances of the **9–027** dispute, by a person:

- who has been refused the grant of a permit under reg.10;
- who has been refused the variation of the conditions of a permit on an application under reg.17;
- who is aggrieved by the conditions attached to his permit following an application under reg.10 or by a variation notice following an application under reg.17;
- whose application under reg.18 for a regulator to give effect to the transfer of a permit has been refused or who is aggrieved by the conditions attached to his permit to take account of such a transfer;
- whose application under reg.19 to surrender a permit has been refused or who is aggrieved by the conditions attached to his permit to take account of the surrender;
- on whom a variation notice is served, other than following an application under reg.17, or on whom a revocation notice, enforcement notice or suspension notice is served.

The powers of the Secretary of State enable him:

- to affirm the decision;
- where the decision was a refusal to grant a permit or to vary the conditions of a permit, to direct the regulator to grant the permit or to vary the conditions as the case may be;
- where the decision was about the conditions attached to a permit, to quash all or any of those conditions;
- where the decision was a refusal to effect the transfer or accept the surrender of a permit, to direct the regulator to effect the transfer or accept the surrender as the case may be.

[10] See reg.32, para.9–031 below.

In each of these cases the Secretary of State may give directions for further conditions to be attached to the permit. He also has powers to quash a variation, revocation, enforcement or suspension notice or to modify it.

In the case of a revocation notice, such revocation shall not take effect pending the final determination or the withdrawal of the appeal. In all other cases, the permits or notices appealed against will continue to have effect pending the outcome of the appeal.

Procedure for appeals

9–028 Schedule 8 to the 2000 Regulations sets down the procedures for any appeals to be made to the Secretary of State. The provisions of s.114 of the Environment Act 1995, which enable delegation of appeals decisions to inspectors appointed by the Secretary of State, are imported into the Regulations.

INFORMATION AND PUBLICITY

9–029 Wide powers are available to the Secretary of State and to the regulator to obtain information relevant to the discharge of the latter's functions. Failure to supply the information to a regulator is an offence.[11]

Public registers

9–030 The regulator has the responsibility to maintain a register under reg.29 which contains the particulars prescribed by Sch.9 to the Regulations. Registers will normally be maintained by local authorities but will also contain any particulars which are contained in a register maintained by the EA relating to Part A facilities. Where information in the register is excluded under regs 30 and/or 31 (see para.9–011 above) the register must make this clear. Registers are required by the regulator to be made available to the public at all reasonable times, without charge. Copies of entries may be taken by the public, on payment of a reasonable charge. There is no specification as to the form in which the register may be kept.

OFFENCES

9–031 Regulation 32 of the 2000 Regulations prescribes the various offences. These include:

- contravention of reg.9(1) (failure to have a permit);

[11] See reg.32, below.

- failure to comply with a permit or a condition;
- failure to comply with reg.16(1) (notice of any change in operation);
- failure to comply with the requirements of an enforcement or suspension notice;
- failure, without reasonable excuse, to comply with any requirement of a notice under reg.28(2) (demand for information);
- making a statement which the offender knows to be false or misleading in any material particular or recklessly making a false or misleading statement in any material particular: in purported compliance with a requirement to furnish information under the regulations, or for the purpose of obtaining the grant of a permit or its variation, transfer or surrender;
- intentionally making a false entry in any record required to be kept under the condition of a permit;
- with intent to deceive, forgery, use or possession of a document issued or authorised to be issued under a condition of a permit or required for any purpose under a condition;
- failure to comply with an order made by a court under reg.35 (remedying of an offence).

Penalties on conviction are substantial:

(a) on summary conviction, a fine not exceeding £20,000 or imprisonment for a term not exceeding six months, or both; or
(b) on indictment, an unlimited fine or imprisonment for a term not exceeding five years, or both.

However, in respect of offences relating to the provision of information under reg.16 (notification of change), compliance with a requirement under reg.28 (information), making a false statement or false entry, or forging a document the penalties are:

(a) on summary conviction a fine not exceeding the statutory maximum (presently £5,000); or
(b) on conviction on indictment an unlimited fine or imprisonment for a term not exceeding two years, or both.

Where an offence committed by a body corporate is proved to have been committed with the consent or connivance or is attributable to neglect on the part of a director, manager, secretary or other similar officer or any person purporting to act in such capacity, that individual, as well as the body corporate, may be found guilty of the offence and punished accordingly. Similar provisions apply where the body corporate is managed by its members.

On rare occasions, proceedings for breach of an enforcement or suspension notice may be thought by the regulator to be inadequate. In these circumstances the regulator is free to take proceedings in the High Court to ensure compliance with the notice. The powers of the High Court include the right to impose mandatory and other injunctions, breach of which will be a contempt of court where almost unlimited powers of enforcement are available.

Evidence

9–032   Regulation 34 provides that where, by virtue of a condition of a permit granted by a local authority regulator, an entry is required to be made in any record as to compliance with a condition and the entry has not been made, that fact shall be admissible as evidence that the condition has not been observed.

Power of court to order cause of offence to be remedied (reg.35)

9–033   The conviction of a person for an offence of failing to:

(a) have a valid permit;
(b) comply with its conditions; or
(c) comply with the requirements of an enforcement notice or suspension notice,

empowers the court to order remedial steps to be taken by the offender. The order must specify the time scale and the steps to be taken and this can only be made where it is within the offender's power to undertake the remedy. An order can be imposed either in substitution for or in addition to any other punishment authorised by the Regulations.

CHAPTER 10

WASTE ON LAND

INTRODUCTION

The main regulatory provisions of Pt II of EPA 1990 (waste on land) came **10–001** into force on May 1, 1994, replacing the provisions of COPA 1974. There are sections in the Public Health Acts 1936 and 1961 which provide that statutory nuisance procedures (see p. 00) can be applied in the case of deposits of noxious matter, polluted ponds, pools, ditches, gutters, or watercourses or canals. Section 34 of the 1961 Act enables the local authority to take steps for removing from land in the open air any rubbish which is seriously detrimental to the amenities of the neighbourhood. A notice must be served on the owner and occupier of the land before such action can be taken and there are rights of counter-notice.

Just as the provisions of COPA 1974 were replaced by Pt II of EPA 1990, so the latter is intended to be substantially replaced by the provisions of PPCA 1999 and the subsidiary regulations of 2000 (as amended)—see Ch.9. However, not all waste management activities will be the subject of control under the 1999 Act; for example, landfills accepting inert waste only, not exceeding 25,000 tonnes and certain small incineration and treatment plants.[1]

CONTROL OF POLLUTION ACT 1974

Before the coming into force of COPA 1974, the control of waste on land **10–002** rested almost exclusively on the statutory nuisance provisions of the Public Health Act 1936 and such conditions as could be imposed under the Town and Country Planning Acts. It became apparent that this legislation was inadequate to control the activities of a fast-growing industry which was, in turn, to deal with the disposal, usually by landfill, of the rapidly increasing quantities of waste produced by an affluent British post-war society.

COPA 1974 brought into force a new system of control of waste disposal. Subject to some amendments this remained the appropriate Act, until its replacement by EPA 1990. There will be occasions when licences and other documents fall to be interpreted by reference to COPA 1974. This commentary is, therefore, retained.

---

[1] For further clarification see Appendix 4.

The definition of "waste"

10–003   "Waste" was defined by s.30(1) of COPA 1974 as including:

(a) any substance which constitutes a scrap material or an effluent or other unwanted surplus substance arising from the application of any process; and

(b) any substance or article which requires to be disposed of, has been broken, worn out, contaminated or otherwise spoiled,

but does not include a substance which is an explosive within the meaning of the Explosives Act 1875.

There have been a number of cases concerned with the definition of "waste". The general principle is that it must be interpreted by reference to the person disposing of the material. Accordingly, an occupier may need a licence for the disposal even of top soil from a building site, and may be convicted of an offence of tipping this material on another's land without a licence.[2]

"Controlled waste"

10–004   The regulation of the disposal of waste was mainly by reference to "controlled waste". Thus, by s.3 of COPA 1974, except in prescribed cases, a person could not:

(a) deposit controlled waste, or cause or knowingly permit controlled waste to be deposited, on any land; or

(b) use any plant or equipment, or cause or knowingly permit any plant or equipment to be used, for the purpose of disposing of or of dealing in a prescribed manner with controlled waste

unless the land on which the waste was deposited or, as the case may be, which forms the site of the plant or equipment was occupied by the holder of a licence issued in pursuance of s.5.

A licence under (a) and (b) above would authorise the deposit or use in question and such deposit or use had to be in accordance with the conditions, if any, specified in it. Failure to comply with s.3 was an offence, with substantial penalties including, on indictment, liability to imprisonment for up to two years. Indeed, in the case of waste which was poisonous, noxious or polluting or gave rise to an environmental hazard and was deposited in a way that could be assumed to involve abandonment, imprisonment might be up to five years.

"Controlled waste" was defined as household, industrial and commercial waste which, in turn, had three separate definitions,[3] as follows.

---

[2] *Long v Brooke* [1980] Crim. L.R. 109. The definition is examined in further detail below (see para.10–031).

[3] COPA 1974, s.30(3).

(a) "Household waste" consisted of waste from a private dwelling or residential home or from premises forming part of a university or school or other educational establishment or forming part of a hospital or nursing home.

(b) "Industrial waste" consisted of waste from any factory within the meaning of the Factories Act 1961 and any premises occupied by a body corporate established by or under any enactment for the purpose of carrying on under national ownership any industry or part of an industry or any undertaking, excluding waste from any mine or quarry.

(c) "Commercial waste" consisted of waste from premises used wholly or mainly for the purposes of a trade or business or the purposes of sport, recreation or entertainment, excluding:

(i) household and industrial waste; and

(ii) waste from any mine or quarry and from premises used for agriculture within the meaning of the Agriculture Act 1986; and

(iii) waste of any other description so prescribed.

The Secretary of State had powers under s.30(4) to modify these definitions and some modifications were provided in the Collection and Disposal of Waste Regulations 1988[4] and the Control of Pollution (Special Waste) Regulations 1980, as amended, (see below).

Licences

Given the provisions of s.3 of COPA 1974, it was necessary in most cases to **10–005** ensure that the disposal of controlled waste was the subject of a licence issued by the disposal authority. For regulatory purposes the disposal authority was:

- in Greater London, the London Waste Regulation Authority;
- in Greater Manchester, the Greater Manchester Waste Disposal Authority;
- in Merseyside, the Merseyside Waste Disposal Authority;
- elsewhere in England, the county council or the metropolitan district council;
- in Wales, the district council.

A disposal licence was not required for any process when an authorisation under the IPC provisions of Pt I of EPA 1990 was in force.

Outline of application procedure

An application for a waste disposal licence was dealt with in the Collection **10–006** and Disposal of Waste Regulations 1988.[5]

---

[1] For further clarification see Appendix 4.
[5] SI 1988/819.

The application was required to be made by the occupier of the land. The disposal authority was bound to grant the application (assuming that it was technically in order) unless rejection was necessary for the purpose of preventing pollution of water or danger to public health. A planning permission for the activity had to exist under TCPA 1990 or its predecessors before a disposal licence could be granted. The single exception to this provision was where planning permission was not required for the activity in question. A licence granted in the absence of an adequate planning permission would appear to be void.[6]

Conditions of a licence

10–007   Section 6 of COPA 1974 provided the extent to which conditions could be imposed on any disposal licence. These concerned:

  (a) the duration of the licence;
  (b) the supervision by the holder of activities to which the licence related;
  (c) the kinds and qualities of waste which could be dealt with in pursuance of the licence, the methods of dealing with them and the recording of information;
  (d) precautions to be taken on the land to which the licence related;
  (e) the steps to be taken to facilitate compliance with conditions of the planning permission on which the licence was based;
  (f) the hours of working; and
  (g) any works to be carried out in connection with the land, plant or equipment to which the licence related, before the activities authorised by the licence were begun or while they were continuing.

Department of the Environment Circulars

10–008   Helpful information about the grant of licences and conditions may be found in DoE Circulars 55/76, "Control of Pollution Act 1974—Part I (Waste on Land) Disposal Licences" and 13/88, "Control of Pollution Act 1974: The Collection and Disposal of Waste Regulations" (now replaced).

Waste management papers

10–009   From time to time the DoE (now the DETR) has published a series of policy statements and guidance notes relating to technical and administrative aspects of waste management and control. There is now a large number

---

[6] See *R. v Derbyshire CC Ex p. North East Derbyshire DC* [1979] 77 L.G.R. 389.

of waste management papers, some of which have been revised. A full list of these papers is in Appendix 3 below. Careful attention should be paid to these papers since they give useful technical guidance and also demonstrate the standards and policies which the DETR would expect to see applied in the regulatory processes.

Appeals

An appeal could be made to the Secretary of State on: **10–010**

  (a) the refusal of a site licence;
  (b) the grant of a site licence subject to unacceptable conditions; or
  (c) the failure by the local authority to reach a decision on an application within the time permitted which, unless extended by agreement, was two months.

The procedure for appeals was set out in the Collection and Disposal of Waste Regulations 1988[7] However, procedures were not specified in detail. The Secretary of State has power to hold a public inquiry under s.290 of the Local Government Act 1972. While it was within his power to make a decision on the appeal, he effected this by a direction to the authority, which was then required to issue any appropriate licence or decision in accordance with his direction.

Modification and revocation of licences

It was open to a holder of a disposal licence to seek its modification. An   **10–011** application to the authority was required and an appeal process was available in the event that the holder was not satisfied with the decision.

It was also open to the authority to seek a modification of a licence or revocation. In either case such modification or revocation could be pursued at any time during the currency of the site licence. Again, an appeal could be made by the holder. Where the appeal was against modification of conditions of a licence or against its revocation, a decision of the authority was held in suspension until the appeal was dismissed or withdrawn,[8] except where:

  (a) the authority's notice was served in pursuance of s.7 (variation and revocation) or 9(4)(b) (revocation after failure to comply with notice to comply with a condition); and
  (b) the authority included in its notice a statement that in its opinion it was necessary for the purpose of preventing pollution of water or danger to public health that the suspension of revocation provisions should not apply.

[7] SI 1988/819.
[8] COPA 1974, s.10(2).

Where this statement had been included in the variation or revocation notice, the waste disposal licence remained varied or revoked until the decision on appeal of the Secretary of State was made. However, there was an interim arrangement set out in s.10(3) which allowed the holder to apply to the Secretary of State to determine that the authority had acted unreasonably in including such a statement in the notice. The Secretary of State had powers to lift the suspension, which then lasted until such time as the appeal itself was determined. In these circumstances the holder was entitled to recover compensation from the authority in respect of any loss suffered by him in consequence of the statement. Disputes over the amount of compensation were determined by arbitration (Arbitration Act 1950).

Approvals relating to local authority sites

10–012   Where waste operations were being undertaken by the disposal authority itself the procedures appropriate to applications, modifications etc. were dealt with in s.11 of COPA 1974. Special procedures protected the interests of the NRA (now the Environment Agency) and public safety. However, for the most part, these procedures were rendered obsolete once local authorities divested themselves of their operational responsibilities (*e.g.* by local authority waste disposal companies—see para.10–027 *et seq.* below).

Register of licences

10–013   All licences, once granted under the 1974 Act, and all modifications and other changes, had to be available for public inspection. The procedure was that copies of all relevant documents were maintained by the waste disposal authority in a register kept at its offices. This register was open to inspection by the public free of charge at all reasonable hours and copies of entries in the register could be obtained on payment of a reasonable charge.

Transfer and surrender of licences

10–014   Under COPA 1974, the holder of a waste disposal licence could transfer such licence by giving notice to the authority. He was required to state the date of transfer and details of the transferee's name and address. The authority had the right, which it had to exercise no later than eight weeks from the receipt of the original notice, to give a counter-notice to the transferee that it declined to accept him as holder of the licence. Two weeks thereafter the licence ceased to have effect. There appears to have been a right to appeal under s.10(1)(a).

The surrender of a licence by its holder was a simple procedure, effected by delivery of the document to the authority and notice that the holder no longer required the licence. Thereupon, it would appear that all obligations under the licence came to an end and enforcement had to rely upon any planning permission or its conditions and other matters of general law (*e.g.* statutory nuisance, WRA 1991). However, note that this right of simple cancellation was brought to an end when Pt II of EPA 1990 was brought fully into force (see para.10–055 below).

Special wastes

More stringent controls apply to a category of wastes described in COPA 1974 as "special" waste. These are wastes which, by their nature, are dangerous or intractable. The regime of control is now set out in s.62 of EPA 1990, as amended, and the Special Waste Regulations 1996[9] which came into force on September 1, 1996. The definition of "special waste" is set out in reg.2 of and Sch.2 to the Regulations. The schedule replicates definitions of hazardous waste in Annex III to the EC Council Directive 91/689/EEC on hazardous waste. Regulation 4 obliges the EA to assign specific codes to consignments of special waste. The codes are required to be shown, together with other information, on consignment notes accompanying the waste when transported. There are also provisions for the form of the notes, as well as pre-notification to the EA concerning consignments. The mixing of special waste with other waste or different categories of special waste is forbidden by reg.17, unless there is specific authorisation or exemption. Failure to comply with the Regulations is an offence and carries penalties.[10]

    The 1996 Regulations have been amended by the Special Waste (Amendment) (England and Wales) Regulations 2001.[11] Most of the provisions came into force on November 1, 2001. The amendments mainly relate to procedures for dealing with special waste but it should be noted that there are further obligations on consignees who have rejected deliveries. In those circumstances, consignees must identify those deliveries to the Environment Agency and a new consignment note must be prepared showing where redirection has arisen.

10–015

CONTROL OF POLLUTION (AMENDMENT) ACT 1989

The Control of Pollution (Amendment) Act 1989 (brought into force on April 1, 1992) imposes a requirement that carriers of controlled waste must be registered with the EA. Some carriers are exempt.

10–016

---

[9] SI 1996/972.
[10] Further guidance is provided in DoE Circular 6/96, "Environmental Protection Act 1990 Pt II. Special Waste Regulations 1996". See also "Special Waste: A technical guidance note on their definition and classification", published by the EA for England, Wales and Scotland (available from the Stationery Office.
[11] SI 2001/3148.

Subject to certain provisions set out in the Act, transport of controlled waste without registration is an offence.

Registration

10–017 In general, registration is required by any person who transports controlled waste to or from any place in Great Britain in the course of any business of his or otherwise with a view to profit. "Transport" includes the use of road, rail, air, sea or inland waterway. The EA must establish and maintain a register of waste carriers. For further information, see the Controlled Waste (Registration of Carriers and Seizure of Vehicles) Regulations 1991[12] and DoE Circular 11/91. Significant modifications have been made to the Act and the regulations by the Waste Management Licensing Regulations 1994.[13]

Limits on rejection of application

10–018 The EA may not refuse an application for registration except on two specific grounds:

(a) that the application is procedurally faulty; or
(b) that the applicant or another relevant person has been convicted of certain offences and in the EA's opinion is undesirable to be authorised.

Under (b) above, in general this means that registration is at risk if any of a range of offences set out in Sch.1 to the 1991 Regulations, as amended from time to time, has been committed by the applicant or certain persons associated with him. The offences relate mainly to public health, environmental and transport contraventions. The definitions of associated persons and organisations are described in detail in s.3(5) of the 1989 Act. However, conviction is not an automatic bar to registration. There remains a discretion with the EA.

Appeals against refusal of registration

10–019 Appeals lie to the Secretary of State if the application is refused or not dealt with, usually within two months. There is a 28-day period for appeal, running from the date of refusal or the end of the two-month or extended period.

Production of certificate of registration

10–020 A policeman or duly authorised officer of the EA is entitled to require the production of the authority for transporting waste. It is, therefore, desirable that a copy of the appropriate registration certificate (or exemption) should

[12] SI 1991/1624.
[13] SI 1994/1056; see para.10–022 below.

be carried with each vehicle. Seizure and disposal of vehicles may be authorised by a magistrate in circumstances of actual or anticipated offences (see s.6).

Registers

The EA is required to maintain registers giving details of applications, **10–021** variations and other documents. This register is open to public inspection.

Registration of professional collectors, transporters and brokers of waste

The 1994 Regulations (see para.10–017 above) make important modifica- **10–022** tions to the 1989 Act and 1991 Regulations. The need for this arises because of the requirements of art.12 of the Framework Directive on Waste,[14] as amended. As a result, certain gaps and exceptions from registration under the 1989 Act are closed. Paragraph 12 of Sch.4 to the 1994 Regulations provides a simple registration requirement for those previously exempted. These include waste collection and disposal author-ities, charities and voluntary organisations. Guidance on the modifications can be found in paras 1.70–1.84 of Annex 1 to DoE Circular 11/94.

ENVIRONMENTAL PROTECTION ACT 1990

EPA 1990 introduced a stricter regime of control of waste on land. **10–023** Virtually all of Pt I of COPA 1974 was repealed and replaced by Pt II of EPA 1990. In its turn, Pt II has been substantially modified by the provisions of the PPCA 1999—see Ch.9. This provides that a large number of landfills, incinerators and other waste treatment plants will be controlled under that Act. As a result, only a limited number of smaller landfills and plants will be caught by Pt II of EPA 1990.

Administratively, the arrangements were initially much the same. The same authorities which were waste disposal authorities under COPA 1974 were largely waste regulation authorities within the meaning of s.30 of EPA 1990. Section 32 of EPA 1990 effectively takes away from the authorities operational powers to run waste disposal sites themselves. The details are dealt with in the section concerning local authority waste disposal com-panies (see para.10–027 below). The main changes to COPA 1974 are:

- the separation of regulatory and operational functions of the waste disposal authority;
- the extension of control to essentially all types of handling of waste;

---

[14] 75/442/EEC.

- the imposition of a duty of care on all persons who produce, handle or dispose of waste;
- tighter control on transfer and surrender of licences;
- the imposition of fees for applications for, and the subsistence of licences;
- a requirement that a licence holder should be "fit and proper".

Administrative matters

10–024 The practical effect of EPA 1990, so far as waste disposal authorities were concerned, was to split their functions into three distinct types.

Regulation

10–025 The waste regulation authority exercised the functions of the grant and supervision of licences and licensed sites and pursued the enforcement of the Act generally, with particular regard to unauthorised operations both under the Act itself and the Control of Pollution (Amendment) Act 1989. It acted as registration authority under the 1989 Act. The regulation authority also shouldered the duties of s.50 of EPA 1990 (now repealed), which required, *inter alia*, the preparation of a waste disposal plan designed to identify the arrangements needed to treat or dispose of controlled waste situate in its area.

As a result of the coming into force of the Environment Act 1995, most waste regulatory duties now lie with the EA, which took on its new responsibilities from April 1, 1996.

Disposal

10–026 This responsibility is with the waste disposal authority and is defined in s.51 of EPA 1990. The authority must arrange for the disposal of the controlled waste collected in its area by the waste collection authorities, arrange for places to be provided at which persons resident in its area may deposit their household waste (commonly known as "civic amenity sites"), and arrange for the disposal of waste so deposited. In simple terms the waste disposal authority is the "organiser", ensuring that all waste arising in its area is disposed of either by the council's own operational arm, by the waste collection authority or through the private sector. It also has recycling powers (see para.10–029 below).

As a result of various phases of local government reorganisation, unitary authorities (usually absorbing the powers of both county and district councils) are established for many mainly urban areas. Where unitary authorities are set up, the disposal and collection responsibilities reside in the single authority. Otherwise disposal and collection remains separately administered, usually at county and district level.

Operation

The powers for a waste disposal authority to undertake waste disposal **10–027** through its own operational landfill and other sites were removed by s.32 of EPA 1990. Under this section, the Secretary of State was empowered to require disposal authorities either to form or participate in forming waste disposal companies (*e.g.* by joint venture with another authority or the private sector) and to transfer the relevant part of their undertakings in accordance with a scheme made under Sch.2 to the Act. The authority could pre-empt a direction by the Secretary of State by making its own arrangements, either to form a disposal company (known as a "local authority waste disposal company" (LAWDC)) or to make arrangements with the private sector or even another local authority waste disposal company. Many disposal authorities decided not to assign all their operational functions to the private sector, but to form an LAWDC.[15] Schemes of transfer, ensuring that the assets relevant to the LAWDC's operation were transferred by the authority to the new company, were prepared by the authority for submission to and approval by the Secretary of State. There are strict rules set out in s.32 of and Sch.2 to the Act as to the extent to which control of an LAWDC may be exercised by the disposal authority. In short, the LAWDC must be a controlled company at arm's length in accordance with the definition of Pt V of the Local Government and Housing Act 1989.

A LAWDC's activities are limited to the collection, keeping, treatment and disposal of waste and related activities.[16] It effectively competes with other contractors for waste disposal business and is free to seek business from any source, including the private sector. Once formed and operational, it is able to take a transfer (effectively by assignment or otherwise), of all the relevant assets from the disposal authority. For this purpose, any restrictions on assignment, transfer etc. are to be ignored, subject to certain protective provisions as far as third parties are concerned (set out in Sch.2 to the Act). The LAWDC is entitled to inherit all the deemed and actual planning permissions granted to the disposal authority but, once it is operational, all further planning permissions need to be obtained in the usual way. The LAWDC is not able to secure the transfer of any site licences granted under s.11 of COPA 1974 (see para.10–002 above) and it must make fresh applications in the same way as the private sector.[17]

Waste collection authorities

Waste collection authorities remain constituted much as they were under **10–028** COPA 1974, subject to some changes to take account of administrative modifications. They are the unitary and district councils in England and the

---

[15] The procedures for doing this are set out in DoE Circular 8/91, "Competition for Local Authority Waste Disposal Contracts and New Arrangements for Disposal Operations".

[16] EPA 1990, s.32.

[17] Further guidance on LAWDCs is set out in DoE Circular 10/91, "Separation of Local Authority Waste Regulation and Waste Disposal Functions".

county or county borough councils in Wales. In Greater London they are the London borough councils, the Common Council in the City of London, the Sub-treasurer of the Inner Temple and the Under-treasurer of the Middle Temple. The functions of a waste collection authority are described primarily in s.45 of EPA 1990 as including:

- arranging for the collection of household waste in its area except where the waste is in an isolated or inaccessible place where the cost would be unreasonably high to collect and the authority is satisfied that adequate alternative arrangements have been made or can reasonably be expected to be made by the person who controls the waste; and
- collecting any commercial waste from premises or arranging for collection where requested by the occupier (in which case a charge may be made).

It is, therefore, open to a waste collection authority to consign its responsibilities to the private sector and many arrangements of this nature have already been made. Indeed, compulsory competitive tendering requirements imposed by central government demand that any waste collection contracts should be the subject of a competitive tendering process before a preferred method is selected. The waste collection authority is not obliged to use the private sector, but choice of its own organisation, where this is seen to be uneconomic or non-commercial, may be the subject of challenge. See also the requirements of "Best Value" imposed by Pt I of the Local Government Act 1999.

A waste collection authority also has duties of cesspool emptying and the like, for which a reasonable charge may be imposed.

Once waste has been collected by or on behalf of a collection authority, the obligation is to deliver that waste for disposal to such places as the waste disposal authority may direct. There are procedures for resolution of disputes set down in s.48 of EPA 1990.

Waste recycling and minimisation

10–029 The waste collection authority also has the responsibility, under s.49 of EPA 1990, to prepare waste recycling plans, identifying what arrangements are appropriate for dealing with waste by separation, baling or otherwise packaging for recycling purposes. It must give publicity to its plans and ensure that both waste disposal regulation authorities and are advised. A system of payments for recycling and disposal of waste is provided in s.52, and further powers for recycling waste are set out in s.55.

The Waste Minimisation Act 1998 inserted a new s.63A into EPA. This provides that waste collection or disposal authorities shall have powers either themselves or by subcontractor to undertake or contribute towards policies or activities which minimise the quantity of controlled waste generated in their area. The authorities are required to consult one another in carrying out these functions.

Guidance to local authorities on their responsibilities for strategies and plans was published in 1998; see DETR document, "Preparing and Revising Local Authority Recycling Strategies and Recycling Plans".

Prohibition of unauthorised or harmful deposit, treatment, disposal, etc. of waste

Except in relation to household waste at a domestic property and other **10–030** prescribed cases, it is an offence under s.33 of EPA 1990 to:

(a) deposit controlled waste or knowingly cause or knowingly permit controlled waste to be deposited in or on any land, unless a waste management licence authorising the deposit is in force and the conditions of that licence are complied with;

(b) treat, keep or dispose of controlled waste or knowingly cause or knowingly permit controlled waste to be treated, kept or disposed of in or on any land or by means of any mobile plant, except in accordance with a waste management licence;

(c) treat, keep or dispose of controlled waste in a manner likely to cause pollution of the environment or harm to human health.

No licence will be required for any process the subject of the IPC provisions of Pt I of EPA 1990 or of PPCA 1999.

The discharge of liquid waste into underground strata can constitute landfill.[18]

Definitions

"Knowingly cause or knowingly permit"

The term "knowingly cause or knowingly permit" imposes a strict liability **10–031** and essentially incorporates the "ought to have known" principle.[19]

"Environment", "pollution of the environment" and "harm"

The "environment" is defined in s.29 of EPA 1990 as including land, water and the air, and "pollution of the environment" is defined as resulting from the release or escape into any environmental medium from the land on

---

[18] See *Blackland Park Exploration Limited v Environment Agency* (unreported, 2003).
[19] For further guidance see *AlphaCell Ltd v Woodward* [1972] A.C. 24; *Ashcroft v Cambro Waste Ltd* [1981] 3 All E.R. 699; and *Shanks & McEwan (Teeside) Ltd v Environment Agency* [1998] 2 W.L.R. 452. A definitive judgment on the interpretation of this term is to be found in the House of Lords case of *Empress Car Co (Abertillery) Ltd v National Rivers Authority* [1998] 1 All E.R. 481.

which the waste is treated, kept or deposited or from fixed plant by means of which waste is treated, kept or disposed of. "Harm" is defined in s.29(5) as meaning harm to the health of living organisms or other interference with the ecological systems of which they form part and, in the case of man, includes offence to any of his senses or harm to his property.

"Waste"

The definitions of "waste" and "controlled waste" are important elements of the system of regulation under Pt II of EPA 1990. Section 75 provides various definitions. "Waste" includes:

(a) any substance constituting a scrap material or effluent or other unwanted surplus substance arising from the application of any process; and

(b) any substance or article which requires to be disposed of as being broken, worn out, contaminated or otherwise spoiled,

but does not include a substance which is an explosive within the meaning of the Explosives Act 1875.

Anything which is discarded or otherwise dealt with as if it were waste shall be presumed to be waste unless the contrary is proved (s.75(3)). In 1994, the DoE announced its intention to repeal the existing definition of "waste" and to replace it with the definition which appears in EC Council Directive 75/442/EEC (the Framework Directive), as amended by EC Council Directive 91/156/ EEC, so that "waste shall mean any substance or object in the categories set out in Annex I which the holder discards or intends is required to discard". Annex I to the Framework Directive includes a range of 16 general categories of waste.

DoE Circular 11/94, "Environmental Protection Act 1990: Pt II Waste Management Licensing—The Framework Directive on Waste", confirms the intention to repeal the definition in s.75; para.88 of Sch.22 to the Environment Act 1995 does this but, at time of writing, this is not in force. Only those substances or objects which are waste as defined in the Directive shall be subject to the controls which apply to collection, transport, storage, recovery and disposal of waste. This has been achieved by making modifications to Pt II of EPA 1990 by the Waste Management Licensing Regulations 1994.[20] These Regulations are comprehensive, but provide that:

(a) any reference to "waste" in Pt II of EPA 1990 includes a reference to "Directive waste" (Sch.4, paras 9(2) and 10(3));

(b) "Directive waste" means any substance or object in the category set out in Pt II of Sch.4 to the Regulations which the producer or the person in possession of it discards or intends or is required to discard, but with the exception of anything excluded from the scope of the Directive by Art.2 (reg.1(3));

[20] SI 1994/1056.

(c) in the Regulations, "waste" means Directive waste (reg.1(3));

(d) for the purposes of Pt II of EPA 1990, "waste" which is not Directive waste shall not be treated as household, industrial or commercial waste (see below);

(e) the definition of "Directive waste "incorporates not only disposal operations but also recovery operations which are scheduled respectively in Pts III and IV of Sch.4 to the 1994 Regulations.

The DoE Circular makes it clear that the practical effect of these modifications is to transpose into national legislation the Directive's definition of waste so that only "Directive waste" is subject to control as household, industrial or commercial waste (*i.e.* as "controlled waste").

A number of cases have examined the meaning of waste.[21] More importantly, the European Court of Justice case of *Vessoso v Zanetti*[22] considers the definition of "waste" by reference to the Directive and answers in the affirmative the question:

"Whether [Article 1 of the Framework Directive] must be interpreted as meaning that the legal concept of waste must also cover things which the holder has disposed of which are capable of economic reuse and whether the said articles must be interpreted as meaning that the term 'waste' presupposes the establishment of animus dereliquendi (the intention to abandon) on the part of the holder of the substance or object."

Two other European court cases assist in the definition of waste: *Inter-Environment Wallonie ASBL v Region Wallonie*[23] which concerned the definition by reference to industrial production processes; and the *Tombesi*[24] case (below).

Waste or by-product? It is clear from the above cases that the courts will perceive waste from the point of view of the person who is disposing of it, even though such waste, when viewed by the recipients, may be regarded as important and valuable. Nonetheless, there will be examples where a surplus substance or article will also be perceived by the original producer as having value and, therefore, capable of being transferred for that value to the recipient. Under these circumstances, the substance or article may not be waste, particularly where there is no intention to discard on the transferor's part. It will not, therefore, be controlled under the Act. There is clearly a fine line to be drawn between what falls within the definition of waste and otherwise. Each case is likely to turn on its particular merits and there are certain to be circumstances in which a commercial relationship

---

[21] See *Kent CC v Queenborough Rolling Mill Co* [1990] 2 L.M.E.L.R. 28; *Long v Brooke* [1980] Crim. L.R. 109; and *Berridge Incinerators v Nottinghamshire CC* [1987] unreported, but noted in DoE Circular 14/92.

[22] [1990] 2 L.M.E.L.R. 133.

[23] Case C–129/96.

[24] Case C–304/94, ECJ.

will start on the basis that a transferred substance is waste but, through the achievement of value, may remove itself from that category to become, for example, a by-product.

For further guidance, see the *Tombesi* case. Here, the European Court of Justice reviewed the definition of "waste" in the Directive and concluded that objects and substances discarded by their owners, even where there is a commercial value, are still capable of falling into the definition of Directive "waste". See also *Mayer Parry Recycling Ltd v Environment Agency*,[25] which concerned scrap metal recovery operations. On the facts of the case, it was decided that materials which were to be reused and which required no further recovery operation before that use were not waste; materials which were made ready for use by a recovery operation were no longer waste when that operation was complete; and scrap metal capable of being used as a feed stock in a furnace without further processing was a raw material and not a waste.[26]

"Controlled waste"

"Controlled waste" is the main category of waste which is the subject of controls under the Act and is defined as meaning household, industrial and commercial waste, or any such waste. The definition now needs to be read by reference to its modification in the Waste Management Licensing Regulations 1994.[27]

"Household waste" means waste from:

- a domestic property;
- a caravan;
- a residential home;
- an educational establishment;
- a hospital or nursing home.

"Industrial waste" means waste from any of the following premises:

- a factory within the meaning of the Factories Act 1961;
- premises used for or in connection with the provision to the public of transport services by land, water or air;
- premises used for or in connection with the supply to the public of gas, water, electricity or sewerage services;
- premises used for or in connection with public postal or telecommunications services.

---

[25] (1998) *The Times*, December 3.
[26] The *Mayer Parry* case has subsequently been doubted in the case of *Attorney General's Reference (No. 5 of 2000)*, (2000) *The Times*, June 6. For further cases, see also *Arco Chemie Nederland Limited* cases (C–418/97 and C–419/97); *Castle Cement v Environment Agency* [2001] EWHC Admin 224, [2002] J.P.L. 43; and the ECJ case *Abfall Service (AG) v Bundesminster fur Umwelt, Jugend und Familie* (Case C–6/00; *Palin Granit oy v Vehmassalon* [2002] En. L.R. 843 and *Mayer Parry* (Case C–444/00).
[27] SI 1994/1056.

"Commercial waste" means waste from premises used wholly or mainly for the purposes of a trade or business or for the purposes of sport, recreation or entertainment, but excluding:

- household waste;
- industrial waste;
- waste from a mine or quarry or from premises used for agriculture;
- any other excluded waste prescribed by the Secretary of State.

The Secretary of State has taken power to provide that any of the above definitions may be modified to include or exclude types of waste, but he may not impose modifications in the case of waste from any mine or quarry or in connection with agriculture.[28]

ACTIVITIES EXEMPT FROM WASTE MANAGEMENT LICENSING

The main exemptions from the requirement for waste management licens-   **10–032**
ing are now gathered into the extensive Sch.3 to the Waste Management Licensing Regulations 1994,[29] as amended. This provides, in 45 paragraphs, that a large range of waste management activities does not require a licence under EPA 1990. Schedule 3 needs to be read with care, since almost every category of exemption is limited and/or conditional. Furthermore, certain exemptions apply only if the activity is carried on by or with the consent of the occupier of the land in question or if the person carrying on the activity is entitled to do so. The exemptions do not apply to special waste (see para.10–015 above). An activity will only be exempt where it involves the disposal or recovery of waste by an establishment or undertaking (as opposed to an individual) where, in relation to waste and the method of disposal or recovery, certain objectives are attained. These objectives are set down in para.4(i)(a) of Pt I of Sch.4 to the 1994 Regulations. They are described as "relevant objectives" and stem from the Waste Framework Directive (see para.10–030 above). In general, these objectives require that the waste is recovered or disposed of without endangering human health and without using processes or methods which could harm the environment. Certain scrap metal activities do not benefit from the exemptions where authorised by a waste management licence granted on an application made after March 31, 1995 (see reg.17(1A)).

Registration of exemptions

Once a right to exemption is established it is necessary to register such   **10–033**
exemption in accordance with reg.18 of the 1994 Regulations, as amended. Guidance on exemptions and registration is to be found in Annexes 5 and 6 respectively of DoE Circular 11/94.

---

[28] EPA 1990, s.75(8). For details, see the Collection and Disposal of Waste Regulations 1988 (SI 1988/819), the Controlled Waste Regulations 1992 (SI 1992/588) and the Waste Management Licensing Regulations 1994 (SI 1994/1056), as amended.
[29] SI 1994/1056.

THE DUTY OF CARE

10–034 Section 34 of EPA 1990, as amended by the Environment Act 1995, imposes a duty of care on persons involved from production through to final disposal of controlled waste. The duty of care responsibilities came into force on April 1, 1992.

Section 34 imposes a range of responsibilities on anyone who is subject to the duty. That person must take all reasonable steps:

(a) to prevent any other person committing the offences in s.33 (see para.10–030) or in regs 9 and 10 of the Pollution Prevention and Control Regulations 2000 (see Chapter 9);

(b) to prevent the escape of waste from his control or that of any other person;

(c) to ensure that on the transfer of waste such transfer is only to an "authorised person" or to a person for "authorised transport purposes" as defined in s.34; and

(d) when waste is transferred, to ensure that there is also transferred a written description of the waste sufficient to enable each person receiving it to avoid committing any of the offences under s.33 and to comply with the duty of care.

The courts have interpreted responsibilities under s.34, as amended, in various cases.[30]

Application of the duty

10–035 The duty applies to any person who imports, produces or carries waste or, as a waste manager, keeps, treats or disposes of waste or, as a broker, has control of waste.

Note that the responsibility of each person affected by the duty of care is not absolute. That person is only expected to take measures which are:

(a) "applicable to him in that capacity", and

(b) "reasonable in the circumstances".

These terms contemplate that the responsibilities extend only when the waste is in the control of the individual, producer, carrier etc. However, as noted later, the duties are not in watertight compartments and some relate to the circumstances of transfer from one party to another. By the same token, individuals the subject of the duty of care need only act reasonably, although this term may, in practice, prove to be difficult to interpret.

---

[30] For example, see *R. v Hertfordshire CC Ex p. Green Environmental Industries Ltd* [1996] J.P.L. B126; and *Shanks and McEwan (Southern Waste Services) v Environment Agency* (1997) *The Independent*, October 17.

Household waste

Occupiers of domestic property do not have duty of care responsibilities for **10–036** household waste produced on the property. However, this exemption[31] does not apply to someone who is not the occupier of the household in question, such as a builder or decorator who generates waste. That person does have the duty of care.

Penalties for failure to comply

Failure to comply with the duty of care is a criminal offence, punishable by **10–037** a fine.

The code of practice

The DoE has published a code of practice,[32] compliance with which will **10–038** normally overcome the responsibilities of the duty of care. It is an important document because of its statutory context. By the terms of s.34(10) of EPA 1990 it is admissible in evidence in any court proceedings and may be taken into account by the court in deciding any question (*e.g.* of the extent to which the duty of care has been complied with). Thus, while failure to comply with the code is not a crime, such failure may be taken into account by the court in deciding whether there has been a failure to comply with the duty. This distinction is important because the code does not lay down an exclusive method of compliance with the duty. Provided that duty is complied with, an operator may employ quite different procedures and practices.[33]

Some definitions

A "producer" is not defined either by EPA 1990 or by the Environmental **10–039** Protection (Duty of Care) Regulations 1991.[34] The code of practice suggests that the term includes a person whose actions give rise to controlled waste, including deciding to discard an article, material or substance. Some further assistance is provided by DoE Circular 19/91.

The definition of "keeper" is absent from the Act and the Regulations and is, therefore, likely to be interpreted in its normal meaning. However, it is a wide description and may well cover all elements of storage, even temporary.

---

[31] EPA 1990, s.34(2).
[32] 2nd ed. The code of practice is obtainable from the Stationery Office.
[33] DEFRA has also published a summary of the code of practice, "Waste and Your Duty of Care" (March 2003).
[34] SI 1991/2839.

A person who "treats" waste is defined in s.29(6) of EPA 1990. The term relates to any process including reuse, reclamation and recycling. The Secretary of State has taken power to make regulations to define the term further.

An "authorised person" includes the waste collection authority, a licence holder or a person who is exempt from holding a licence, a registered carrier under the Control of Pollution (Amendment) Act 1989 or a person exempted under that Act (see para.10–016 above) and a waste disposal authority in Scotland. A list of exempt carriers is set out in the Controlled Waste (Registration of Carriers and Seizure of Vehicles) Regulations 1991.[35]

"Authorised transport purposes" relates mainly to transport by a person within the same premises and will also include the carriage of waste relating to import and export to and from Great Britain.

The duty of care in practice

10–040 In simple terms the duty of care applies in different ways according to the type of holder of the waste. The following are examples of individual responsibilities.

The producer's duty

10–041 The producer's duty is to:

    (a) identify the composition of waste;
    (b) prepare and supply a consignment note;
    (c) (pack the waste safely for consignment;
    (d) store safely; and
    (e) transfer to the right person.

In regard to responsibilities (a) and (b), the producer must ensure that an adequate description of the waste is provided, with sufficient detail to foresee any problems etc. He must also take into account the type of premises where the waste is or might be kept. In the consignment note he should name the waste and the process from which it is derived. A full analysis will be appropriate in some circumstances. A copy of the consignment note is set out in DoE Circular 19/91 and in the code of practice; it will not be applicable in every case. On consignment, the waste must be contained and packed by reference to its whole journey (*e.g.* where it will be disposed of or used for some other purpose). On transfer it will be important to check the credentials of the person to whom the transfer is made, particularly with regard to any need for a licence. A receipt for the consignment is desirable.

---

[35] SI 1991/1624, as amended.

The carrier's duty

The carrier's duty is to: **10–042**

(a) check the waste and its source;
(b) check that the consignment is accurate and correct;
(c) check the packing;
(d) deliver the waste correctly; and
(e) be registered, as necessary, under the Control of Pollution (Amendment) Act 1989.

It would be proper for him to make his registration certificate available for inspection.

The waste manager's duty

The waste manager's duty is to: **10–043**

(a) check the source of waste and the consignment note;
(b) check the composition of the waste and its packing by reference to the consignment note and other information;
(c) satisfy himself that the transfer note is accurate;
(d) satisfy himself that the carrier is registered; and
(e) ensure that he is licensed to take the waste in question.

The waste manager's responsibility may be as a collector or an operator of transfer stations (in the private sector) and he is likely to be the most vulnerable of the various categories of waste handlers. It will be most important, therefore, to ensure careful adherence to the code of practice or an equal standard.

The documentation requirements

The following documentation is required: **10–044**

(a) a full description of the waste, its quantity and packing;
(b) details of the "holder";
(c) details of the collector; and
(d) details of the transfer/collection (*e.g.* place, time, date).

A record must be made and kept by both transferor and transferee for two years. It may not be necessary to provide a transfer/consignment note for each load of waste. There is no reason why transfers cannot be "batched" for record purposes if what are being dealt with are the same wastes, the same parties etc. In these circumstances it would be suitable for one transfer note to be provided for a whole series of similar consignments, for example over a period of one year.

Note that the EA is entitled to see records within a two-year period from creation. Waste holders may want to see records. There appears to be no right, as such, to demand records to be released, but it would probably be appropriate, not to say desirable, to use the EA as an intermediary where information is required. The power to require information is also extended to waste collection authorities by the Environmental Protection (Duty of Care) (England) (Amendment) Regulations 2003.[36]

OFFENCES

10–045   By s.33(6) of EPA 1990 the unauthorised depositing, treatment or disposal of controlled waste without a licence or in contravention of a condition of a licence is an offence. Defences are available under s.33(7), as amended, if the person charged can prove that:

(a) he took all reasonable precautions and exercised all due diligence to avoid the commission of an offence; or

(b) he acted under instructions from his employer and neither knew nor had reason to suppose that he had committed an offence; or

(c) the acts alleged were performed in an emergency to avoid danger to human health in a case where he took all steps as were reasonably practicable in the circumstances for minimising pollution of the environment and harm to human health and particulars of the acts were furnished to the EA as soon as reasonably practicable.

Penalties are now severe, including six months' imprisonment and/or a fine up to £20,000 for summary conviction, or two years' imprisonment and/or an unlimited fine where the proceedings are on indictment in a higher court. Where the waste is special waste the penalties are similar, except that imprisonment following conviction on indictment may be up to five years.

Failure to comply with the duty of care imposed by s.34 of EPA 1990 is an offence which can result in similar substantial fines, but there is no provision for imprisonment.

Directors and senior managers can be personally liable (see paras 16–019 and 16–022 below).

Powers exist[37] for the EA and collection authorities to require the occupier of land to remove waste unlawfully deposited and/or to take other clean-up steps.

[36] SI 2003/63.
[37] EPA 1990, s.59.

APPLICATIONS UNDER THE ENVIRONMENTAL PROTECTION ACT 1990[38]

Unless a permit is required under PPCA 1999 (see Ch.9), a waste **10–046** management licence is required to be granted by the EA which will authorise the treatment, keeping or disposal of controlled waste in or on specified land, or the treatment or disposal by means of a specified mobile plant. An application should be made by:

(a) the occupier, in the case of a licence relating to the treatment, keeping or disposal of waste in or on land; or

(b) the operator, in the case of a licence for the treatment or disposal of waste by means of a mobile plant.

A fee for the application will be payable under a scheme made under the terms of the Environment Act 1995. Such schemes are made from time to time and details may be obtained from the EA.

An application for a licence must be made in accordance with reg.2 of the Waste Management Licensing Regulations 1994,[39] which states only that the application must be in writing. However, close attention must be paid to DoE Circular 11/94 and to Waste Management Paper No. 4, "Licensing of Waste Management Facilities", particularly Chapter 2. It will be seen from the list of waste management papers (see para.10–009 above) that guidance is also available as to specific wastes and their treatment.

No licence may be issued unless planning permission is in force or a certificate establishing the use for the purpose exists under TCPA 1990, as amended by PCA 1991.

The EA is obliged to grant the application unless:

(a) the applicant is not a fit and proper person (see para.10–063 below); or

(b) the rejection is necessary for the purpose of preventing pollution of the environment, harm to human health or serious detriment to the amenities of the locality.

Under (b) above, however, serious detriment cannot be alleged where planning permission is in force for the activity applied for. This means that this ground of refusal will apply only where a certificate relating to the use has been obtained under TCPA 1990 (as amended), no permission exists at all, or the permission falls short of authorising the waste management activity in question.

The EA has four months in which to reach a decision on the application, but a further period is allowed if information from the applicant is missing or if there is agreement with the applicant. In the absence of a decision within the relevant period the EA is deemed to have rejected the

---

[38] This section should be read in conjunction with the requirements of the Landfill (England and Wales) Regulations 2002, SI 2002/1559—see para.10–073.

[39] SI 1994/1056.

application, thereby triggering the appeal provisions (see para.10–060 below).

Consultations on the application

10–047 The EA may not issue a licence until it has referred the proposal to the local planning authority and the Health and Safety Executive. It must consider any representations made within the allowed period of 21 days from the day the proposal is received, but the authorities may agree a longer period.

Further consultation requirements are imposed on the EA in any case where the land in question has been notified under s.28(1) of the Wildlife and Countryside Act 1981 (protection for certain areas of special scientific interest). The EA must consult with the appropriate nature conservation body, which will be English Nature or the Countryside Council for Wales (EPA 1990, s.36(7)).

Conditions of a licence

10–048 Under s.35 of EPA 1990, a licence must be granted on such terms and conditions as appear to the EA to be appropriate. The Act requires that the conditions relate to the activities which the licence authorises, to the precautions to be taken and to works to be carried out in connection with or in consequence of the activities. Conditions may require the licence holder to carry out works or do other things, even though he is not entitled to do so (*e.g.* because he does not own the relevant land). Section 35(4) contains an interesting provision, to the effect that any person whose consent would be required shall grant or join in granting a licence holder such rights in relation to the land as will enable the licence holder to comply with any requirements imposed on him by the licence.

The s.35(4) provisions will often apply where an applicant may need to provide monitoring boreholes or other mechanisms for measuring the transmission of leachate, gas or other potential air pollution. Section 35(4) gave inadequate protection to the owners and occupiers of land required to host such mechanisms. The Environment Act 1995 has corrected this difficulty. Under the terms of ss.35A and 36A of EPA 1990, inserted by the 1995 Act, the EA must now consult owners and other parties having an interest in affected land, before any conditions are imposed in relation to that land. Section 35A provides for compensation to owners and occupiers. See also the Waste Management Licences (Consultation and Compensation) Regulations 1999,[40] which came into force on April 1, 1999.

Regulation 13 of the Waste Management Licensing Regulations 1994 specifically provides that no conditions shall be imposed in any waste

[40] SI 1999/481.

management licence for the purpose only of securing the health of persons at work within the meaning of the Health and Safety at Work etc. Act 1974.

Special considerations for waste oils and groundwater

Regulations 14 and 15 of the 1994 Regulations have imposed further **10–049** obligations in relation to waste oils and ground water respectively. The requirements give effect to EC Directives. As to the provisions relating to ground water, further guidance is available in Annex 7 to DoE Circular 11/94 and waste management paper WMP4, "Licensing of Waste Management Facilities".

Landfill (England and Wales) Regulations 2002

Additional controls on landfills and their operations were set by the EU **10–050** Landfill Directive 1999/31/EC on the landfill of waste. The requirements of the Directive have in part been implemented by the Landfill (England and Wales) Regulations 2002.[41] For detailed commentary see para.10–073.

Variation

There are two separate procedures for variation of a licence under s.37 of **10–051** EPA 1990, as amended by the Environment Act 1995:

(a) By the EA—the conditions of a licence may be varied as may be regarded as desirable by the EA, provided the condition is unlikely to require unreasonable expense on the holder's part.
(b) By the licence holder—the conditions may be varied to the extent requested in the application by the holder, but at the EA's discretion. A fee is payable under a charging scheme required by the Environment Act 1995.

Under s.37A of EPA 1990, inserted by the 1995 Act, the EA has consultation obligations where any modification of a licence would be subject to certain new conditions which the licence holder might not be entitled to carry out (*e.g.* because the works in question would involve land not in his control). In those circumstances the EA must consult with relevant owners, lessees or occupiers of land and give details of the proposed new conditions. Responses are required to be taken into consideration, provided they are made within six weeks. Compensation is payable under s.35A (see above).

Modification

Modification is a step beyond mere variation and may be undertaken by the **10–052** EA under s.37(2) of EPA 1990 where this is required for the purpose of ensuring that the activities authorised do not cause pollution of the

---

[41] SI 2002/1559.

environment or harm to human health or become seriously detrimental to the amenities of the locality affected by the activities. The Secretary of State will make regulations under s.35(6) to control these responsibilities. Modification is effected by notice served on the licence holder and it shall state the time when the modification is to take effect. Both variation and modification by the EA may be subject to appeal by the licence holder.[42]

The consultation requirements of s.37A (see above) also apply to proposals for modification in certain circumstances.

Revocation and suspension

10–053 Under the terms of s.38 of EPA 1990, revocation and suspension of a licence may be undertaken by the EA in the following circumstances:

    (a) where the holder has ceased to be a fit and proper person by reason of a conviction for a relevant offence—these are prescribed by reg.3 of the Waste Management Licensing Regulations 1994 (see para.10–063);

    (b) where the continuation of the licensed activities would cause pollution to the environment, harm to human health or serious detriment to the amenities of the locality affected; and

    (c) where the pollution, harm or detriment cannot be avoided by modification.

Additionally, revocation (to the extent specified) may be exercised by the EA where the holder has ceased to be a fit and proper person by reason of the management of the activities authorised by the licence having ceased to be in the hands of a technically competent person. As to technical competence—see para.10–063.

The definition of "fit and proper person" is set out below (see para.10–063). Once a licence is revoked in part it will cease to have effect to authorise the carrying on of the activities specified, but it is open to the EA to retain further requirements imposed by the licence which it believes should continue to bind the licence holder. This could arise in circumstances where the right to continue to dispose of waste ceases, but the obligation to prevent pollution caused by earlier disposals of waste may be required to continue.

The EA also has power to suspend a licence on much the same grounds as revocation can take place. The effect of notice is that the rights to undertake those activities approved by the licence, or some of them as specified by the EA, are suspended. The notice may require the licence holder to take measures to deal with or avert the pollution or harm. Failure to comply is an offence (EPA 1990, s.38(10)). Such measures may include a

---

[42] For further information on variation and modification procedures see DoE Circular 11/94 and WMP4.

requirement on the holder to carry out works or do other things notwithstanding that he is not entitled to undertake them. These circumstances are the subject of s.38(9A)–(9C); these provisions, inserted by the Environment Act 1995, have the effect of bringing into play the provisions of s.36A (see para.10–046, above).

Notice of revocation or suspension

The EA must serve notice on the licence holder of any revocation or **10–054** suspension. The notice must state the time when any requirement is to take effect and may also specify when the suspension is to cease and in what circumstances. For a case providing guidance on how a notice suspending a waste management licence may be formulated, see *R. v Secretary of State Ex p. Premiere Environment Ltd*.[43]

Surrender of licence

Whereas a licence under COPA 1974 could be surrendered by the holder at **10–055** any time without further liability under the licence, the position was substantially changed when the relevant provisions of EPA 1990 came into force in May 1994. Section 39 provides that neither site licences originally granted under COPA 1974 nor waste management licences under EPA 1990 may be surrendered, except under special circumstances.

Applications for surrender

Licences, whether originally granted under COPA 1974 or under EPA **10–056** 1990, will be capable of being surrendered under s.39 of EPA 1990 only if the EA accepts such surrender. An application is required to comply with reg.2 of the Waste Management Licensing Regulations 1994.[44] Sch.1 to the Regulations specifies the information and evidence required. Further guidance can be found in Annex 4 to DoE Circular 11/94, paras 4.50–4.54. A fee is payable. The Regulations identify standards and criteria to be met by the licence holder and deal with matters concerning pollution and health and safety at the site, including long-term provision for the control of gas and leachate, as well as aftercare of the restored site. In many cases considerable periods of time will elapse before surrender can be accepted, notwithstanding closure of all operations and completion of restoration.

Action on application for surrender

Upon receipt of an application for surrender the EA is required to inspect **10–057** the land and seek any further information or evidence (EPA 1990, s.39). It must then decide whether it is likely or unlikely that there will be any more

---

[43] [2000] EGCS 12.
[44] SI 1994/1056.

pollution of the environment or harm to human health. Only when it is satisfied that pollution or harm will not occur may it accept surrender and then it may do this only after referring the proposal to the local planning authority and considering any representations. Some guidance on the proper approach to surrender applications is set out in WMP4, WMP26A, "Landfill completion" and WMP26E, "Landfill restoration and post-closure management" (draft).

Certificate of completion

10–058 Once the EA is prepared to agree to surrender, it must issue to the applicant a certificate of completion and only upon the issue of that certificate does the licence cease to have effect. See *In re Wilmott Trading Ltd*[45]; *Re Wilmott Trading Ltd (No. 2)*[46] and *In re Mineral Resources Ltd*[47]: all these cases concern surrender on insolvency.

Transfer of licences

10–059 With effect from May 1994, controls on the transfer of licences were brought into force by s.40 of EPA 1990. The EA has power to ensure that transfer is only to be made to a "fit and proper person" (see para.10–063 below). An application for transfer is required by reg.2 of the Waste Management Licensing Regulations 1994,[48] to be made in writing and to include the information prescribed by Sch.2 to the Regulations. The information mainly concerns the details of the proposed transferee and of the persons who will be managing the activities the subject of the licence. The information needs to be sufficient for the EA to make a judgement about whether the proposed transferee is a "fit and proper person". If it cannot be so satisfied, then the application is to be refused, without prejudice to a right of appeal. Further explanation is available in Annex 4 to DoE Circular 11/94, paras 4.55 and 4.56.

Appeals under Pt II of EPA 1990

10–060 A range of rights of appeal is available to applicants and others under s.43 of EPA 1990. Appeals may be made in respect of decisions (or failures to make decisions) in circumstances, where:

- an application for a licence or modification of conditions is rejected

[45] (1999) *The Times*, April 28.
[46] (1999) *The Times*, June 17.
[47] [1999] 1 All E.R. 746.
[48] SI 1994/1056.

- a licence is granted subject to conditions
- the conditions of a licence are modified
- a licence is suspended
- a licence is revoked
- an application to surrender a licence is rejected
- an application for the transfer of a licence is rejected.

The procedure for an appeal requires the Secretary of State to appoint an inspector (to whom he may delegate the determination). Any party to the appeal may request, or the Secretary of State may decide, that a hearing should be undertaken. Once the appeal is determined the EA is given a direction by the Secretary of State to give effect to that determination.

Detailed procedures for appeals are set out in the regs 6–10 of the 1994 Regulations, as amended (see above).

Interim arrangements pending determination

Different interim arrangements arise, depending on the type of appeal, as follows. **10–061**

(a) if the appeal relates to the modification of conditions of a licence or to revocation, the decision under appeal is ineffective and becomes effective only on the appeal decision;
(b) if the appeal relates to the suspension of a licence, the making of an appeal has no effect on the decision in question.

However, in the case of (a) above, a decision under appeal is not ineffective if a statement was included in the notice conveying the EA's decision that, in its opinion, the required action is necessary for the purpose of preventing or, where that is not practicable, minimising pollution of the environment or harm to human health. Such statement and its effect and any suspension can be challenged by the current or former holder of the licence on the grounds of unreasonableness. The challenge is to the Secretary of State.

In both cases (a) and (b), unreasonable behaviour on the EA's part can lead to the licence holder's entitlement to recover compensation in respect of any loss suffered from suspension.

Further guidance on appeals is set out in Annex 10 to DoE Circular 11/94. The Planning Inspectorate in Bristol will also provide a guide.

Further challenge to the High Court

EPA 1990 provides for no further appeal from a decision of the Secretary of State, but there are limited circumstances where an appeal may lie to the High Court. The most likely route for this will be by way of judicial review by the Administrative Court Division of the High Court. **10–062**

Judicial review is available to challenge not only decisions of the Secretary of State, but also those of other public bodies, including the EA. It is important to bear in mind that judicial review is not available except to challenge the decision-maker's administrative action. In other words, mere disagreement of the court on the merits of an appeal decision is not sufficient. An example of a judicial review of a waste management matter is *R. v Vale Glamorgan BC and Associated British Ports Ex p. James.*[49] The court will not normally interfere by way of judicial review where the complainant has a statutory alternative, such as an appeal under the EPA 1990, unless that route is frustrated, *e.g.* by long delays on the part of the regulator or the Secretary of State—see *R. v Environment Agency Ex p. Petrus Oils Limited.*[50]

Meaning of "fit and proper person"

10–063   A licence under Pt II of EPA 1990 may not be granted by the EA, nor may it be transferred, unless the applicant or the transferee respectively qualifies as a "fit or proper person" in accordance with the definition in s.74. Moreover, any fit or proper person who ceases to justify that category may be required to forfeit the licence. The EA must consider whether an applicant or a transferee is or is not a fit and proper person to hold the licence and it may determine this in the context of the carrying on by the applicant or transferee of the activities authorised by the licence and the fulfilment of the requirements of that licence. A person will fail to qualify as a fit and proper person if it appears to the EA that:

(a) he or another relevant person has been convicted of a relevant offence; or

(b) the management of the activities which are or are to be authorised by the licence are not or will not be in the hands of a technically competent person; or

(c) the person who holds or is to hold the licence has not made and either has no intention of making or is in no position to make financial provision adequate to discharge the obligations arising from the licence (s.74). The Environment Agency has published a revised policy on financial provision for non-landfill waste management licences which applies from July 1, 2003.

The definition of "another relevant person" is not mentioned specifically in the Act, but, by reference to s.74(7), it is clear that another convicted person will be relevant, if convicted of a relevant offence:

(a) if he is employed by the holder; or

---

[49] [1996] Env L.R. 102.
[50] [1999] Env L.R. 732.

(b) if he is in partnership with the holder; or

(c) where the holder or proposed holder is a director, manager, secretary or other similar officer of a body corporate (*e.g.* limited company); or

(d) where the holder or proposed holder is, in fact, a body corporate, and a director, manager, secretary or other similar officer has been convicted of a relevant offence or was in the above capacity when the body corporate was convicted.

Under reg.3 of the Waste Management Licensing Regulations 1994,[51] the Secretary of State has defined what is a "relevant offence". In the main, relevant offences are convictions under EPA 1990 or other public health or relevant environmental legislation. From March 14, 1997, an offence against the landfill tax provisions of the Finance Act 1996 (see section below) is also to be regarded as a "relevant offence". See the Waste Management (Miscellaneous Provisions) Regulations 1997,[52] Environment Agency guidance on relevant convictions is available from the Environment Agency.

It is important to note that, in relation to offences, the EA is given a discretion whether to overlook these and grant the licence notwithstanding. However, it has no such discretion where technical competence or financial capability is in dispute.

Technical competence is defined by regs 4 and 5 of the 1994 Regulations, as amended by the Waste Management Licensing (Amendment) Regulations 1997.[53] See, particularly, Table 1 introduced by reg.4 (as amended) of the 1994 Regulations, but see below.

Guidance generally on fit and proper persons and standards for technical competence can be found in DoE Circular 11/94, Annex 4, paras 4.65–4.80. Transitional provisions for dealing with the assessment of technical competence are dealt with in these paragraphs. Further guidance is also available, particularly regarding the approach to financial provision, in WMP4, "Licensing of Waste Management Facilities". For further guidance on technical competence, including certificates issued to individuals by the Waste Management Industry Training and Advisory Board, see the 1994 Regulations, as amended by the Waste Management Regulations 1996[54] and the 1997 Regulations (see above).

Technical competence requirements have been amended, with effect from April 1, 2003, by a new schedule inserted by the Waste Management Licensing (Amendment) (England) Regulations 2003.[55] Corresponding provisions for Wales are to be found in the Waste Management Licensing (Amendment) (Wales) Regulations 2003.[56] The effect of the new regu-

[51] SI 1994/1056.
[52] SI 1997/351.
[53] SI 1997/2203.
[54] SI 1996/634.
[55] SI 2003/595.
[56] SI 2003/780.

lations is to replace reg.4 of the 1994 Regulations and to insert a new Sch.1A in those regulations. See also Environment Agency Guidance "Technical Competence for Operators of Authorised Waste Facilities".

Public registers

10–064 Under s.64 of EPA 1990, as amended, the EA is required to maintain a register containing details of all current licences and the applications relating to them, applications and other documents relating to modification, revocation, suspension, details of appeals and certificates of completion under s.39, details of notices imposed on licence holders under s.42 and notes of convictions of licence holders etc. In some circumstances information may be excluded from a register if the Secretary of State so decrees. He may do this only if the inclusion in the register of any information would be contrary to the interests of national security. Section 66, as amended, allows other information to be excluded from the register if the EA accepts or, on appeal, the Secretary of State decides that the information is commercially confidential and may be excluded. Commercially confidential information may only be protected from disclosure for a period of four years, at the end of which a renewal application must be made. "Commercially confidential information" applies by s.66(11) if, in relation to any individual or person, its inclusion in the register would prejudice, to an unreasonable degree, the commercial interests of that individual or person. Note also that the Secretary of State may specify certain information which, regardless of its commercial confidentiality, must, nonetheless, be included in the register.

Regulation 10 of the 1994 Regulations[57] specifies the particulars to be entered in public registers, while reg.11 both prevents the registration of information about criminal proceedings not yet concluded and requires that monitoring information more than four years old should be excluded. Detailed guidance on public registers is available in Annex 9 to DoE Circular 11/94. Annex 10 contains guidance on appeals in relation to commercial confidentiality.

Special and non-controlled waste

10–065 Sections 62 and 63 of EPA 1990, as amended, provide the Secretary of State with powers to make regulations to deal with the regime of control in respect of special waste and to bring under control certain wastes which derive from agricultural and mines and quarries industries (see as to special waste para.10–015).

The enforcement powers of inspectors

10–066 Section 108 of the Environment Act 1995 provides power to the EA to appoint authorised inspectors who have wide-ranging powers noted in that section. These include powers to enter land and buildings, take samples and obtain documents and records.

[57] SI 1994/1056.

The EA also has power under the 1995 Act to serve a notice on any person requesting information it reasonably needs. It is an offence to fail to comply with a notice without reasonable excuse. See *In re Green Environmental Industries Ltd and another.*[58]

Power in the case of imminent danger

Section 109 of the Environment Act 1995 gives powers to the EA to deal   **10–067** with articles or substances believed to be a cause of imminent danger to or of serious pollution of the environment, or serious harm to human health.

Code of enforcement practice

The EA has published an "Enforcement and prosecution policy". Copies   **10–068** are obtainable from the EA. The policy deals with the basis upon which enforcement will be undertaken, relying on the principles of proportionality, consistency, transparency and targeting in relation to enforcement action.

Obstruction of an inspector

Obstruction of an inspector is an offence which may be dealt with either   **10–069** summarily or on indictment. In the latter case the fine may be unlimited or there may be imprisonment for a term not exceeding two years or both (Environment Act 1995, s.110).

Transition from COPA 1974 to EPA 1990

The EPA 1990 provides a number of transitional arrangements, which   **10–070** apply as a consequence of the replacement of COPA 1974. The main provisions are as follows.

   (a) On the coming into force of the waste management licensing system on May 1, 1994, a disposal licence granted under s.5 of COPA 1974 was to be treated as a site licence unless it had expired or ceased to have effect (EPA 1990, s.36). At that point it is liable to variation, revocation and suspension and subject to the restrictions on surrender or transfer as set out in EPA 1990.
   (b) Resolutions of local authorities made under s.11 of COPA 1974 (disposal of waste on local authority land) are preserved.
   (c) Certain transitional arrangements apply, relating to LAWDCs formed under s.32 of EPA 1990.

[58] [1998] Env L.R. 153.

Modifications required to licences

10–071   There are two important practical aspects of the transition arrangements, both arising because of the extent and responsibilities imposed by EPA 1990. First, where a disposal licence was held under COPA 1974 for a waste facility which carries on activities not previously regulated but now the subject of control under EPA 1990, the licence holder must make a prompt application to vary. This needs to be done to cover all the site activities. For example, management or treating of waste as well as disposal may have become licensable under EPA 1990.

Secondly, where a COPA 1974 licence holder did not meet the criteria which would normally satisfy the provisions of s.74 of EPA 1990 for the purposes of a grant of a waste management licence, the transitional arrangements provided that the waste regulation authority (now the EA) must treat the operator of a site as a fit and proper person, despite the new obligations of EPA 1990, until such time as circumstances relating to the operation of the site change (*e.g.* the management changes or a relevant person is convicted of a relevant offence). Further guidance is available in DoE Circular 11/94, Annex 4, paras 4.74 and 4.75.

Pollution Prevention and Control Act 1999

10–072   This Act is not yet fully in force but, together with the Pollution Prevention and Control Regulations 2000,[59] will materially affect and amend the provisions of Pt II of EPA 1990. For details of the provisions of the Regulations see Ch.9. Once the 1999 Act and the subsidary regulations are fully in force, applications for permits will be made under those provisions. The distinguishing features for waste activities are as follows:

> (a) Regulation 4 of the 2000 Regulations largely replicates the provisions of s.74 of EPA 1990 (see para.10–063).
> (b) Regulation 10(4) replicates the requirement of s.36(2) of EPA 1990 that certain waste management activities must benefit from planning permission and that a permit under PPCA 1999 may not be issued unless the regulator is satisfied that the applicant is a fit and proper person to carry out the activity.
> (c) On the transfer of any licence, reg.18 has the effect of requiring the regulator to satisfy himself that the transferee is also a fit and proper person.
> (d) Paragraphs (11) and (12) of reg.19 provide for special requirements in the case of surrender of a permit relating to specified waste management activities.
> (e) Regulation 21 provides for special arrangements in the case of revocation of permits, arising where an operator has ceased to be a fit and proper person.

---

[59] SI 2000/1973.

Note from Appendix 4 that virtually all waste installations will be the subject of control by the EA, as applies to Pt II enforcement under EPA 1990.

The EU Landfill Directive and the Landfill Regulations

Coincidentally with bringing into force the new regime for waste control   **10–073**
under the 1999 Act, the requirements of the EU Landfill Directive[60] will be incorporated. Implementation of the directive has been secured in England and Wales by the Landfill (England and Wales) Regulations 2002.[61] The regulations came into force on June 15, 2002. Some landfills will continue to be the subject of the Waste Management Licensing Regulations 1994[62] but the majority will be caught by the 1999 Act and the 2000 Regulations. The Landfill Regulations introduce complex transitional provisions which will require some care in interpretation. With few exceptions, noted above, the regulations will apply to all landfills including, generally, temporary storage of waste longer than a period of a year, or more than three years where recovery or treatment is in contemplation. There are exemptions for the spreading of sludges and similar material, inert wastes and where the landfill no longer accepts wastes since July 16, 2001. The discharge of liquid waste arising from oil production into underground strata constitutes landfill—see *Blackland Park Exploration Limited v The Environment Agency* [2003].

The Environment Agency must classify landfills in three categories, for

(a) hazardous waste (defined in the Hazardous Waste Directive 91/689/EEC);
(b) non-hazardous waste;
(c) inert waste as defined.

Certain wastes are banned at landfills. These include waste in liquid form (but not sludges), dangerous waste, certain clinical and research waste, tyres including, after July 16, 2006, shredded tyres except those from bicycles and very large tyres, and waste which does not fulfil the appropriate acceptance criteria. Waste acceptance criteria are set out in Sch.1 to the regulations. They apply generally and there are additional criteria for hazardous, non-hazardous and inert landfills. Subject to limited exceptions, all waste will be subject to prior treatment before landfilling may take place. This is intended to reduce the hazardous nature of the waste as well as its volume, to facilitate handling or to improve recovery. Waste acceptance procedures are laid down in the regulations but are subject to further guidance from the Environment Agency (see below).

The regulations also provide for control and monitoring of operational sites, closure and after care. A new enforcement procedure, involving a

[60] 19991/31/EC.
[61] SI 2002/1559.
[62] SI 1994/1056.

closure notice, is available to the Environment Agency where a reasoned decision about closure has been taken by them.

Schedule 4 to the regulations establishes a procedure for operators of landfills intended to be used after July 16, 2002. Conditioning plans should have been in place by that date. In their absence, non-compliant sites are liable to be closed. For the remainder, new permits will be granted within a transitional period up to March 31, 2007.

Technical guidance

Technical guidance on the directive and the regulations has been published by the Environment Agency and supplements general guidance on the directive issued at the end of 2001. The guidance issued to date includes:

- Landfill Directive: General Regulatory Guidance to Landfill Operators/Licence holders;
- Regulatory Guidance Note 1—classification of sites;
- Regulatory Guidance Note 2 (Version November 4, 2002) Interim Waste Acceptance Criteria and Procedures;
- Regulatory Guidance Note 3 (Version 4.0 December 02) ground-water protection: locational aspects of landfills in planning consultation responses and permitting decisions;
- Regulatory Guidance Note 4: defining existing landfill site;
- Regulatory Guidance Note 5: Habitats Regulations and the Landfill Directive, information and guidance for landfill operators;
- Regulatory Guidance Note 6: Interpretation of the Engineering Requirements of Annex 1 of the Landfill Directive;
- Regulatory Guidance Note 7 (Version 1.1) requirements for landfills that stop operating;
- Regulatory Guidance Note 8: guidance for pet cemeteries and pet crematoria;
- Regulatory Guidance Note 11 (Version 1.2 August 2003): the disposal in landfills for non-hazardous waste of: stable non-reactive hazardous waste, asbestos wastes and wastes with high sulphate or gypsum content;
- Regulatory Guidance Note 14: duty of care and European Waste Catalogue;
- Regulatory Guidance Note 15; applicability of the Landfill Directive to the deposit of waste in lagoons;
- Regulatory Guidance Note 16: establishing the area to be covered by a PPC permit for a landfill;
- Regulatory Guidance Note 17: the ban on the landfilling of whole used and shredded used tyres in accordance with the requirement of the Landfill (England and Wales) Regulations 2002.

Designed to coincide with the application of the IPPC regime but also covering non-IPPC regulation of waste management, the Environment Agency have issued, "Best Practice Guidance: Recovery and Disposal of

Hazardous and Non-hazardous Waste". The document is intended to be a statement of the expectations of the Agency as to standards to be expected in waste management operations and is aimed primarily at the industrial waste treatment sector. The Environment Agency have also published Technical Guidance WM2, "Interpretation of the Definition and Classification of Hazardous Waste". This guidance deals with methods for identifying hazardous waste, by reference to definitions in the 1991 Directive and other supporting measures. It should be read with Regulatory Guidance Note 14 (see above).

Waste incineration

Special attention should be paid to the Waste Incineration (England and Wales) Regulations 2002[63] which came into force on December 28, 2002. They make amendments to the 2000 Regulations in order to provide for implementation of the EU Directive 2000/76/EC on the incineration of waste. The 2002 Regulations:

- require IPPC applications for existing plants to be made between January 1 and March 31, 2005;
- set down the information required for the purposes of an application, particularly concerning design, heat generation and residues;
- prohibits some incinerators from being put into operation until the application has been determined;
- provide enforcement provisions;
- provide that change in operation of an incinerator which involves the disposal of hazardous waste is to be regarded as a substantial change (see above para.9–007), requiring a prior application for an adjustment of a permit.

Waste and Emissions Trading Act 2003

Two main environmental initiatives are provided for by the Waste and Emissions Trading Act 2003. For comments on emissions trading see para.8–038.   **10–074**

Waste trading

The scheme provided by the Act is intended to offer waste disposal authorities some flexibility to meet the stringent and progressively rigorous targets for reducing the amounts of biodegradable municipal waste sent to landfill. Assuming that the government takes up the four year derogation made available under the Landfill Directive, by 2010 landfill of this waste must be no more than 75 per cent of that produced in 1995 and, by 2020,

[63] SI 2002/2980.

the figure must be down to 35 per cent. The scheme envisages that landfill allowances will be allocated to each waste disposal authority. If the authority can beat its target, the balance of the allowance can either be banked (for further use) or traded to another local authority with a lower performance. It is the intention of the government to progressively reduce the allowances. The new Act also attends to the difficulties which arise where there are both district and county authorities. By April 2005, a joint strategy will be required to ensure that a collection authority must deliver their waste in a separated form, thereby facilitating recycling and landfill reduction.

WASTE STRATEGY 2000 AND TRANSFRONTIER SHIPMENTS

Waste Strategy 2000

10–075　EU and UK legislation has, for some time, required the production by the Government of a nation-wide waste strategy document. Only in 2000 has this document finally appeared, in the form of "Waste Strategy 2000—England and Wales". It is in two parts: Pt I deals with general policy matters, particularly in relation to changes in policies, while Pt II applies the strategy to specific issues including the decision-making framework, waste stakeholders, waste management options, handling of hazardous waste, packaging and packaging waste. There is a chapter which describes progress with various waste streams. The document is fundamental to waste regulation in the future as well as development planning and development control under the town and country planning legislation. It is published by the Stationery Office.

The Waste Strategy 2000 proposed the preparation of municipal waste management strategies in order to achieve the objective of sustainable waste management. Guidance on the preparation of the strategies was published by DETR in 2001. The guidance includes statutory targets for all local authorities to significantly increase composting rates.

The corresponding Waste Strategy for Wales was published in 2002.

Transfrontier shipment of waste

10–076　The EU's waste management policy concerns the movement of hazardous waste across frontiers. Council Regulation (EEC) 259/93 and Council Directive 75/442/EEC provide for a system of prior notification and authorisation of the import and export of waste both within the EU and by way of trade between the EU and other states. As far as the United Kingdom is concerned, detailed provisions are included in the Transfrontier Shipment of Waste Regulations 1994.[64]

---

[64] SI 1994/1137.

The DoE has published Circular 13/94 on the subject. For guidance on the interpretation of Regulation 259/93, see *R. v Environment Agency Ex p. Dockgrange Ltd.*[65]

Regulation 259/93 has been modified by Council Regulation (EC) 120/97, which came into effect on January 1, 1998. From that date there is a ban on all exports for recovery of waste of a hazardous nature, except where there are special agreements made in accordance with the Basel Convention on the control of transboundary movements of hazardous wastes and their disposal. See the "UK Management Plan for Exports and Imports of Waste" (1996). In 2000, in light of the Convention, a new protocol was signed by the UK. The effect of this protocol is that any export of hazardous waste must be insured to cover any damage that may be caused on the journey to a recycler of a disposer of that waste. The protocol provides not only for liability but also to ensure adequate and prompt compensation in the event that damage results from the trans-boundary movement of waste.

LANDFILL TAX

Sections 39—71 of and Sch.5 to the Finance Act 1996 introduce a tax on   **10–077**
the disposal of waste in landfill sites throughout the United Kingdom. The tax came into force on October 1, 1996. A tax is applied if there is a disposal of material as waste by way of landfill at a landfill site. Disposal is "by way of landfill" if the material is deposited on the land's surface, in a structure on the land or under the land's surface. A landfill site is defined by reference to a waste management licence in force for the site (see para.10–046). "Waste" has the same meaning as in EPA 1990, as amended (see para.10–031).

The Landfill Tax Regulations 1996

The Landfill Tax Regulations 1996[66] came into force on August 1, 1996 and   **10–078**
provide for general administration, including provisions for registration of bodies who are liable to be taxed. The Regulations have been amended from time to time.

Liability

The tax must be paid to HM Customs & Excise by "the landfill site   **10–079**
operator", who holds a waste management licence. Tax is payable by reference to the weight of the waste deposited, at a rate subject to annual

---

[65] [1997] Env L.R. 575.
[66] SI 1996/1527.

increase. A reduced rate of £2 per tonne applies for certain types of waste, mainly inactive or inert (s.42). The categories are defined in the Landfill Tax (Qualifying Material) Order 1996,[67] as amended. For a case on the liability to tax in respect of the deposit of soil on a landfill site, see *Customs & Excise Commissioners v Darfish Limited*.[68]

Exemptions

10–080   There are a number of categories of waste which are not subject to any charge. These include dredgings, naturally occurring materials arising from mining or quarrying operations, burials of domestic pets at pet cemeteries and waste resulting from the clearing up of historically contaminated land. However, this last category is the subject of conditions, set out in the Landfill Tax (Contaminated Land) Order 1996.[69] See HM Customs & Excise Information Note LF2, "Reclamation of Contaminated Land". See also *Taylor Woodrow v Customs & Excise*.[70] A further exemption is available by virtue of the Landfill Tax (Site Restoration and Quarries) Order 1999.[71] This Order provides for two exemptions, namely inert waste disposed of in a landfill site but used for the purposes of restoring the site and inert waste used for the purposes of filling in existing or old quarries. These exemptions are effected by inserting further ss.43C and 44A into the Finance Act 1996. Each exemption is subject to certain conditions. For cases on liability for tax in respect of recycled and restoration materials, see *Parkwood Landfill Limited v Customs & Excise Commissioners*[72] and *Ebbcliff Limited v Customs & Excise Commissioners*.[73]

Calculating the weight of waste

10–081   Methods for calculating the weight of waste are in s.68 of the Finance Act 1996 and regs 41—44 of the Landfill Tax Regulations 1996.[74] Normally an available weighbridge at a landfill site will be expected to be used, but otherwise an alternative method of calculation will be agreed with local Customs officers. Landfill site operators may discount the water content of waste where it is added to enable the material to be transported for disposal, for the extraction of minerals or where it is present as part of an industrial process and the water constitutes 25 per cent or more of the disposal by weight. It may also be discounted when added to sewage or effluent, treated at a water treatment plant. No discount for water content

[67] SI 1996/1528.
[68] *The Times*, March 28, 2000.
[69] SI 1996/1529.
[70] November 1998.
[71] SI 1999/2075.
[72] November 28, 2002.
[73] July 30, 2004, CA.
[74] SI 1996/1527.

is allowed where it has the potential to pollute ground water, where it is naturally present in the waste or where it is present as a consequence of rain or snow. Written approval of HM Customs & Excise is required to any scheme for discounting water.

Tax-free areas

There is no liability for tax if waste is sorted, pending use or disposal, recycled (including compost) or incinerated at a landfill site. An application for exemption must be made by the site operator to HM Customs & Excise. See the Landfill Tax Regulations 1996.[75] **10–082**

Registration

It is the obligation of the landfill site operator to register for landfill tax with HM Customs & Excise within 30 days of the date when the operator decides to carry out "taxable activities". A registration certificate will be issued. **10–083**

Offences

Schedule 5 to the Finance Act 1996 provides for offences and penalties for failure to pay the tax, etc. With effect from March 14, 1997, offences under Sch.5 are prescribed offences for the purposes of the provisions relating to "fit and proper persons" under s.74 of EPA (see para.10–063). **10–084**

Environmental bodies

Section 53 of the Finance Act 1996 entitles a landfill taxpayer to certain credits if he pays the sum of money to "a body whose objects are or include the protection of the environment" (environmental bodies). Tax credits of up to 90 per cent of any contribution may be claimed, subject to a limit of 20 per cent of the landfill tax bill in any 12-month period. The contribution must be spent by the body on approved environmental purposes, set out in the Landfill Tax Regulations 1996, as amended. These include the promotion of more sustainable waste management practices, education, restoration and the creation of wildlife habitats or conservation areas. The regulating body responsible for monitoring and control of environmental bodies under the Act is known as ENTRUST, a private sector body, independent of government but nonetheless, bound by the Act (see the Landfill Tax (Amendment) Regulations 1999).[76] **10–085**

[75] SI 1996/1527.
[76] SI 1999/3270.

Changes to landfill tax credit scheme

10–086   Changes to the landfill tax credit scheme came into force from April 1,
2003. The Landfill Tax (Amendment) Regulations 2003[77] give effect to
these changes. Two-thirds of the funding which currently goes through the
scheme is to be allocated to public spending projects involving research,
development and education on sustainable waste management or development of the market for recycled waste. A new tax credit scheme will receive
about a third of the funding currently available to the existing scheme. This
will be spent on community environmental projects not falling within those
noted above. Landfill site operators were enabled to make continuing
contributions towards qualifying projects until March 31, 2003 or until the
particular project is completed or the funding exhausted, provided certain
criteria are met. These arrangements will come to an end at March 31,
2004.

 As to the continuing tax credit system, the 20 per cent limit on claims for
credits is reduced to 6.5 per cent from April 1, 2003. Further changes to the
credit scheme were made by the Landfill Tax (Amendment) (No. 2)
Regulations 2003[78] and came into force on October 1, 2003. These
regulations allow the disbursement of credit for the support of biological
diversity in natural habitats. However, the entitlement to provide funding
under the scheme does not apply where works involved are already the
subject of a statutory obligation or are carried out with a view to profit.

 HM Customs & Excise have issued a landfill tax information note dated
February 21, 2003.

PRODUCER RESPONSIBILITY

10–087   Under Pt V of the Environment Act 1995, the Government has powers
to impose producer responsibility obligations for the promotion of reuse,
recovery and recycling of products or materials (EA 1995, ss.93–95).

 The main provisions relating to producer responsibility concern packaging recycling and recovery. The Producer Responsibility Obligations (Packaging Waste) Regulations 1997[79] as amended, came into force on March 7,
1997. They place the responsibility on companies with a turnover of £1
million, handling over 50 tonnes of packaging annually, to recover and
recycle a proportion of their packaging waste. The term "packaging"
includes cardboard, glass, plastics and metals together, since 2000, with
wood and other packaging products.

 The level of obligation depends upon a company's use of packaging
products, expressed as a percentage of the weight of packaging handled.
The present percentages are as follows:

[77] SI 2003/605.
[78] SI 2003/2313.
[79] SI 1997/648.

raw material manufacturer	6 per cent
converter	9 per cent
packer/filler	37 per cent
retailer	48 per cent

Importers bear the percentages of the preceding links in the chain but end consumers do not incur any obligations. Thus, using transit packaging will incur an 85 per cent obligation, combining the packer/filler and retailer obligations. Exports are exempt from the packaging regulations.

National targets for recycling and recovery have progressively increased, by reference to the European Packaging and Packaging Waste Directive (94/62/EC). The national targets for 2002 were 59 per cent recovery and 19 per cent recycling of packaging waste. Those figures remained in force for 2003—see Producer Responsibility Obligations (Packaging Waste) (Amendment) (England) Regulations 2002[80] which came into force on March 21, 2002. The Producer Responsibility Obligations (Packaging Waste) (Amendment) (England) Regulations 2003[81] came into force on January 1, 2004. They serve to provide compliance with EU Directive 2004/12/EC which amends the original directive noted above. The new regulations make significant changes to packaging waste targets and must be implemented by August 2005. Recovery targets for 2004 now extend to 63 per cent of the tonnage of packaging waste, increasing to 70 per cent by 2008. Likewise, recycling targets for a range of materials are the subject of significant increases, *e.g.* glass from 49 per cent in 2004 to 71 per cent in 2008, aluminium from 26 per cent to 35.5 per cent in those years.

Compliance is ensured by one of two methods: either businesses may deal with re-processors directly, annually providing to the EA estimates of packaging handled, certificates of compliance and returns, or they may join a collective scheme which will, for a fee, bear the burden of compliance on behalf of its members. However, by the 2003 Regulations mentioned above, a producer of packaging waste continues to be liable for compliance with the regulations notwithstanding he has joined a scheme. Businesses were required to register with the EA or with a collective scheme. To have failed to do so is an offence, as is a failure to register recovered and recycled packaging waste and failure to supply a certificate of compliance. Conviction in the magistrates' court can result in a fine up to the statutory maximum and, on indictment, an unlimited fine. A user's guide to the Packaging Regulations is available from DEFRA.

Packaging standards

The Packaging (Essential Requirements) Regulations 1998[82] implement **10–088** parts of the European Directive 94/62/EC on packaging and packaging waste. Specific requirements for the design and manufacture of packaging

---

[80] SI 2002/732.
[81] SI 2003/3294.
[82] SI 1998/1165.

are laid down by the Regulations, having regard particularly to the need for reuse. See Department of Trade and Industry guidance, "Packaging (Essential Requirements) Regulations".

End of Life Vehicles Regulations

10–089   At the end of 2003, the End of Life Vehicles Regulations 2003[83] came into force. They partially implement the EU Directive 2000/53/EC which requires vehicles to be designed, constructed and destroyed in such a way as to facilitate recycling and re-use. For the most part, the regulations are specific to the vehicle manufacturing industry. However, Pts V to VII, also relate to the waste industry. Part V introduces the certificate of destruction which will normally be issued by an authorised treatment facility—usually one holding a site licence under the EPA 1990. Such certificates will normally be issued to the last holder or owner of the vehicle and a charge for this certificate is prohibited.

Part VI of the regulations provides for the treatment of vehicles (*i.e.* those put on the market after June 2002). Reception of a vehicle may not be the subject of a charge and producers are expected to be responsible for the meeting the costs of break up and other treatment. Part VII of the regulations provides for amendment of all existing site licences where the keeping or treatment of waste motor vehicles is authorised to be modified. Modifications will following Sch.5 to the regulations which relate to responsibilities in respect of these vehicles. The importance of this part is that recovery operations, exempt from the need for a site licence to take on vehicle destruction and recycling, will now require such a site licence. However, there is an exception where the only treatment undertaken is of de-polluted vehicles. De-pollution involves the removal of potentially polluting components such as batteries, fuel and/or antifreeze or other fluids.

Household Waste Recycling Act 2003

10–090   This Act came into force on October 30, 2003. Under its terms, all authorities with a duty to collect waste must, by the end of 2010, collect at least two recyclates separate from the remainder of household waste.

The obligations are effected by adding a s.45A to the EPA 1990 and a s.45B in respect of Welsh waste collection obligations.

---

[83] SI 2003/2635.

CHAPTER 11

CONTAMINATED LAND

INTRODUCTION

Until the end of the 1980s, law and policy relating to contaminated land **11–001** was not directly addressed by the UK Government. The obligations of landowners and occupiers to avoid contamination rested on the civil law of tort[1] and the indirect provisions of the Public Health Act 1936 (*e.g.* abatement of nuisance) and water pollution (*e.g.* the Water Resources Act 1963). In other words, at such times as land was used so as to create contamination, such use brought with it liabilities in circumstances where that contamination caused nuisance or pollution. However, the existence of unknown contaminated land can represent a significant problem, particularly for an innocent purchaser who, despite reasonable investigations of the land, only later discovers a latent problem which may well have a disastrous effect upon his investment. His remedies against previous owners and/or the perpetrator of the contamination may be extremely limited because of the passing of time or the principle of caveat emptor (let the buyer beware). Furthermore, the contamination may be continuing and may attract fresh liabilities as a result. A typical example is the plight of the first-time buyer of a dwelling built on a landfill site. Despite his detailed enquiries he may acquire his interest innocently, only later to discover significant landfill gas problems, the emergence of leachate, subsidence etc.—a likely disaster scenario. However, the provisions of the Environment Act 1995 may be of assistance (see para.11–004 below).

The problem was brought into sharp focus as a result of the investigation by the House of Commons Environment Committee published in January 1990, which drew a generally supportive response from HM Government.

ENVIRONMENTAL PROTECTION ACT 1990, s.143

Section 143 of EPA 1990 was intended to enable the Secretary of State to **11–002** establish registers of contaminated land to be kept by local authorities. However, during a number of consultation exercises it became clear that practical difficulties attended the making and maintaining of registers, such that in March 1993 the Secretary of State for the Environment announced

[1] See Ch.16.

that it was no longer intended to bring s.143 into force. At the same time he set in train a further study, which has resulted in the consultation paper "Paying for Our Past". This discusses a wide range of issues pertaining to contaminated land, including liability, the need for rationalisation of existing legislative arrangements, standards to which clean-up should be pursued and strategy for proceeding to a programme of clean-up. During 1994 the Government's conclusions were published in "Framework for Contaminated Land". This has been followed by proposals in the Environment Act 1995, although implementation was delayed until April 2000. The 1995 Act inserts a new Pt IIA into EPA 1990.

OTHER RELEVANT LEGISLATION

11–003   By no means is there a lack of powers available to both central and local government to secure clean-up. For provisions controlling the interaction of other legislation with the Environment Act 1995, see s.78YB of EPA 1990 (para.11–014 below)).

Pt I of EPA 1990 gives the EA wide powers to impose conditions on authorisations. These powers can be sufficiently extensive to prevent ongoing pollution and possibly to require clean-up. When it comes fully into force, PPCA 1999, together with the Pollution Prevention and Control Regulations 2000, will replace Pt I and will provide enhanced powers which make clear that clean-up will be required in respect of any installation and activity the subject of the Act (see Ch.9).

Part II of EPA 1990, as amended by PPCA 1999, enables the EA both to require clean-up of contamination through conditions of a waste management licence or permit and to refuse to allow the surrender of that licence or permit because the condition of the land continues to offer the potential of pollution or harm to human health (see para.10–056).

Contaminated land can be a statutory nuisance. Under Pt III of EPA 1990, environmental health authorities have powers to require abatement of nuisance and/or the execution of works (see para.12–008). However, note that, with effect from April 1, 2000, the definition of statutory nuisance has been amended so as to delete reference to most contaminated land (see EPA 1990, s.79(1A) and (1B)).

The EA has powers under ss.161–161D of WRA 1991 to control and remedy pollution from contaminated land in circumstances where it is a threat to controlled waters (see para.7–033 above). With the coming into force of the new contaminated land controls, there is potential for overlap with the EA's powers. Guidance on this is to be found in the EA policy statement "Environment Agency policy and guidance on the use of anti-pollution works notices" and in DETR Circular 2/2000, "Contaminated Land: Implementation of Pt IIA of the EPA 1990".

Other powers are available to the Health and Safety Executive under ss.21 and 22 of the Health and Safety at Work etc. Act 1974. Furthermore, by s.215 of TCPA 1990, the local planning authority may serve notices requiring the remedying of the condition of land adversely affecting the amenity of a locality.

These powers offer to the regulator the opportunity to bring proceedings against the polluter, landowner or occupier, as the case may be. In each case there are powers for the regulators themselves to enter the land to carry out necessary works, recovering the cost from the person responsible. Furthermore, the requirement for planning permission for redevelopment of land which is or may be contaminated offers opportunities for clean-up. It is open to the local planning authority to impose conditions on any planning permission which require this work to be undertaken. PPG23, "Planning and Pollution Control", published by the former DoE, contains a section on contaminated land.

Environment Act 1995 and Pt IIA of EPA 1990

Comprehensive powers to deal with contaminated land were approved by Parliament in the Environment Act 1995. Section 143 of EPA 1990 was repealed. Section 57 of the 1995 Act inserted a substantial number of additional sections as Pt IIA of EPA 1990. The legislation came into force on April 1, 2000. Substantial statutory and other guidance on the operation of the regime is to be found in DETR Circular 2/2000 (see above). **11–004**

Regulations

Besides Pt IIA of EPA 1990, the Contaminated Land (England) Regulations 2000[2] provide detailed systems of control and procedure for the operation of the Act's requirements. These Regulations came into force on April 1, 2000. They: **11–005**

(a) specify the types of land required to be designated as a special site (see below);

(b) prescribe the content of a remediation notice and the parties upon whom copies are to be served;

(c) provide for compensation for rights of entry, etc; and

(d) prescribe grounds of appeal against a remediation notice and procedures for appeals both to magistrates' courts and to the Secretary of State.

There are also provisions relating to the suspension of a remediation notice and providing for registers to be kept (see below).

Administration

Administration obligations under the legislation are imposed largely on local authorities, but some special sites are the EA's responsibility (see below). The obligation is on local authorities to inspect their area from **11–006**

[2] SI 2000/227.

time to time to determine whether land is contaminated. "Contaminated land", for the purposes of EPA 1990, is land which by reason of substances in, on or under it is, or has a significant possibility of, causing significant harm or is causing, or is likely to cause, pollution of controlled waters (see s.78A(2)). Guidance published by the Secretary of State will assist authorities in making a decision about whether land is contaminated. However, the judgement must be determined on the basis of a risk assessment, identifying a source of pollutants, a pathway by means of which the pollutant is conveyed and a receptor (*i.e.* land or other target which is exposed or could be exposed to the pollutant). The guidance is to be found in DETR Circular 2/2000 (see above) and in "Contaminated Land Inspection Strategy: Technical Advice for Local Authorities" (DEFRA, 2002).

Special sites

11–007 The procedure for the identification by local authorities of special sites is set out in s.78C of EPA 1990. Again, guidance in Circular 2/2000 assists local authorities in reaching conclusions about whether land is a special site. The local authority will take advice from the EA before making a decision. In cases of dispute between a local authority and the EA about whether a site is a special site, s.78D provides for the conclusion to be reached by the Secretary of State.

Duty of enforcing authorities: "appropriate persons"

11–008 Section 78E of EPA 1990 imposes on the enforcing authority the responsibility to require the remediation of contaminated land in circumstances where a site has been identified as such. Section 78F provides for the identification by the regulator of "appropriate persons" who are liable to be given notice, called a "remediation notice". This specifies what that person is to do by way of remediation and the periods within which he is required to undertake the necessary steps. The guidance, in Circular 2/2000, illustrates how conclusions are to be reached by local authorities as to the appropriate person or persons to bear responsibility for remediation. The basic provisions are in s.78F of the Act but, for the most part, decisions on the identification of appropriate persons will rely heavily on the guidance. The scheme of the Act is that the primary party to be held responsible is the polluter, but if that party cannot be found after reasonable enquiry then the owner or occupier for the time being is to be regarded as the appropriate person. The Act provides for procedures, which are specified in the guidance, illustrating how liability is to be shared between more than one responsible party. The polluter is defined generally as any person who caused or knowingly permitted the substances in any of them, by reason of which the land is contaminated, to be in, on or under the land (s.78F(2)). See para.7–029 for interpretations of "caused" and "knowingly permitted".

The voluntary route

Section 78H of EPA 1990 provides that a remediation notice is not to be   **11–009**
served until the enforcing authority has made every reasonable endeavour
to confirm whether the responsible parties will undertake remediation on a
voluntary basis.

Liability for the escape of contamination to other land

Section 78K of EPA 1990 provides for special rules to apply in circum-   **11–010**
stances where contamination has passed from one person's land to another.
A person who has caused or knowingly permitted any substances in land
shall be presumed to have caused or knowingly permitted those substances
to be in land to which they appear to have escaped. In these circumstances
the owner or occupier of the receptor land (onto which the contamination
has flowed), provided that he has not caused or knowingly permitted the
substances to be on the land, is generally not liable to receive a remediation
notice. Further provisions in s.78K control the position where there is a
transfer of contamination from one piece of land to another and where
ownerships or occupation are in different hands.

Appeals

There are rights of appeal against a remediation notice. This may be made   **11–011**
within a period of 21 days from the date of service of the notice by a local
authority. The appeal is usually made to a magistrates' court. Any
remediation notice served by the EA is to be the subject of an appeal to the
Secretary of State (s.78L). Procedures are described in the Contaminated
Land (England) Regulations 2000.[3]
   The grounds of appeal are set out in reg.7. They include:

- whether the land is contaminated land as defined;
- a challenge to what is required to be done by way of remediation;
- whether an appellant is an appropriate person (see above) and
  therefore responsible for remediation;
- whether another person is also an appropriate person;
- whether the appellant should have been excluded from responsibility (see Chapter D of Annex 3 to Circular 2/2000);
- challenge of the proportion of cost to be borne by the appellant;
- whether the notice complies with restrictions in EPA 1990 on the
  serving of notices (see *e.g.* s.78H);
- whether the case is one of imminent danger of serious harm (see
  s.78H(4));

---

[3] SI 2000/227.

- where the remediation is taking place on a voluntary basis;
- where the remediation requirements breach restrictions on lia-bility for pollution of controlled waters (see s.78J);
- where remediation requirements breach restrictions on liability relating to escaping substances (see s.78K);
- whether the authority has itself agreed to carry out remediation (see s.78N);
- whether hardship on the part of the responsible party applies (see Chapter E of Annex 3 to Circular 2/2000);
- whether the authority's powers to remediate were exercisable having regard to the hardship;
- whether regard has been had to specific guidance from the EA (see s.78V);
- whether enough time was allowed for remediation;
- whether the notice would make personally liable an insolvency practitioner, an official receiver or other receiver or manager (see s.78X);
- whether certain powers under other legislation apply;
- whether there is some informality, defect or error in the notice, but an appeal on this ground must be dismissed if the informality, defect or error was not material.

A remediation notice is suspended pending the final outcome of the appeal.

Penalties

11–012   Failure to comply with the remediation notice, without reasonable excuse, is an offence. There are special rules in s.78M which deal with circum-stances where there is a shared liability. The penalty on conviction for failure to comply with the remediation notice is a fine not exceeding £20,000. A daily fine of up to £2,000 can be imposed, applying until such time as the remediation notice has been complied with.

Section 78N gives powers to the enforcing authority to undertake the remediation required by the notice itself. However, the section contains a detailed system of control of the powers which may be exercised. Recovery of the cost of remediation by the enforcing authority is the subject of provisions in s.78P. See also the guidance in Annex 2 to Circular 2/2000.

Registers

11–013   Each enforcing authority is required to maintain a register containing a wide range of information arising from the service of remediation notices. This information includes details of any appeals, remediation statements or declarations, designation of any site as a special site, convictions and other information. Where national security is involved (s.78S) or where information is confidential (s.78T), the information may be excluded from the registers, subject to conditions.

Interaction of the Environment Act 1995 with other legislation

Section 78YB of the 1990 Act, as amended, makes various provisions which **11–014** seek to avoid duplication of controls as between the 1995 Act and other "clean-up" legislation (see para.11–003 above). The provisions are as follows.

No remediation notice may be served where the EA has powers under s.27 of EPA 1990 (see para.8–029 above) to remedy harm arising from an offence under Pt I of that Act.

The contaminated land provisions do not apply to any land where there is a site licence in force under Pt II of EPA 1990 (waste on land—see para.10–030 above), except to the extent that any significant harm or pollution of controlled waters has been caused other than by breach of the conditions of the licence or the carrying on in accordance with the licence of any activity so authorised.

No remediation notice shall be served in a case where waste has been deposited in contravention of s.33(1) of EPA 1990. The powers of s.59 (see para.16–020 below) are available to the responsible authority.

A remediation notice may not require any person to do anything which would have the effect of impeding or preventing the making of a discharge in pursuance of a consent given under Chapter II of Pt III of WRA 1991 (pollution offences—see para.7–042 above).

The contaminated land provisions do not apply if and to the extent that any significant harm or pollution of controlled waters is attributable to the final disposal on land of controlled waste. Enforcement action may instead be taken under the Pollution Prevention and Control (England & Wales) Regulations 2000.[4]

A remediation notice is not to be served in respect of contaminated land where such land is attributable to an activity (other than the final disposal by deposit in or on land of controlled waste) where enforcement action may instead be taken under the Pollution Prevention and Control (England and Wales) Regulations.

---

[4] SI 2000/1973.

CHAPTER 12

NOISE AND STATUTORY NUISANCE

NOISE

The control of noise in relation to waste management sites is likely to be **12–001** dealt with mainly in the context of the controls available to the local planning authority (by conditions of any planning permission) under TCPA 1990 (see *e.g.* PPG24, "Planning and Noise", and MPG11, "The Control of Noise at Surface Mineral Workings") or by the EA by conditions of any authorisation or permit under EPA 1990 or PPCA 1999 (see Ch.9). However, there are other duties and responsibilities of local authorities to which attention should be drawn.

CONTROL OF POLLUTION ACT 1974

Control of noise on construction sites

During the time that waste management facilities are being constructed, **12–002** noise from the activity can represent a potential cause of noise complaint to the public health authority. Section 60 of COPA 1974 provides the authority with a power to serve a notice indicating how construction works are to be carried out. The definition of "construction works" includes not only the activities of erection, repair or maintenance, but also the breaking open of roads, demolition and engineering construction. A notice may specify the works to be carried out, the hours of operation and the plant and machinery to be used or not used. The requirements of a notice may be the subject of an appeal to the magistrates' court.

An alternative course available to the developer is set out in s.61. This allows an application for prior consent for work intended to be carried out on a construction site. Once consent is granted, and provided that activities are carried on within the terms of the consent and its conditions, there is immunity from any prosecution under s.60. Compliance is not, of itself, a defence to proceedings for statutory nuisance (see below). Nonetheless, the availability of a prior consent would be a useful defensive mechanism.

The Control of Noise (Codes of Practice for Construction and Open Sites) (England) Order 2002[1] approves Pts I, III and V of British Standard

---

[1] SI 2002/461.

BS5228:1997 and Pt IV of BS5228: 1992 as suitable for giving guidance on appropriate methods for minimising noise and for vibration control from construction and other open sites. Parts I, III and V relate to basic information and procedures for noise and vibration control, surface coal extraction and other surface mineral extraction.

Noise abatement zones

12–003   A further anticipatory or reactive power is available under s.63, by which a local authority may designate all or any part of its area as a noise abatement zone. The procedure for doing this is set out in Sch.1 to COPA 1974, as revised by Sch.2 to the Local Government Planning and Land Act 1980.

Noise level registers

12–004   Once a noise abatement order is made there are responsibilities on the local authority to take steps, as soon as practicable, to record the level of noise arising from premises as designated in the order. Measurements will be recorded in a register, with copies of entries served on relevant owners and occupiers. Such owners and occupiers may appeal to the Secretary of State against the record within 28 days if they wish to object to its accuracy. This may be important, because in the absence of a challenge by way of appeal, the validity or accuracy of any entry is not subsequently to be questioned in any proceedings under this part of COPA 1974. The register is open to public inspection.

Effect of registration

12–005   Once registration of a recorded level of noise is made it may not be exceeded except with the local authority's consent. Applications for consent are dealt with under s.65 of COPA 1974.

Reduction of noise levels

12–006   The establishment of a noise abatement zone brings with it a second consequence. The local authority is empowered to take steps to reduce noise deriving from any premises. This is achieved by serving a notice under s.66 of COPA 1974 on any person responsible, requiring reduction in the level of noise and the prevention of any subsequent increase without consent. It may also require the taking of steps to achieve these purposes. This notice, described as a "noise reduction notice", will set a time limit, being not less than six months, within which the noise level is to be reduced. There is a right of appeal against the notice to the magistrates' court, within three months.

Noise and Statutory Nuisance Act 1993

Additional controls are imposed by the Noise and Statutory Nuisance Act 1993. Noise created by certain vehicles, machinery or equipment in the street, which is prejudicial to health or a nuisance, is to be regarded as a statutory nuisance. The Act also gives powers for local authorities to adopt s.9 which applies to their area relating to audible intruder alarms (s.3). Thereby, an officer of the local authority may have access to any premises where any audible alarm gives reasonable cause for annoyance to persons living or working in the vicinity. Where there is excessive noise, a warning notice can be served which can require action within as little as 10 minutes. Failure to comply is an offence. For further guidance, see DoE Circular 9/97, "Noise and Statutory Nuisance Act 1993".   **12–007**

STATUTORY NUISANCES

The law relating to statutory nuisances is set out in Pt III of EPA 1990. The local public health authority is provided with a procedure for dealing with nuisances if it is satisfied that a statutory nuisance exists or is likely to occur or recur. In simple terms, the action to be taken includes the service of an abatement notice, in respect of which the person served may appeal to the magistrates' court within 21 days. The court has power to support, modify or dismiss the abatement notice. Assuming its confirmation, failure to comply, without reasonable excuse, with an abatement notice is an offence which can result in liability on summary conviction to a fine not exceeding £20,000. As to what constitutes reasonable excuse, see *Polychronakis v Richards and Jerrom Ltd*.[2] Upon conviction the local public health authority may itself take the necessary action and recover its costs. Since the coming into force of the Noise and Statutory Nuisance Act 1993, costs recoverable from an owner may be a charge on the premises.   **12–008**

What is a statutory nuisance?

Statutory nuisance is defined by s.79 of EPA 1990 as: **12–009**

(a) any premises in such a state as to be prejudicial to health or a nuisance;

(b) smoke emitted from any premises so as to be prejudicial to health or a nuisance;

---

[2] [1998] Env L.R. 346.

(c) fumes or gas emitted from premises so as to be prejudicial to health or a nuisance;

(d) any dust, smell, steam or other effluvia arising on industrial, trade or business premises and being prejudicial to health or a nuisance;

(e) any accumulation or deposit which is prejudicial to health or a nuisance;

(f) any animal kept in such a place or manner as to be prejudicial to health or a nuisance;

(g) noise emitted from premises so as to be prejudicial to health or a nuisance; and

(h) any other matter declared by any enactment to be a statutory nuisance.

The above list is qualified in a number of ways:

(i) Item (b) does not apply to smoke emitted from a chimney of a private dwelling within a smoke control area (Clean Air Act 1993), dark smoke emitted from a chimney either of a building or serving the furnace of a boiler or industrial plant attached to a building for the time being fixed to or installed on the land (Clean Air Act 1993), smoke emitted from a railway locomotive or steam engine, or dark smoke emitted otherwise than as mentioned above from industrial or trade premises.

(ii) Item (c) only applies to private dwellings.

(iii) Item (d) does not apply to steam emitted from a railway locomotive engine.

(iv) Item (g) does not apply to noise caused by aircraft, except models.

(v) In item (h), examples of enactments establishing other statutory nuisances are the Public Health Act 1936 (insanitary systems, watercourses, tents, vans, etc) and the Mines and Quarries Act 1954 (fencing of disused mines).

(vi) With effect from April 1, 2000, land which is contaminated land within the meaning of Pt IIA of EPA 1990 is excluded from the list in s.79 above (see s.79(1A) and (1B)).

(vii) Section 2 of the Noise and Statutory Nuisance Act 1993 amended EPA 1990 so that a further category of statutory nuisance, noise that is prejudicial to health or a nuisance and is emitted from or caused by a vehicle, machinery, or equipment in a street, has been added. However, s.2 does not apply to noise made by traffic, naval, military or air forces or arising from a political or similar demonstration.

(viii) A smoke nuisance could include the smell of smoke (see *Griffiths v Pembrokeshire CC*.[3]

---

[3] Divisional Court, March 31, 2000.

The definition of "statutory nuisance" has been considered over a considerable period of years. The following cases are relevant:

- *Pontardawe RDC v Moore-Gwyn*[4] (premises)
- *National Coal Board v Thane*[5] (nuisance)
- *Coventry City Council v Cartwright*[6] (prejudicial to health)
- *Wivenhoe Port v Colchester BC*[7] (dust)
- *Tower Hamlets LBC v Manzoni and Walder*[8] (noise)
- *Southwark LBC v Ince*[9] (noise)
- *R. v Bristol City Council Ex p. Everett*[10] (potentially dangerous staircase)
- *Haringey LBC v Jowett*[11] (traffic noise)
- *Wandsworth LBC v Raltrack PLC*[12] (bird nuisance).

Summary proceedings

The first step in summary proceedings by a local authority is usually the **12–010** service of an abatement notice. This can require the nuisance to be stopped or reduced and, where necessary, seek prevention of its occurrence or recurrence. It was established in the case of *R v Falmouth and Truro Port Authority Ex p. South West Water Limited*[13] that in all cases the local authority can, if it wishes, leave the choice of means of abatement to the perpetrator of the nuisance. However, where the means of abatement are identified by the local authority then those means must be specified with sufficient clarity so that the recipient/person with responsibility has a clear understanding of what is required. The notice must normally provide for time limits within which the necessary actions are to be taken. The notice will be served normally on the person responsible for the nuisance, but where that person cannot be found it is served on the owner or occupier of the premises in question. The owner of the premises where there is a defect of structural character is also required to be served.

Certain proceedings may not be started by the local public health authority without the Secretary of State's approval. This applies where smoke, fumes, gas, dust, steam, smell or other effluvia are emitted from premises the subject of Pt I of EPA 1990 or, when it comes into force, PPCA 1999. These matters are often the EA's responsibility. The intention is to avoid duplication of controls.

---

[4] [1929] 1 Ch. 656.
[5] [1976] 1 W.L.R. 543.
[6] [1975] 1 W.L.R. 845.
[7] [1985] J.P.L. 175.
[8] [1984] 148 JP 123.
[9] [1989] 21 H.L.R. 504.
[10] [1998] 3 All E.R. 603.
[11] [1999] *The Times*, May 20.
[12] July, 31 2000, DC.
[13] [2003] All E.R. 306.

A special defence is available in cases of abatement notices served in respect of industry, trade or business premises where the nuisance relates to paras (a), (d), (e), (f) and (g) of s.79 (see (1) and (5)–(7) above). The defence is also available in respect of para.(b), but not where the nuisance constitutes smoke emitted from a chimney (see "Best practicable means" at para.12–014 below).

Appeals

12–011   Under s.80 of EPA 1990, anyone in receipt of a notice may appeal to the magistrates' court within 21 days of the date of service. If there is no appeal and no compliance with the notice then prosecution may follow.

The procedures for appeal are set out in the Statutory Nuisance (Appeals) Regulations 1995.[14] An appeal may be made on one or more of the following grounds:

(a) the abatement notice is not justified by s.80;

(b) there has been some informality, defect or error with the notice;

(c) the authority unreasonably has refused to accept compliance with alternative requirements or the requirements for the abatement notice are otherwise unreasonable in character or extent, or are unnecessary;

(d) the time given by the abatement notice for compliance is not reasonably sufficient;

(e) the best practicable means (see below) have been used to prevent or counteract the effects of the nuisance (this ground of appeal is not available in respect of fumes, gas or smoke, unless smoke is emitted from a chimney)—the best practicable means ground of appeal is also available in respect of a notice alleging noise emitted from or caused by a vehicle, machinery or equipment, being used for industrial, trade or business purposes;

(f) in the case of a nuisance relating to noise, that the requirements are more onerous than those in force as a result of notices relating to the control of noise levels, served under ss.60—67 of COPA 1974 (see para.12–002 above);

(g) in the case of noise emitted from or caused by vehicles, machinery or equipment, the requirements are more onerous than those for the time being in force as the result of a notice served under para.1 of Sch.2 to the Noise and Statutory Nuisance Act 1993 (loud speakers in streets); and

(h) the abatement notice should or might have been served on some other person, besides or in addition to the appellant. In most cases under this ground the appellant is required to serve a copy of his notice of appeal on that other person, who will then be joined in the proceedings.

[14] SI 1995/2644.

Appeal hearing

On the appeal hearing, the magistrates' responsibility is either to quash the **12–012** abatement notice, vary it (if this can be done in favour of the appellant) or dismiss the appeal. While the appeal is pending, the abatement notice is suspended, except in the special case where it alleges injury to health or that the nuisance is or is anticipated to be of limited duration.

Complaint by member of the public

Any member of the public may make a complaint direct to the magistrates' **12–013** court under s.82 of EPA 1990 on the ground that he is aggrieved by the existence of a statutory nuisance. It is unnecessary for him to proceed through the public health authority, but he is under the same restrictions concerning premises the subject of Pt I of EPA or PPCA 1999 (see para.12–010 above). The interim process of abatement notice is not required here. However, s.82(6) of EPA 1990 requires the complainant to give notice of his intention to bring the proceedings. This notice must be in writing and addressed to the person against whom the complaint is made. It must also specify the complaint. The court's obligation is to make an order on the defendant to abate the notice if it is satisfied with the complaint. It may also prohibit the occurrence and order the execution of any necessary works, and has power to fine the defendant. The "best practicable means" defence can be available. The court has power to order compensation under the Powers of Criminal Courts (Sentencing) Act 2000.[15] As to a landlord's liability for noise nuisance, see *Baxter v Camden LBC (No. 2)*.[16] With effect from April 1, 2000, these provisions are not available in respect of contaminated land within the meaning of Pt IIA of EPA 1990.

Best practicable means

In the case of certain appeals or prosecutions the defence of "best **12–014** practicable means" is available in respect of industrial, trade or business premises and in relation to the nuisances listed above (see para.12–010). Thus, the court is able to balance the environmental factors with the consequences on the economic operation of the business activity. The term "best practicable means" is explained in s.79(9) of EPA 1990 as follows:

(a) "practicable" means reasonably practicable having regard, among other things, to local conditions and circumstances, to the current state of technical knowledge and to the financial implications;

(b) the means to be employed include the design, installation, maintenance and manner and periods of operation of plant and machinery, and the design, construction and maintenance of buildings and structures;

[15] *Botross v Hammersmith and Fulham LBC* [1994] *The Times*, November 7.
[16] [1999] 2 W.L.R. 566.

(c) the test is to apply only so far as compatible with any duty imposed by law; and

(d) the test is to apply only so far as compatible with safety and safe working conditions and with the exigencies of any emergency or unforeseeable circumstances.

Some guidance in the interpretation of the definition of "best practicable means" can be found in codes of practice which have been published under s.71 of COPA 1974.

Injunctions

12–015 A local authority has powers under EPA 1990 to dispense with an abatement notice in respect of a nuisance and to proceed direct to a High Court injunction application under s.81 or civil proceedings under s.222 of the Local Government Act 1972. See *Vale of White Horse DC v Allen*.[17] However, it is unlikely to pursue this course unless a particularly intractable nuisance exists.

[17] High Court, October 4, 1996.

Chapter 13

LANDFILL GAS

Introduction

Landfill gas (including methane) is an almost inevitable consequence of decomposition, particularly of household waste, in any given site. The scale and method of waste disposal in the past did not produce major problems other than odour nuisance associated with the leakage of gas. With the demise of the era of the domestic solid fuel boiler (when household waste tended to comprise cinders and burnt fuel), the "organic" content of waste rose considerably. It is the biodegradation of this type of waste, coupled with greatly increased quantities, which have now substantially raised the landfill gas profile in environmental terms. Landfill gas sites which are inadequately controlled are likely to produce problems of odour nuisance, danger from explosion and asphyxiation, and will be inimical to plant life at and in the vicinity of the site. Nonetheless, landfill gas has significant energy characteristics, particularly after treatment, and is being used currently for industrial and other energy purposes, either by direct firing or after conversion to electricity. The purpose of this chapter is to describe the main legislation relating to control and exploitation.

13–001

Town and country planning

Planning permission is required for the activities of control and exploitation of landfill gas. A reasonably modern planning permission for landfill is likely to be sufficiently widely drawn as to authorise control and even exploitation as an ancillary activity to the landfill operations. Each case will turn on its differing facts and on the terms and conditions of the planning permission itself. First, it is unlikely that the planning permission will be silent about requirements for the control of landfill gas (although detailed matters are likely to be deferred to the site licence under EPA 1990 or permit under PPCA 1999—see below). Thus, drilling wells and laying pipelines within land which is the subject of planning permission are not likely to require any further authority, beyond compliance with conditions of the consent seeking detailed plans and methods to be approved.

13–002

The erection of buildings or plant used in connection with the permitted landfill development may benefit from planning permission granted by the Town and Country Planning (General Permitted Development) Order

(GPDO) 1995[1] (see Sch.2, Pts 2 (minor operations), 4 (temporary buildings and uses), 8 (industrial development), 19 (development ancillary to mining operations) and 21 (waste tipping at a mine)). However, caution must be exercised, since many planning permissions impose conditions reducing or removing rights under GPDO 1995. Even if such rights are available it is important to check the conditions which are imposed in the Order. Furthermore, ancillary legislation may have to be obeyed.

In respect of completed sites, where activities relating to landfill may have ended many years ago, but landfill gas has emerged as a problem or opportunity, it may well be that such planning permissions which did exist for the landfill operation are inadequate for any new development related to landfill gas control or exploitation. Again, each case will turn on its individual circumstances and the precise terms of planning permissions granted. (For further consideration of these matters, see Ch.4.)

ENVIRONMENTAL PROTECTION ACT 1990 AND POLLUTION PREVENTION AND CONTROL ACT 1999

13–003   Waste management licences and permits under EPA 1990 and PPCA 1999 respectively will exercise much of the environmental control of gas collection and exploitation. Insofar as the licences do not deal adequately with these matters, the EA can achieve variation quite simply (see paras 9–016 and 10–051 above).

The position is somewhat more complicated in the case of the closed site which requires to be reopened for gas control, etc. Insofar as a site licence under COPA 1974 was ever in existence, this is likely to have been surrendered. In general terms, a licence under COPA 1974 was required only where a person was depositing controlled waste on land or using any plant or equipment for the purpose of disposing of controlled waste, or of dealing in a prescribed manner with controlled waste. The term "in a prescribed manner" relates to regulations made by the Secretary of State under the Act *i.e.* the Collection and Disposal of Waste Regulations 1988.[2] By reg.8 of and Sch.5 to those Regulations, a disposal licence is required for the use of plant or equipment but only in specified circumstances. One of these (reg.8, para.5) is the production of fuel from waste. It follows, therefore, that if the provision of plant is for this purpose (as opposed to mere controlling) then a licence, previously under COPA 1974 and now under EPA 1990 or PPCA 1999, is expected to be required.

The position is different now that Pt II of EPA 1990 is in force. First, the definition of activities requiring to be licensed is extended beyond mere depositing to include treating, keeping or disposing. It is at least possible that the control and particularly the exploitation of gas will require a licence under s.33 of EPA 1990. This is certain to be the case where, for

---

[1] SI 1995/418.
[2] SI 1988/819.

example, plant for treatment of gas is required. Secondly, a licence which existed at the time or is granted after s.39 of EPA 1990 (surrender of licences) came into force (May 1994) will continue to subsist until such time as the EA is satisfied that pollution of the environment or harm to human health is unlikely to ensue because of the site's condition. Clearly, the generation of gas from such site will mean that the licence will remain extant and can be made capable of controlling all activities related to the gas.

As part of its series of waste management papers the DoE provided useful guidance in WMP27, "A Technical Memorandum on the Monitoring and Control of Landfill Gas: 1991".

STATUTORY NUISANCES

While, to a large extent, the control of a landfill gas site will be based upon **13–004** the provisions of TCPA 1990 and Pt II of EPA 1990, the operator will need to take account of other legislation, of which Pt III of EPA 1990, relating to statutory nuisances, will be relevant. Any dust, steam, smell or other effluvia arising on industrial, trade or business premises and being prejudicial to health or a nuisance is within the definition of statutory nuisance (EPA 1990, s.79). (For further details see the section on statutory nuisance in Ch.12 above. See also the references to contaminated land control in Ch.11.)

WATER RESOURCES ACT 1991

If the operation of the landfill gas site produces any pollution (such as **13–005** effluent from gas dewatering plant) or any poisonous, noxious or polluting matter, or any solid waste matter is allowed to enter into any controlled waters (*e.g.* groundwaters, rivers and streams etc), then an offence is normally committed unless a licence is obtained. (For further information see Ch.7.)

HEALTH AND SAFETY AT WORK ETC. ACT 1974

Provisions relating to the protection of employees, visitors and others **13–006** arising from landfill gas control and exploitation are contained in the Health and Safety at Work etc. Act 1974 and in regulations made under that Act. (For further details see Ch.14.)

EXPLOITATION

Consideration must be given to further legal requirements, once it is **13–007** decided that the gas is of sufficient quantity and quality to justify commercial exploitation. Notable among these are the Pipelines Act 1962 (mainly in respect of the transport of gas by pipeline from the waste site to the customer or other facility), the Gas Acts 1986 and 1995 (supplies of gas to be authorised), and the Electricity Act 1989 (licensing of supply of electricity).

Non-fossil fuel obligation

13–008 By s.32 of the Electricity Act 1989, public electricity suppliers may be required by the Secretary of State to make arrangements to secure that a proportion of their supplies is obtained from non-fossil fuel generating stations, of which landfill gas generators are an example. Orders have been made from time to time (see, *e.g.* the Electricity (Non-fossil Fuel Sources) (England and Wales) Order 1990.[3]). The provisions are useful to non-fossil fuel generators because they provide for certain advantageous price opportunities, designed by the Government to attempt to shift the balance away from fossil fuel energy sources.[4] The non-fossil fuel obligation scheme aims to ensure that, by 2010, 10 per cent of the United Kingdom's electricity comes from renewable sources.

Environmental Protection Act 1990 and Pollution Prevention and Control Act 1999

13–009 Major electricity generating plants fuelled by landfill gas may require to be authorised under Pt I of EPA 1990 (see para.8–007 above) or under PPCA 1999 (see Ch.9).

---

[3] SI 1990/263.
[4] For further orders see SIs 1991/2490, 1994/3259, 1997/248 and 1998/2353.

PART IV

HEALTH AND SAFETY ISSUES, EU LEGISLATION, COMMON LAW AND REMEDIES

CHAPTER 14

HEALTH AND SAFETY AT WORK

INTRODUCTION

An employer owes a general responsibility to an employee for the health **14–001** and safety of that employee. This liability can arise under statute, but also by the operation of civil law. Note that the responsibility is to an employed person and, therefore, it is not usually owed to an independent contractor unless there are special circumstances. For example, there may be liability to an independent contractor as a result of the contract between the employer and that contractor. Furthermore, the court has held that where the relationship between the employer and the independent contractor is, in effect, a contract of employment, then common law liability may apply.[1] The common law position is altered by the Health and Safety at Work etc. Act 1974. Note also the employer's responsibility to the disabled, eg the Disability Discrimination Act 1995.

DUTY OF CARE

For an employee to succeed against an employer at common law he must **14–002** establish a claim of negligence (*i.e.* that the employer owed him a duty of care, that he was in breach of that duty and, as a result, that the employee suffered damage). The duty of care is to take reasonable care for the safety of workmen. What is reasonable is dependent on the circumstances in each case, but the court has stated that it means taking reasonable care to provide proper plant and premises, to maintain them in proper condition and to carry on operations so as not to subject those employed by the employer to unnecessary risk.[2] In *Wilsons and Clyde Coal Co v English*,[3] the employer's obligation was put in a different way (*i.e.* the provision of a competent staff of men, adequate material, a proper system and effective supervision).

In emphasising the duty of an employer to an employee, it is important not to lose sight of the fact that in circumstances of waste management

---

[1] See *e.g. Ferguson v John Dawson & Partners (Contractors) Ltd* [1976] 1 W.L.R. 1213; and *Kitson Calder v H Vickers & Sons (Engineers) Ltd* [1988] I.C.R. 232.

[2] See *Smith v Baker* [1891] A.C. 325.

[3] [1938] A.C. 57.

operation a duty of care is also owed to all others who are likely to be affected by the operation and, again, that duty is to act reasonably.

The duty of care does not extend so far as to require the employer to be responsible for dangers which he neither knew nor ought reasonably to have known.[4]

Statutory safety provisions

14–003 The existence or absence of a particular safety provision in, for example, legislation or a code of practice can normally be considered in order to ascertain whether the employer has met the standard of care required by common law. However, as with waste management, there are a number of industries where an employee's required operations carry certain risks. If these are ordinary risks of the employment ordinarily found or accepted in the waste management business then the employer will not, generally, be liable for injury or damage to an employee. For example, a properly trained employee operating properly maintained mobile plant on the uneven terrain of a landfill site cannot expect an employer to be legally responsible for the overturning of that vehicle if the employee has driven it negligently and contrary to his training and instructions.

Protective equipment

14–004 It is inherent in the employer's responsibility to the employee that, where appropriate, the correct protective equipment should be provided and maintained. In the case of employees with special disabilities which might create a greater risk of injury, a higher standard of care in the provision of protective equipment is expected. The employer's duty extends to the taking of reasonable steps to ensure that protective equipment is used.

Negligence of fellow employee

14–005 Often, injury and damage to one employee will arise as a result of the negligence of another employee. An employer is liable usually for those negligent acts undertaken in the course of employment and the standard of care is essentially that of reasonable prudence.[5] Horseplay amongst employees or practical joking will not result in liability on the employer, except, perhaps, where there has been inadequate supervision or failure to take reasonable steps to prevent such unauthorised activities (*e.g.* if it has happened regularly in the past). Foreseeability applies in the case of negligence of employees.

---

[4] See *Quinn v Cameron and Robertson* [1958] A.C. 9.
[5] See *Vincent v PLA* [1957] 1 Lloyds's Rep. 102.

Defences for the employer

It may be possible for the employer to argue that the employee has **14–006** contributed to his own injury or damage by negligent acts. In those circumstances the amount of damages recoverable from the employer may be reduced by the proportion of negligence on the part of the employee. It may also be possible to argue that an employee accepts a risk voluntarily, with the full knowledge of that risk. This defence is rare where an employee is carrying out his usual tasks, but if, for example, he takes on a responsibility for which he is not qualified or where he has been expressly forbidden to do so by his employer, he will not be able to claim successfully.

Where injury or damage is suffered by an employee from a defect in the manufacture of a tool or other piece of equipment, the employer remains liable if he is under a duty of care to provide safe plant and appliances. However, he may be able to pass on his liability to the manufacturer of the tool or equipment.

Breach of statutory duty

Not only is the employer liable to an employee in common law, but he also **14–007** has extensive responsibilities for the safety, health and welfare of employees as a result of a range of statutes. If he is in breach of those statutes then it is likely that he will be liable to be prosecuted, but, in addition, he is also liable to the employee in respect of that specific breach of statutory duty. Thus, it is common for an employee who has been injured to claim both on the basis of negligence at common law and the breach of statutory duty. However, the statutory duty of an employer extends beyond the employee and can often embrace other persons entitled to be on the premises. See, for example, ss.3 and 4 of the Health and Safety at Work etc. Act (HSWA) 1974 (at para.14–020 below). Statutory duty can extend, therefore, not only to employees of the employer himself, but also to employees of an independent contractor working on the premises.

Defence to breach of statutory duty

The defences available to an employer will be similar to those arising in the **14–008** case of a claim under common law, but with some modifications. For example, sometimes the employer will properly delegate the performance of his statutory duty to the employee. Thus, negligence on the part of the employee in undertaking that duty will not usually cause liability to arise with the employer. An employer cannot normally delegate his statutory duty to a third party or independent contractor. He will remain liable in the event of a breach.

In the case of a breach by the employer which arises, in effect, by the failure of the employee (*e.g.* where the danger arising from a breach of statutory duty is so obvious that he ought to be regarded as solely responsible, or where the breach was caused solely by an act of the employee), the employer will be likely to escape liability to the employee on the grounds of breach of statutory duty. See, for example, *McGuiness v Key Markets Ltd*[6] and *Norris v Syndic*[7] (employee removed a safety guard and was injured). The defence of contributory negligence is also available as with the common law claim.[8]

SAFETY, HEALTH AND WELFARE LEGISLATION

Administration

14–009 The administration of legislation relating to health and safety at work is delegated to the Health and Safety Commission (HSC), which has general overseeing research, advice and information responsibilities. The duty of ensuring compliance with and regulating the legislation is placed with the Health and Safety Executive (HSE), to whose Director General a number of chief inspectors report, including the Chief Inspectors of Mines, Quarries and Factories and the Director of Agricultural Safety. Powers of the HSE may be transferred to local authorities.

The main legislation

14–010 The primary statutes are:

- the Mines and Quarries Act 1954
- the Factories Act 1961
- the Offices, Shops and Railway Premises Act 1963
- HSWA 1974.

Of these, only the first two are discussed here. HSWA 1974 is dealt with separately below.

Mines and Quarries Act 1954

14–011 This Act contains a number of provisions of relevance to waste management, particularly landfill in disused or partly used quarries. The general duties of mine and quarry owners are laid down by s.1, to the effect that the operation is managed and worked in accordance with the Act and various orders made thereunder, particularly in regard to the health and safety of persons at the quarry. There are similar obligations in respect of mines

[6] [1972] 13 KIR 249.
[7] [1952] 2 Q.B. 135.
[8] See para.14–006 above.

(defined as mainly underground operations). The obligations of managers and owners include the requirement to keep plans and geological maps. In respect of quarries, Pt IV of the Act specifies the requirement to establish an adequate management system by way of appointments and notification to the Quarries Inspectorate. The provisions for the safety, health and welfare of workmen and others in quarries is laid down by Pt V. There are requirements for records, returns and information to be provided, which all normally confirm compliance (Pt IX). Part XIII requires fencing of abandoned and disused mines and quarries and Pt XIV details offences, penalties and legal proceedings.

The Act should be considered together with the Mines and Quarries (Tips) Act 1969 and the Mines Management Act 1971.

Factories Act 1961

What is a "factory"?

The definition of "factory" is in s.175 and is extensive. There will be cases **14–012** where waste management premises fall within that definition. This includes any premises in which, or within the close or curtilage or precincts of which, persons are employed in manual labour in any process for or incidental to the making, altering, repairing, ornamenting, finishing, cleaning or washing or the breaking-up or demolition of any article, being premises in which or within the close or curtilage or precincts of which the work is carried on by way of trade or for purposes of gain and to or over which the employer of the persons employed therein has the right of access or control. The definition also extends to premises where persons are employed in manual labour (*i.e.* any premises in which the business of sorting any articles is carried on as a preliminary to the work carried on in any factory or incidentally to the purposes of any factory).

Obligations in relation to a factory

The responsibilities under the Factories Act are split into various groups, as **14–013** follows.

Health

The premises must be kept clean and free from refuse. They must not be **14–014** overcrowded or operated at unreasonable temperatures. They must be adequately ventilated and lit and provided with sufficient and suitable sanitary conveniences.

Safety

Safety provisions relate mainly to the protection of employees from the **14–015** machinery which they may be operating or where they may be in the vicinity. There are provisions in this section for fencing. There is also a requirement to protect employees from dangerous substances where the danger might result from heat, corrosion etc. There are special provisions in relation to lifting equipment, including cranes, the safety of floors and stairs and general safety, and the avoidance of dangerous fumes, explosives or inflammable dusts and gases.

Welfare

14–016   There are requirements for the supply of adequate and wholesome drinking water, for washing facilities and for the storage of clothing. Employees are required to have protection in appropriate circumstances and they must not be employed to lift, carry or move any load so heavy as to be likely to cause injury or harm.

Offences and penalties

14–017   Section 155 imposes a liability on an occupier (and sometimes an owner) of a factory to prosecution for offences. Part VII of the Act provides for penalties and consequential matters.

HEALTH AND SAFETY AT WORK ETC. ACT 1974

14–018   The primary aim of HSWA 1974 was the reorganisation of the administration and control of health and safety at work, which, before the Act came into force, had become distributed among a number of separate items of legislation, such as the Explosives Act 1875, the Alkali etc. Works Regulation Act 1906, the Mines and Quarries Act 1954, the Factories Act 1961, the Offices Shops and Railway Premises Act 1963, and the Employment Medical Advisory Service Act 1972. In other words, the 1974 Act was designed to rationalise the legislation, to create a more integrated administration and to set down with greater clarity the respective responsibilities of employer and employee.

General purposes of the Act

14–019   HSWA 1974 sets out to secure the health, safety and welfare of persons at work, the protection of other persons against risks to health or safety related to the activities of persons at work, the control and keeping of explosives and other dangerous substances and the control of emission of noxious and other substances from premises. This last objective is now largely replaced by Pt I of EPA 1990 and PPCA 1999 (see Ch.9). HSWA 1974 sets down general rules but, equally importantly, establishes responsibility on the Secretary of State for Work and Pensions, the HSC and the

HSE to provide detailed controls, which may be effected by regulations, approved codes of practice and other provisions.

General duties

The first part of the Act lays down the general duties to others of those **14–020** involved with health and safety at work. Section 2 imposes a duty on every employer to ensure, so far as is reasonably practicable, the health, safety and welfare at work of all his employees. Section 3 imposes a duty on every employer to conduct his undertaking in such a way as to ensure, so far as is reasonably practicable, that persons not in his employment who may be affected thereby are not exposed to risks to their health and safety. Section 3 also requires that every self-employed person must conduct his undertaking in such a way as to ensure, so far as is reasonably practicable, that he and other persons (not his employees) who may be affected thereby are not exposed to risks to their health and safety.

Section 4 imposes on persons duties in relation to those who are not their employees but who use non-domestic premises as a place of work or where they may use plant or substances provided for their use there. In general, the duty requires any person who has any control of such premises or the means of access thereto or egress therefrom, or is responsible for any plant or substance in those premises, to take reasonable measures, so far as is reasonably practicable, that such premises, access, egress, plant or substances are safe and without risks to health.

Section 5 imposes a general duty on persons having control of any premises to use the best practicable means for preventing emission into the atmosphere from the premises of noxious or offensive substances and for rendering harmless and inoffensive such substances as may be so emitted. This provision has been largely superseded by the requirements of Pt I of EPA 1990 and PPCA 1999 (see Ch.9).

Section 6 places duties on designers, manufacturers, importers or suppliers of any article for use at work to ensure, so far as reasonably practicable, that the article is so designed and constructed that it will be safe and without risks to health at all times when it is being set, used, cleaned or maintained by a person at work. There are secondary responsibilities on the manufacturer concerning testing and the provision and maintenance of training and information about the manufactured articles or substances.

Finally, s.7 extends to the duties of employees at work, who must take reasonable care for the health and safety of themselves and of any other persons affected by their acts or omissions at work.

Health and safety regulations and approved codes of practice

Besides the statement of the general duties of employers and others, the **14–021** main thrust of HSWA 1974 is in the generation of detailed regulations and approved codes of practice. Sections 15–17 of the Act deal with these responsibilities. While HSWA 1974 and regulations have the full force of law, note that failure to observe any provision of an approved code of practice does not, itself, create liability to civil or criminal proceedings. However, a failure to comply with a code is admissible evidence in criminal proceedings for contravention of a provision for which an approved code is in force. Thus, proof of any failure to comply with the code will be enough generally for the court to convict, unless it is established that the actual matter to which the code applied was dealt with satisfactorily in another way.

The European influence

14–022   Increasingly, initiatives for the introduction of standards of health and safety have passed from UK Government to the EU. The pattern now established is for legislation to be passed by the EU which, where necessary, then involves implementation by each member state, mainly according to its own legislative structure. In the main, requirements of EU legislation have been accommodated in the United Kingdom by a series of sets of regulations.

Regulations relevant to the waste management industry

14–023   For regulations to which the waste management industry is subject, see Appendix 6.

Codes of practice and other HSE guidance

14–024   For a list of codes of practice appropriate to the waste management industry, see Appendix 5. Note that a substantial number of other relevant documents, too lengthy for this book, are noted in a list of current publications, available from the HSE. The HSE maintains web pages on the internet under the general heading "Heath and Safety in the Waste Management and Recycling Industries"—see www.hse.gov.uk/waste.

Enforcement

14–025   Enforcement of HSWA 1974 is generally delegated to inspectors appointed under the terms of s.19. The powers of an inspector are set out in s.20 and are extensive, including rights:

    (a) at any reasonable time (which, in an emergency, may be at any time) to enter any premises, taking with him a police officer if he expects any serious obstruction;

(b) to bring any equipment or materials with him for his purposes;

(c) to make any examination and investigation as necessary;

(d) to require any part of any premises or anything within those premises to be left undisturbed for as long as is necessary for examination or investigation;

(e) to take measurements, photographs, recordings and samples;

(f) in the case of any article or substance which is a danger to health or safety, to require it to be dismantled and tested and, in some cases, to order destruction and, in appropriate cases, to take possession and retain for as long as necessary any such article or substance for examination, protection from tampering and maintenance for use as evidence;

(g) to seek information from any person, to inspect and copy any books or documents; and

(h) to require facilities, assistance and general co-operation from the person in charge of any premises or others.

Improvement and prohibition notices

Among additional powers available to an inspector is power to serve an improvement notice where he is of the opinion that there is contravention of statutory requirements and that that contravention will be continued. This notice states the facts, the offence alleged to be committed and requires remedies to be undertaken within a time scale. A prohibition notice arises where the inspector is of the opinion that activities at any premises either already involve or will involve a risk of serious personal injury. The prohibition notice states the opinion and the facts giving rise to that opinion, as well as directing that the activities in question will be brought to an end within a period to be specified, or immediately if the circumstances justify this.   **14–026**

In the case of improvement and prohibition notices there is a 21-day period for appeal. Rules of procedure of employment tribunals to deal with appeals are set out in the Employment Tribunals (Constitution and Rules of Procedure) Regulations 2001.[9] While an appeal suspends an improvement notice pending final disposal, this does not happen in the case of a prohibition notice unless the appeal tribunal so directs.

Offences

Section 33 of HSWA 1974 sets out a long list of offences which include: **14–027**

(a) failure to discharge a duty under ss.2–7;

(b) contravention of any health and safety regulations;

---

[9] SI 2001/1170.

(c) obstruction of an inspector or failure to comply with his requirements;

(d) contravention of any prohibition or improvement notice;

(e) the making of any false or reckless statement or a false entry in any register, book or other document;

(f) falsification of any document with intent to deceive or falsely pretending to be an inspector; and

(g) failure to comply with a court order following conviction for an offence, where the court also orders other remedies and/or forfeiture of articles or substances.

In general, the institution of proceedings under HSWA 1974 in England or Wales can be by an inspector only or by or with the consent of the Director of Public Prosecutions. This, thereby, limits severely the right of employees and the public to proceed in the criminal courts.

Offences by bodies corporate

14–028   In common with most modern environmental and safety legislation there are provisions in the case of offences by bodies corporate also to make liable to criminal proceedings any director or senior officer, if it can be proved that the offence was committed with the consent or connivance of the person in question (see para.16–019 below).

CHAPTER 15

EUROPEAN UNION LEGISLATION

EU ENVIRONMENTAL POLICY

Since the Treaty of Rome and the United Kingdom's accession to Europe, **15–001** the legislation approved by the European Community (now the European Union) and applying within its boundaries has been significant. While the UK Government has developed its waste management control programme with some vigour during the past 25 or so years, nonetheless there is no doubt that this has been partly as a result of the quest for much higher standards sought and achieved by some of the north European member states, particularly Germany and Holland. The two major statutes dealing with environmental standards, WRA 1991 and EPA 1990, accommodated and, to a certain extent, anticipated what has emerged from Brussels during the 1990s.

There is no doubt that the adoption by the European Community of the 1973 Programme of Action on the Environment and subsequent programmes have had a marked effect upon the making of UK policy in this area and, in particular, the speed with which that policy has been applied. Just as the UK administration has had difficulty aligning itself with EC policy in a number of economic areas, so a rationalisation of environmental law and policy has been no exception. The understandable tendency of the United Kingdom to rely upon its island status and its "remote" geographical location compared with the rest of Europe has brought it into conflict with the aspirations of some mainland countries. Nonetheless, the EC/EU as a whole has subscribed to a substantial number of directives and other legislative measures, representing the basis for the equalisation of policy. There is no doubt that the practitioner needs to be alert to the continuous development in this area.

HOW EU LEGISLATION WORKS IN PRACTICE IN THE UNITED KINGDOM

Only in exceptional cases do European measures operate directly to impose **15–002** obligations on individuals within member states. For the most part they set down criteria and standards, together with procedures which the member state is required to obey and secure that its subjects obey. How the member states secure this objective is up to them, but in the United Kingdom this will usually require an act of Parliament or subsidiary legislation. Sometimes the necessary legislation is already in place, in which case minor adjustments of policies promulgated (*e.g.* by departmental circulars) are all that is required. For a leading case on the necessity of compatibility of UK law with European legislation, see *R. v Secretary of State for Transport Ex p. Factortame Ltd and others*.[1]

A member state's failure to transpose a European directive within the period laid down represents a serious breach of EU law and will give rise to a right in damages from the state for individuals who suffer injury as a consequence.[2]

Principal EU measures

Directives

15–003   The majority of EU law has been set down in directives. For the most part they simply set objectives, and only exceptionally will they become directly effective under s.2(1) of the European Communities Act 1972.[3] Framework directives set general standards, followed by "daughter" directives, which deal with specific subjects.

Regulations

These have effect as law and may be enforced in the UK courts without the need for any further steps to be taken by legislative or administrative action (see European Communities Act 1972, s.2(1)). However, regulations are rare and there are only some 30 relating to environment policy, many of which deal with special circumstances such as the aftermath of the Chenobyl nuclear accident. These include supervision and control of shipments of waste (259/93), substances that deplete the ozone layer (3093/94), export from and import into the community of certain dangerous chemicals (1734/88), the establishment of the European Environment Agency and the European environment information and observation network (1210/90), the Community eco label awards scheme (880/92), shipments of waste (1420/1999), substances that deplete the ozone layer (2037/2000).

Decisions

Decisions are legally binding in the United Kingdom, but so far they have tended to be so specific to a particular set of circumstances as to have little effect upon UK law generally.

Recommendations

Recommendations represent the lowest level of EU legislation and have no legally binding effect, being merely advisory.

[1] (1996) 1 C.M.L.R. 889.
[2] See *Dillenkofer and others v Germany* [1997] 2 W.L.R. 253.
[3] See article in the Law Society's Gazette, February 14, 1990, p.27).

The EU's enforcement powers

Enforcement remains devolved to member states, but they are answerable to the EU as a whole for the steps that they take to implement EU legislation. There is considerable debate about the extent to which the EU should be given much stronger policing powers. This is likely to become more important as European environment policy develops and becomes more complicated and specific. A small step in this direction was taken in 1990 with the establishment of the European Environment Agency, but its present role is simply to collect and analyse data on environmental matters. Given that the United Kingdom has a well-developed pollution control administration (*e.g.* the EA) and that the more influential member states have similar arrangements, it seems unlikely that in the near future much action will be taken in this enforcement area.

For the most part, therefore, the individual can expect little, if any, direct contact with the European institutions, particularly with regard to enforcement. He has a right of access to the European Court of Justice in certain circumstances, particularly where he protests against the action of a member state and cannot obtain redress in the domestic court.

Principal EU legislation

Water framework directive

The Water Framework Directive (2000/60/EC) will require significant **15–004** changes to the way in which water is protected and controlled in the UK. The key objectives include:

- the prevention of further deterioration of water resources and the protection and enhancement of the status of aquatic eco-systems and associated wetland;
- the promotion of sustainable water consumption;
- contribution to mitigating the effects of flood and drought.

The directive will apply to all inland surface waters, groundwaters, transitional water, *e.g.* estuaries and coastal lagoons and coastal waters. Deriving from this framework directive will be a number of "daughter" directives which will repeal a range of existing measures including those referred to below. However, this period of transition is expected to extend over some 15 years.

Pollution of inland waters

The control of pollution of surface and groundwater has received the closest attention of EU legislators, commencing with directives in 1973 on detergents. The other main areas the subject of directives are quality of drinking and bathing water, the discharge of dangerous substances into water and the quality of water required for freshwater fish and shellfish.

Detergents

The directives are:

- Council Directive 73/404/EEC on detergents
- Council Directive 73/405/EEC on the control of the bio-degradability of anionic surfactants
- Council Directive 82/242/EEC on the testing of the bio-degradability of non-anionic surfactants.

These directives secure that member states forbid the sale and use of anionic, cationic, non-ionic and ampholytic detergents where the average level of biodegradability of the surfactants is less than 90 per cent. Relaxations were permitted in 1982.

Drinking water

The directives are:

- Council Directive 75/440/EEC on the quality of surface water for drinking
- Council Directive 79/869/EEC on the sampling and analysis of surface water for drinking
- Council Directive 80/778/EEC on the quality of water for human consumption
- Council Directive 98/83/EC on the quality of water for human consumption.

The approach to drinking water is to categorise surface water into three types and to require treatment as specified to ensure fitness for drinking. Water that falls outside the categories is forbidden to be used for drinking water. The sampling and analysis Directive 76/868/EEC provides for the method and frequency of sampling. Directive 80/778/ EEC extends both to water for direct human consumption and water used in connection with the preparation of foodstuffs. This Directive goes further than its predecessors to regulate toxic and other substances to be added to water. However, it is replaced by Directive 98/83/EC with effect from December 25, 2003, when higher and more comprehensive standards will be imposed.

The European Court of Justice published, in July 1990, an important interpretation of the 1980 Directive on drinking water quality in *Commission v Kingdom of Belgium*.[4] Proceedings had been brought against Belgium as a consequence of an alleged breach of the Directive. The court concluded that the Directive did not apply to private water supplies (*i.e.* water used by private individuals for their household purposes).

---

[4] Case C–42/89.

Bathing water

The single directive in this category is Council Directive 76/160/EEC on the quality of bathing water, which deals with bathing, both in the sea and in inland waters specifically authorised or where it has occurred by tradition. It has no effect upon swimming pools.

Waste water

Council Directive 91/271/EEC concerning urban waste water treatment provides for collection, treatment and discharge of domestic sewage, as well as the treatment and discharge of types of industrial waste water. Compliance is required by targeting 2000 and 2005. In the main, secondary treatment is required.

Dangerous substances

In this category there are framework directives supplemented by subsidiary measures dealing with specific discharges (*e.g.* of titanium oxide and waste cadmium). The main framework directives are:

- Council Directive 76/464/EEC on pollution caused by the discharge of certain dangerous substances into the aquatic environment
- Council Directive 80/68/EEC on the protection of groundwater against pollution caused by certain dangerous substances
- Council Directive 91/676/EEC concerning the protection of waters against pollution caused by nitrates from agriculture sources.

Framework Directive 76/464/EEC contains a list of a range of substances which, of themselves, represent persistent and difficult pollutants. Examples include mercury, mineral oils and synthetic substances. A system of licensing has been established by member states, by reference to daughter directives setting specific standards. Directive 80/68/EEC extended protection to groundwater. There is a separate list, but this is very similar and contains much the same substances as are to be found in the 1976 Directive. Member states are required by the 1980 Directive to take all necessary steps to prevent or limit the introduction of the listed substances into groundwater.

The DoE issued Circular 20/90, setting out arrangements for compliance with Directive 80/68/EEC. It describes the steps which are to be taken by controlling authorities in classifying substances between Lists I and II. List I refers to substances which must be prevented from entering groundwater, while List II contains substances where input must be limited to avoid pollution.

Quality of water required for freshwater fish and shellfish

The directives are: **15–005**

- Council Directive 78/659/EEC on the quality of fresh water as needed to support fish life
- Council Directive 79/923/EEC on the quality required of shellfish waters.

Directive 78/659/EEC seeks to protect and enhance the quality of freshwaters (excluding fish farming ponds) which are inhabited by salmon, trout and coarse fish. The designation of waters by member states was required, followed by programmes to reduce pollution to the prescribed standards within a five-year period. Directive 79/923/ EEC effectively extended responsibility of member states to designate coastal waters and the like, so as to ensure capability to support shellfish.

Atmospheric pollution

15–006   There are three main categories of EU measures relating to air pollution, but it will be appreciated that these categories are interlinked. They are measures relating to motor vehicles, chlorofluorocarbons (CFCs) and halons, and general air quality particularly related to industrial pollution.

Motor vehicles

15–007   The main directives are:

- Council Directive 70/220/EEC on air pollution by motor vehicles
- Council Directive 72/306/EEC on the emission of pollutants from diesel engines for use in vehicles
- Council Directive 77/537/EEC on the emission of pollutants by diesel engines for use in tractors
- Council Directive 88/77/EEC on measures to be taken against the emission of gaseous pollutants from diesel engines for use in vehicles
- European Parliament and Council Directive 94/63/EC on the content of volatile organic compound (VOC) emissions resulting from the storage of petrol and its distribution from terminals to service stations
- European Parliament and Council Directive 97/68/EC on measures against the emission of pollutants from internal combustion engines in non-road machinery
- European Parliament and Council Directive 98/70/EC on the quality of petrol and diesel fuels
- Commission Recommendation 1999/125/EC on the reduction of CO_2 emissions from passenger cars.
- European Parliament and Council Directive 99/94/EC on consumer information on fuel economy and CO_2 emissions for new passenger cars.

Directive 70/220/EEC established standards to control the emission of gaseous pollutants, particularly carbon monoxide, hydrocarbons and nitrogen oxides, and it did this by reference to the design of petrol and diesel engines. The Directive dealt with cars and light vehicles up to three-and-a-half tonnes. The primary purpose was trade harmonisation, essentially to prevent higher standards for vehicles being imported from one member state to another. While free trade was its primary purpose, nonetheless compliance with pollution standards was a significant secondary purpose. It will be appreciated that there have been a number of amendments (*e.g.* to reduce permitted levels of emission of the main pollutants). Directive 88/77/EEC dealing with diesel engines covers those in vehicles over three-and-a-half tonnes. Directive 98/70/EC is in effect an overhaul of earlier directives as to content of petrol of diesel fuels.

Chlorofluorocarbons and halons

The main measures are: **15–008**

- European Parliament and Council Regulation (EC) No 2037/2000 on substances that deplete the ozone layer;
- European Parliament and Council Directive 2002/3/EC on ozone in ambient air.

The reader will recall the stronger enforcement characteristics of regulations compared with directives (see para.15–003). That such measures have been applied to chlorofluorocarbons and the like is an indication of the extent to which the EU has adopted a precautionary approach to the protection of the ozone layer.

Increasing concern at the deterioration of the earth's ozone layer has led to more stringent controls over gases which deplete that layer, hence the 2000 Regulation which replaces a less stringent control which had been approved in 1991 and 1994.

Air quality

The main measures are: **15–009**

- Council Directive 80/779/EEC on air quality limit values for sulphur dioxide and suspended particulates
- Council Directive 84/360/EEC on the combating of air pollution from industrial plants
- Council Directive 85/203/EEC on air quality standards for nitrogen dioxide
- Council Directive 88/609/EEC on the limitation of emissions of certain pollutants into the air from large combustion plants

- Council Directive 89/369/EEC on the prevention of air pollution from new municipal waste incineration plants
- Council Directive 89/429/EEC on the reduction of air pollution from existing municipal waste incineration plants
- Council Directive 96/62/EC on ambient air quality assessment and management
- Council Directive 1999/13/EC on emissions of volatile organic compounds
- Council Directive 1999/30/EC on limit values for sulphur dioxide, etc. in ambient air
- European Parliament and Council Directive 2000/69/EC on limit values for benzine and carbon monoxide in ambient air
- European Parliament and Council Directive 2001/80/EC on limitation of emissions of certain pollutants in the air from large combustion plants
- European Parliament and Council Directive 2001/81/EC on national emissions ceilings for certain atmospheric pollutants.

The approach of Directive 80/779/EEC was to establish limits and guideline values for sulphur dioxide and other particulates, including smoke concentrations in the atmosphere for different times of the year. A target of April 1, 1983 was set for the reduction to certain limit values, but there were loopholes. Air quality standards for nitrogen dioxide were the subject of Directive 85/203/EEC. The intention was to secure reduction of nitrogen dioxide to specified limits by July 1, 1987 and to provide for monitoring.

Directives which specified the source of air pollution have developed since 1984 following the Directive 84/360/EEC (industrial plants). Member states are required to establish a regime of authorisations for various processes including those relating to the energy, metals, minerals, chemicals, waste and paper industries. The measure is designed specifically to deal with processes in an effort to secure the general aims of the air quality directives mentioned above. A similar approach was adopted in 1988 with Directive 88/609/EEC on limitation of emissions of certain pollutants into the air from large combustion plants. This seeks to require reduction in overall emissions of sulphur dioxide from combustion plants, such as power stations, by stages, designated as 1993, 1998 and 2003. The two 1989 directives on municipal waste incineration plants once again set emission limit values and the general improvement of standards. Towards the end of the 1990s there has been much activity and movement towards upgrading and making more rigorous all directives on air pollution, particularly those which have an effect upon global problems such as ozone depletion and global warming; the 1999 directives are aimed particularly at these problems. See also directives on the incineration of hazardous waste (below). The 2000 and 2001 Directives adopt more specific policies, in the first case concentrating on particular pollutants and in the second, targeting perceived significant polluters.

Waste on land

The main measures relating to waste on land are: **15–010**

- Council Directive 75/442/EEC on waste
- Council Directive 91/689/EEC on hazardous waste
- Council Regulation (EEC) 259/93 on the supervision and control of shipments of waste
- Council Directive 94/67/EC on the incineration of hazardous waste
- European Parliament and Council Directive 94/62/EC on packaging and packaging waste
- Council Directive 96/59/EC on the disposal of polychlorinated byphenyls and polychlorinated terphenyls (PCB/PCT)
- Council Directive 1999/31/EC on the landfill of waste
- Council Regulation (EC) 1420/1999 on shipments of waste to non-OECD countries
- Commission Regulation (EC) 1547/1999 on control procedures under Council Regulation (EEC) 259/93 on shipments of waste to countries not subject to OECD decision C(92)39
- Commission Decision 2000/532/EC on a list of wastes
- European Parliament and Council Directive 2000/53/EC on end of life vehicles
- European Parliament and Council Directive 2000/76/EC on the incineration of waste
- Council Directive 2002/96/EC on waste, electrical and electronic equipment.

Framework Directive 75/442/EEC defines waste, requiring member states to establish waste disposal authorities, prepare waste disposal plans and secure a regime of control by permits and supervision. Directive 91/689/EEC has the effect of replacing most of the Framework Directive and has updated many of the obligations. Both the 1975 and 1991 measures required a comprehensive list of wastes to be prepared and this is now available in Commission Decision 94/3/ EEC. Special categories of waste are the subject of other directives and examples of these are waste oils[5] and PCB/PCT.[6]

As the United Kingdom's waste strategy becomes skewed away from landfill toward greater incineration of hazardous waste and recycling/reuse, the relationship of Directive 94/67/EC on incineration of hazardous waste with the Directive on landfill[7] is understood. The latter requires very stringent reductions in the quantity of waste to be consigned to landfill. Furthermore, Directive 94/62/EC on packaging and packaging waste sets the basis upon which significant controls and requirements for recycling and reuse are laid down (see para.10–087).

[5] 75/439/EEC.
[6] 96/59/EC.
[7] 1999/31/EC.

The Landfill Directive[8] was adopted on April 26, 1999. Member states have two years to transpose it into national legislation. The landfill of waste from municipal sources must be reduced to 75 per cent of 1995 levels within five years, to 50 per cent within eight years and to 35 per cent within 15 years. A range of wastes which do not satisfy environmental and health standards set out in Annex II to the Directive are banned. Annexes to the Directive identify what these are and concern chemical manufacturing and processes. The Directive requires member states to impose regimes of control so that the operator of the process is obliged to take all the necessary measures to prevent major accidents and to limit consequences, both for humans and their environment. Preventative measures such as safety programmes are required and supervision responsibilities are imposed on member states. See Ch.10 for the UK implementation provisions.

Regulation (EEC) 259/93 on the shipment of waste has been brought into force in the UK by regulations (see para.10–087).

Hazardous substances

15–011 Relevant measures appropriate to this work are:

- Council Directive 79/117/EEC prohibiting the placing on the market and use of plant protection products containing certain active substances
- Council Directive 90/219/EEC on the contained use of genetically modified micro-organisms
- Council Directive 91/157/EEC on batteries and accumulators containing certain dangerous substances
- Council Directive 93/75/EEC on minimum requirements for vessels carrying dangerous or polluting goods
- Council Directive 94/55/EC on the transport of dangerous goods by road
- Council Directive 96/49/EC on the transport of dangerous goods by rail
- Council Directive 96/82/EC on the control of major accident hazards involving dangerous substances
- European Parliament and Council Directive 2001/18/EC on the deliberate release into the environment of genetically modified organisms.

Directive 79/117/EEC prohibited the placing on the market and use of plant protection products containing certain active substances. These were categorised in the annex to the Directive as mercury and persistent organochlorine compounds. Directive 96/82/EC on major accident hazards

[8] 1999/31/EC.

replaced a 1982 directive, also known as the Seveso Directive after the major accident in Italy. This controls industrial activities at installations which involve the use or presence of dangerous substances. Directives in 1994 and 1996 apply to the transport of certain wastes having dangerous characteristics: these directives are upgrades of earlier measures and concern both health and safety and environmental standards.

Council Regulation (EEC) 1734/88 seeks to establish a system to ensure that third-party states are advised of the export to that third-party state of any chemicals listed in the Annex to the Regulation. A reciprocal arrangement is required to be in place. Directives 90/219/EEC and 2001/18/EC dealing with genetically modified organisms make provision for a system of notification of operations and containment, and deal with accidents and waste management. Other aspects dealt with include research and development and safeguards. The provisions have been embodied in Pt VI of EPA 1990.

Noise

The main thrust of Council directives on noise has been specific to the source of such noise. There exists a range of directives on noise from particular machines and activities. The following are examples: **15–012**

- Council Directive 70/157/EEC on noise from motor vehicles
- Council Directive 78/1015/EEC on noise from motor vehicles
- European Parliament and Council Directive 2000/14/EC on the approximation of the laws of member states relating to the noise emission in the environment by equipment for use outdoors
- European Parliament and Council Directive 2003/49/EC on the assessment and management of environmental noise.

There are also directives relating specifically to sound power levels of compressors and tower cranes, welding generators, power generators, powered hand-held concrete breakers and picks, and lawnmowers. It will be appreciated that the EU approach has been to attack noise "at source", usually by requiring the problem to be dealt with by design rather than by enforcement during use of the product in question. This will mean that enforcement of EU legislation at the consumer level is usually unnecessary.

Environmental assessment

The two measures within this category are Council Directive 85/337/EEC on the assessment of the effects of certain public and private projects on the environment and European Parliament and Council Directive 2001/42/EC on the assessment of the effects of certain plans and programmes on the environment. The application of these directives is mainly a matter for   **15–013** town and country planning legislation. However, they are worthy of mention, in the light of the requirements in EPA 1990 to provide an environmental assessment in connection with applications under Pt I. The directives oblige member states to secure the assessment of the effect of projects upon human beings, fauna, flora and other aspects of the environment. The assessment procedure is the responsibility of the proposed developer. Categories of development caught by the directives are specified in the annexes, but these categories are split between those where an assessment is obligatory and those where a requirement is at the discretion of the member state. The 2001 directive addresses the assessment of the effects of strategic environmental plans or programmes, usually produced by member states and delegated authorities. These plans might relate to agriculture, forestry, energy, transport, waste management, town and country planning and the like. Under the terms of the directive an environmental assessment of the consequences of these plans and programmes is required to be produced as part of any public consultation exercise.

CHAPTER 16

AN OUTLINE OF THE COMMON LAW AND OTHER LIABILITIES AND REMEDIES

INTRODUCTION

The control of pollution and other activities associated with waste manage- **16–001**
ment relies, generally, upon the system of statute law and regulation. While
responsibility for enforcement rests with waste regulation authorities and
other bodies, themselves created by statute, there remain a number of
options, both statutory and created by the common law, which are designed
specifically to protect an individual's rights.

It is likely that an individual who has a complaint against a waste
management operation will take this to the responsible authority, either the
EA or the local planning authority. This approach is unlikely to put the
individual at risk of the cost of pursuing a complaint in the courts, since
that responsibility would be taken over by the relevant enforcement agency.
As a result, the number of civil actions in the courts are necessarily limited,
although by no means eliminated. Indeed, the position of the individual
under, for example, EPA 1990 has been enhanced by rights of public access
to information (see para.16–002 below) and even rights to bring prosecutions without reference to the enforcement agency itself. The formidable
extent of criminal procedures available against polluters needs to be
distinguished from the civil remedies which continue to exist in common
law, albeit that a number of remedies now are to be found in the more
modern statutes. Not only will the individual take advantage of these
remedies, but groups of individuals may undertake "class" actions, as
bodies such as the Friends of the Earth and Greenpeace have shown in
recent years.

Member states' obligations to ensure public participation in respect of
plans, programmes and decisions relating to the environment have existed
since 1985. See Directive 85/337/EEC and 96/61/EC. With effect from June
25, 2003, a further Directive 2003/35/EC on public participation imposed
new obligations on member states.

ACCESS TO ENVIRONMENTAL INFORMATION

"The Government believes that the public should have a right of access **16–002**
to information held by pollution control authorities."

This statement of Government policy, appearing as it did in the Environment White Paper, "This Common Inheritance" (DoE, 1990), comes towards the end of a significant period of change in the aspirations of individual members of the public and special interest groups for information on environmental issues. Successive governments have long held the view that the all-pervading influence of human activity on the environment must be met by ensuring that society as a whole has a satisfactory means of securing balance between development and natural protection. Thus, since the 1960s there has been an acceleration of statutory provision of public rights to information concerning the environment, as a means to this end.

Routes to public access

16–003 Rights of access to public information are achieved in one of two ways. First, most environmental acts of Parliament or their derivative regulations provide for public registers of information. Secondly, these are now augmented by the implementation in the United Kingdom of Directive 90/313/EEC on freedom of access to information on the environment. Implementation of the Directive has been achieved by the Environmental Information Regulations 1992,[1] as amended by the Environmental Information (Amendment) Regulations 1998.[2] These amendments brought the 1992 Regulations fully into line with the exceptions set out in the Directive. The Directive provides that in certain circumstances environmental information can be treated as confidential, so that it covers information:

- affecting international relations, national defence or public security
- affecting matters in legal proceedings and certain investigations
- affecting confidentiality of the deliberations of any relevant person
- involving the supply of yet incomplete documents or internal communications of a relevant person
- affecting commercial or industrial confidentiality.

For guidance on the operation of the regulations see *R. v British Coal Corp Ex p. Ibstock Building Products Ltd*.[3]

Public registers

16–004 The extent and range of information held on public registers will depend upon the individual legislative requirements but, typically, a register entry will be likely to hold the following information:

- applications for consents and, possibly, details of responses received as a result of consultation

[1] SI 1992/3240.
[2] SI 1998/1447.
[3] [1994] J.P.L. B40.

- consents, licences etc., with details of their conditions
- details of variations, revocations and similar notices
- records of monitoring data concerning licensed premises and processes
- information relating to any appeals (*e.g.* against refusal of any consent etc)
- details of convictions for offences under the statute concerned.

Registers are, in all cases, open to public inspection at reasonable hours, free of charge. A reasonable charge may be made for copies of documents.

The value of information

An individual lay member of the public or a special interest group usually **16–005** will not be able to appreciate fully the operation of industrial premises or processes and the environmental impacts caused by them. However, properly used, the registers represent a major step forward in obtaining information toward such an understanding. Such information can be used for challenging proposals for new or modified development and, in particular, for checking on the performance of a process against given standards. The range of information now required to be placed on registers represents a potent weapon in the hands of the public. The public is enabled not only to force the operators of premises or processes to face up to their responsibilities, but can also challenge the performance of the regulators in ensuring compliance with the law and any consents and authorisations granted thereunder.

The different registers

Waste management

Waste management registers are maintained by the EA and, in England, **16–006** waste collection authorities under Pt II of EPA 1990.

Waste carriers

Waste carrier registers are maintained by the EA under the Control of Pollution (Amendment) Act 1989 and the Controlled Waste (Registration of Carriers and Seizure of Vehicles) Regulations 1991.[4]

Integrated pollution and local authority pollution control

These registers are maintained by the EA and local authorities under s.20 of EPA 1990 and reg.15 of the Environmental Protection (Applications, Appeals and Registers) Regulations 1991.[5] In the case of Pt A prescribed

---

[4] SI 1991/1624.
[5] SI 1991/507.

processes, copies of the IPC entries are maintained for that area by the local authority.[6]

Similar register provisions are to be found in regs 29 to 31 of the Pollution, Prevention and Control (England and Wales) Regulations 2000.[7]

Water

Registers on discharge consents are maintained by the EA regional offices under s.190 of WRA 1991 and the Control of Pollution (Applications, Appeals and Registers) Regulations 1996. Registers on trade effluent consents are maintained by sewerage undertakers at their offices under s.196 of WIA 1991. Registers on water resources, abstraction, etc. are maintained by the EA under s.197 of WRA 1991.

Radioactive Substances Act 1993

These registers are maintained by the EA under s.39 of the 1993 Act; copies are also held by local authorities. Registers have only been maintained since January 1991 and do not deal with registration made before then. See also DoE Circulars 21/90 and 22/92.

Town and country planning

Registers are maintained by local planning authorities. A range of information concerning planning matters is entered mainly under TCPA 1990, the GDPO 1995,[8] the Planning (Hazardous Substances) Regulations 1992,[9] and the Town and Country Planning (Control of Advertisements) Regulations 1992.[10]

Local land charges registers

These are maintained by unitary and district councils under the provisions of the Local Land Charges Act 1975 and the Local Land Charges Rules 1977.[11] These registers will disclose, for example, information about statutory nuisances.

Noise abatement zones

These registers are maintained by local authorities which have exercised powers of designation under s.63 of COPA 1974 and reg.64 of the Control of Noise (Measurement and Registers) Regulations 1976.[12]

Atmospheric pollution

Registers are maintained by local authorities under Pt V of the Clean Air Act 1993.

[6] reg.16.
[7] SI 2000/1973.
[8] SI 1995/419.
[9] SI 1992/656.
[10] SI 1992/666.
[11] SI 1977/985.
[12] SI 1976/37.

Litter control

Registers are maintained by principal litter authorities (*i.e.* all local authorities) under ss.86 and 95 of EPA 1990.

Chemical release inventory

This register is compiled by the EA from public register information held in respect of radioactive substances and prescribed processes subject to control under Pt I of EPA 1990 and PPCA 1999.

Environmental Information Regulations 1992

The Environmental Information Regulations 1992[13] implement Directive 90/313/EEC on freedom of access to information on the environment. The Regulations are wide-ranging and refer to any information concerning a variety of matters. For the information to be accessible it must be held by certain types of bodies defined as "relevant persons". In the main, this description encompasses all public authorities and can include some private bodies which have public-type responsibilities (*e.g.* the water and sewerage companies).

A person who wishes to obtain information from a relevant person simply has to make a request for the release of the data. The relevant person is obliged to respond to that request. See "Guidance on the Implementation of the Environmental Information Regulations 1992" (DEFRA). This gives information on the rights available to the public and on procedures.

A new EU directive 2003/4/EC is intended to replace Directive 90/313/EEC. It maintains the original obligations of public authorities but also obliges them to make information available on electronic databases such as the Internet. Member states must implement the new directive by February 14, 2005. At the time of writing, it is understood that DEFRA are preparing new regulations.

16–007

Local authorities' meetings

In general, local authorities must allow public access to their proceedings and to the relevant papers (see Pt VA of and Sch.12A to the Local Government Act 1972, as amended). The terms on which information is available are set out in s.100H of that Act.

Made under the Local Government Act 2000, the Local Authorities (Executive Arrangements) (Access to Information) (England) Regulations 2000[14] establish a coordinated regime for provision of information to the

16–008

---

[13] SI 1992/3240.
[14] SI 2000/3272.

public. The regulations came into force on January 9, 2001 and apply to county and district councils in England and to London borough councils operating executive arrangements under Pt II of the Act. The general principle of the regulations is to ensure that the public have access to meetings, documents and decisions where a local authority, executive committee or individual take "key" decisions. This means that not only is there access to reports and other documents dealt with by a committee or the council but also to papers which are relevant to any decision which has been delegated to officers. A "key" decision is defined in reg.8 and in general terms means a decision which results in expenditure or savings by a local authority which are significant or which have significance in terms of the effects on local communities.

The regulations also require that the public must have a longer term advance notification of key matters. To achieve this, authorities are required to prepare a forward plan, detailing key decisions to be made over the following four months and this must be published, with notification of availability, in a local newspaper. There are exceptions for key decisions which might arise in emergency or where a forward notice would be difficult or impossible.

Exempted information

16–009   It is important to note that there will be some circumstances, albeit limited, when the public will not be able to gain access to information. There are two main occasions when access may be denied. First, the operator of a process or owner of premises may make a claim for confidentiality of information supplied on the grounds that they wish to protect commercial or industrial secrets. For the most part this claim needs to be supported by evidence to the regulator (on a confidential basis). If the claim is supported, whether by the regulator or, on appeal, by the Secretary of State, the information to be protected is excised from the register. Secondly, information may also be excluded from registers where it affects national security. The provisions whereby exclusion is secured will vary, depending upon the relevant statutory provision, but see, for example, ss.21 and 22 of EPA 1990.

COMMON LAW LIABILITIES

16–010   In a handbook of this type it would be inappropriate to examine in detail the laws of tort, particularly trespass, nuisance and negligence, which are the prime "civil offences" for which remedies are open to the private individual. A claimant is enabled to take action for damages or other remedies, such as injunction, in the event that the defendant is responsible for actions which fall within the definitions of trespass, nuisance or negligence. The rule in *Rylands v Fletcher*[15] assists a claimant in that it

---

[15] [1868] LR 3 HL 330.

imposes more limited duties on him to prove negligence or responsibility on the part of the defendant. However, the rule has been somewhat modified in recent times.[16]

REMEDIES

Common law

Such remedies include the right to an injunction and/or damages. Where an **16–011** individual wishes to proceed against a statutory authority, orders of the court such as mandamus or certiorari may be available.

Note that it is a defence to a common law action in nuisance that statutory authority exists. However, that authority must be certain, insofar as it authorises the commission of a nuisance.[17]

The following cases should also be noted, which clarify the extent to which the courts will go in dealing with nuisance claims and the awards of damages: *Walter v Selfe*[18] (smoke); *Halsey v Esso Petroleum Co Ltd*[19] (noxious smells); *West v Bristol Tramways*[20] (fumes); *Murdock and another v Glacier Metal Co Ltd*[21] (noise from factory); *Arscott v The Coal Authority and Another*[22] (Limits on flooding liability).

The tort of negligence may be a basis for a claim.[23]

Action based on statutory liability

The environmental legislation, particularly EPA 1990 and WRA 1991, **16–012** provides a strong basis for actions in negligence, particularly where failure to comply with the statutory requirements is proved. In other words, a failure to comply with the legislation may give rise not only to criminal penalties, but also to damages and other action in civil law. Both sets of proceedings will rely upon the same breaches and essentially the same evidence. For example, the unlawful deposit at a landfill site which damages the claimant's interests, say as a result of offensive smells or wind- or waterborne deterioration, could lead to prosecution under either of the Acts, as well as civil proceedings for any resulting damages which the claimant may have suffered.[24] In *Blue Circle Industries plc v Ministry of Defence*,[25] the Court of Appeal awarded damages for breach of statutory

---

[16] *e.g.* by *Cambridge Water Co v Eastern Counties Leather* [1994] 1 All E.R. 53.
[17] *Allen v Gulf Oil Refining Ltd* [1981] A.C. 101; *Sturges v Bridgman* [1879] 11 Ch D 852.
[18] [1952] 19 LTOS 308.
[19] [1961] 2 All E.R. 145.
[20] [1908] 2 K.B. 14.
[21] [1998] Env L.R. 732.
[22] QBD July 16, 2003.
[23] *Tutton v AD Walter Ltd* [1985] 3 All E.R. 757; *Tysoe v Davies* [1941] RTR 88.
[24] see *Leakey v National Trust* [1980] 1 All E.R. 17; *Smith v Great Western Railway* [1926] 42 TLR 391.
[25] [1998] 3 All E.R. 385.

duty under the Nuclear Installations Act 1965. The damages included a component for loss of value of the land. However, the House of Lords has held in the case of *Marcic v Thames Water Utilities* that a claim in common law (that the water company has allowed discharge from sewers) would fail if any ostensible liability under common law was inconsistent with statutory duties.

Other remedies for individuals

16–013   It may be appropriate for a claimant to pursue a claim for an injunction, particularly in those cases where a continuing problem is arising or is likely to recur. The individual has the right to apply to the Attorney General to take proceedings for an injunction to prevent recurrence of public nuisance, but a prior requirement would be that a large number of potential claimants must be affected.[26] An action for an injunction to restrain an anticipated breach would only be available to a private person in circumstances where special harm or damage to a private right was proved.[27]

Environmental Protection Act 1990

16–014   EPA 1990 provides various rights for private persons to bring summary proceedings for statutory nuisance under s.82. A similar right in regard to litter is available under s.91.

Control of Pollution Act 1974

16–015   Section 88 of COPA 1974 provides for civil liability for contravention of s.3(3) of the Act, to the extent that where any damage is caused by poisonous, noxious or polluting waste deposited on land then, insofar as an offence has been committed under s.3, the defendant is also liable specifically in civil law.

Water Resources Act 1991

16–016   In regard to water pollution, a riparian owner has a common law right to receive water in any stream or river on or adjacent to his property without harm to its natural condition. No proof of damage is required where harm arises.[28] The pollution of underground water may also be actionable in common law, for example, by the dumping of waste by the defendant on adjacent land which then pollutes underground resources flowing from the

---

[26] See *Att-Gen v PYA Quarries Ltd* [1957] 2 Q.B. 169.
[27] *Gouriet v Union of Post Office Workers* [1978] A.C. 435.
[28] *e.g.* to livestock or other consumers—see *Young v Bankier Distillery Ltd* [1893] A.C. 691.

defendant's land to the claimant's land. Note that a statutory right to pollute[29] is no defence to civil proceedings.

So far as water abstraction is concerned, an unlawful interference with the supply of surface or underground water to the extent that a claimant's right to abstract is detrimentally affected provides a civil action in tort against the person responsible.

Right of action against the EA

WRA 1991 contains protection for a licensed abstractor of water who has **16–017** suffered as a result of the breach of duty imposed on the EA by s.39 of the Act. Subject to certain conditions and restrictions there is a right of action against the EA under s.60 of the Act where it is in breach of the duty to protect the right of an abstractor who has been granted a licence and who seeks to abstract in accordance with that licence and the conditions imposed. If the EA has taken any action which derogates from a previous protected right, it is in breach of duty and an action may proceed in respect of that breach. Circumstances giving rise to such action are most likely to arise where the EA has granted a second or subsequent abstraction right which interferes with an earlier authorisation.

Statutory provision for civil liability

In some circumstances a statute may modify normal civil liability rules. An **16–018** example of this can be found in s.70 of WRA 1991. Except where the Act provides expressly, restrictions on abstraction, impounding and the construction of wells or boreholes are not to be construed as:

(a) providing any right of action in any civil proceedings, or
(b) derogating from any right of action or other remedy (whether civil or criminal) in proceedings instituted otherwise than under this part of the Act.

THE LIABILITIES OF COMPANY DIRECTORS AND OTHERS

Because it is invariably the case that the waste management role is placed **16–019** in the hands of a corporate body, particularly a private or public limited company, the regulator's attention is turned to that body rather than the individuals which may run it. For example, the holder of a licence to operate a landfill or other waste management site under EPA 1990 will be the operator because that is what the law requires. In those circumstances it is frequently the case that where liabilities of a criminal nature attach, so

---

[29] *e.g.* by ss.88 and 89 of WRA 1991.

responsibility for those liabilities will be focused by the regulators on the licence holder.

Nonetheless, the approach of the legislation to criminal liability in regard to waste management has widened its focus in recent years so that there is taken fully into account, both in regard to the grant of any licence or in the enforcement of liabilities, the role that company directors, managers and others might play in the day-to-day activities leading to responsibility. It is, therefore, all the more important that those who have positions of responsibility in corporate bodies should understand the extent to which they might themselves be called to account by prosecution, financial penalties, imprisonment and even clean-up costs. It should be stressed that in the pursuit of individuals the regulators are not prevented from also bringing proceedings against the corporate body in question.

Statutory provisions

16–020 A typical provision in statutes relating to environmental and health and safety law includes the following:

> "Where an offence under any provision of this Act committed by a body corporate is proved to have been committed with the consent or connivance of, or to be attributable to any neglect on the part of, any director, manager, secretary or other similar officer of the body corporate or any person who was purporting to act in such capacity, he as well as the body corporate shall be guilty of that offence and shall be liable to be proceeded against and punished accordingly."

Such provisions are to be found, for example, in s.37 of HSWA 1974, s.87 of COPA 1974, s.157 of EPA 1990, and s.217 of WRA 1991 and reg.32 of the Pollution Prevention and Control (England and Wales) Regulations 2000.

It may follow from a conviction, whether of the body corporate or the director, manager etc, that an award of clean-up costs will be made. Of particular note to waste managers are the following:

(a) EPA 1990, s.26 (remediation following conviction under Pt I); similar provisions appear in reg.35 of the Pollution, Prevention and Control (England and Wales) Regulations 2000;

(b) EPA 1990, Pt II, s.59 (power of the EA to require the removal of waste unlawfully deposited and to recover the cost from the occupier or any person who deposited or knowingly caused or knowingly permitted the deposit of the waste); and

(c) WRA 1991, ss.161–161D (power of the EA to carry out works of prevention, remedy etc. of pollution of controlled waters and to recover the cost from the person who caused or knowingly permitted the matter to be present in controlled waters).

Definition of "manager"

Guidance on the interpretation of the reference in the above legislation to   **16–021**
"manager" can be found in *R. v Boal*.[30]

Applications for licences etc

Increasingly, the personalities of directors and managers are under scrutiny   **16–022**
in the assessment of suitability of corporate bodies to be granted licences
etc. Thus, under the Control of Pollution (Amendment) Act 1989, corporate applicants for registration as carriers of waste are liable to have the
records of directors and managers scrutinised for relevant convictions,
whereupon registration may be refused. It is also important to bear in mind
that technical, financial and other competence will be tested by the EA in
considering applications for waste management licences under Pt II of EPA
1990.[31]

Civil liability

A detailed discourse on the civil liability of directors and managers is   **16–023**
beyond the scope of this book. However, it is certainly possible for a
director or other officer to incur personal liability in civil law where a
company is responsible for a tort such as negligence, nuisance or trespass.[32]

---

[30] [1992] 3 All E.R. 177.
[31] See the section on "fit and proper person" at para.10–063 above.
[32] See *e.g. The Radiant* [1958] 2 Lloyds's Rep. 596; and *Rainham Chemical Works v Belvedere Fish Guano Co Ltd* [1921] 2 A.C. 465.

PLANNING AND OTHER POLICY GUIDANCE NOTES

Planning policy guidance notes (PPGs) and planning policy statements (PPPs)

1997/PPG1	General Policy and Principles	**A1–001**
1995/PPG2	Green Belts	
1992/PPG4	Industrial and Commercial Development and Small Firms	
2004/PPG7	Sustainable Development in Rural Areas	
2002/PPG8	Telecommunications	
1994/PPG9	Nature Conservation	
1999/PPG10	Planning and Waste Management	
2004/PPS11	Regional Spatial Strategies	
2004/PPS12	Local Development Frameworks	
2001/PPG13	Transport	
1990/PPG14	Development on Unstable Land[1]	
1994/PPG15	Planning and the Historic Environment	
1990/PPG16	Archaeology and Planning	
2002/PPG17	Planning for Open Space, Sport and Recreation	
1991/PPG18	Enforcing Planning Control	
1992/PPG19	Outdoor Advertisement Control	
2004/PPS22	Renewable Energy	
1994/PPG23	Planning and Pollution Control	
1994/PPG24	Planning and Noise	
2001/PPG25	Development and Flood Risk	

Mineral policy guidance notes

1996/MPG1	General considerations and the Development Plan System	**A1–002**
1999/MPG3	Coal Mining and Colliery Spoil Disposal	

---

[1] Problems of subsidence were dealt with in MPG12. However this guidance has now been replaced in favour of a second annex to PPG14. This provides a strategy for dealing with subsidence problems with a special section on coal mining.

1998/MPG2   Applications, Conditions and Permissions
1997/MPG4   Revocation, Modification, Discontinuance, Prohibition
               and Suspension Orders—Town and Country Planning
               (Compensation for Restrictions on Mineral Working and
               Mineral Waste Depositing) Regulations 1997
2000/MPG5   Stability in surface mineral workings and tips
1996/MPG7   The Reclamation of Mineral Workings
1991/MPG8   Planning and Compensation Act 1991: Interim Develop-
               ment Order Permissions
1992/MPG9   Planning and Compensation Act 1991: Interim Develop-
               ment Order Permissions—Conditions
1993/MPG11   The Control of Noise at Surface Mineral Workings
1994/MPG12   Treatment of Disused Mine Openings and Availability of
               Information on Mined Ground[2]
1995/MPG14   Environment Act 1995: Review of Mineral Planning Per-
               missions

Derelict land grant advice

A1–003   1991/DLGAl   Derelict Land Grant Policy

---

[2] Problems of subsidence were dealt with in MPG12. However, this guidance has now been replaced in favour of a second annex to PPG14. This provides a strategy for dealing with subsidence problems with a special section on coal mining.

DEPARTMENT OF THE ENVIRONMENT AND WELSH OFFICE GUIDANCE NOTES (ENVIRONMENTAL PROTECTION ACT 1990)

General (Documents GG1—GG5 relate to local authority air pollution control)

- Integrated Pollution Control—A Practical Guide
- Secretary of State's Guidance—Introduction to Part I of the Act (GG1)   **A2–001**
- Secretary of State's Guidance—Authorisations (GG2)
- Secretary of State's Guidance—Applications and Registers (GG3)
- Secretary of State's Guidance—Interpretation of Terms used in Process Guidance Notes (GG4)
- Secretary of State's Guidance—Appeals (GG5)
- HM Inspectorate of Pollution—Fees and Charges for Integrated Pollution Control 1999/2000

Sector guidance notes

IPR1	Fuel and Power Industry Sector	**A2–002**
IPR2	Metal Industry Sector	
IPR3	Mineral Industry Sector	
IPR4	Chemical industry Sector	
IPR5	Waste Disposal Industry Sector	

(For practical purposes these guidance notes are superseded by more specific process guidance notes that relate to particular processes. They contain all necessary information in greater detail and in a more up-to-date form.)

Fuel production processes and combustion processes (including power generation)

S2 1.01	Combustion processes: large boilers and furnaces 50MW (th) and over	**A2–003**
S2 1.03	Combustion processes: compression ignition engines 50MW (th) and over	

S2 1.04	Combustion processes: waste and recovered oil burners 3MW (th) and over
S2 1.05	Combustion processes: combustion of fuel manufactured from or comprised of solid waste in appliances 3MW(th) and over
S2 1.08	Gasification processes: gasification of solid and liquid feedstocks
IPR1/2	Combustion processes: gas turbines (1994)
PG1/1 (95)	Waste oil burners, less than 0.3 MW net rated thermal input
PG1/2 (95)	Waste oil or recovered oil burners, less than 3 MW net rated thermal input
PG1/3 (95)	Boilers and furnaces, 20–50 MW net rated thermal input
PG1/4 (95)	Gas turbines, 20–50 MW net rated thermal input
PG1/5 (95)	Compression ignition engines, 20–50 MW net rated thermal input
PG1/10 (92)	Waste derived fuel burning processes less than 3 MW net rated thermal input
PG1/11(96)	Reheat and heat treatment furnaces. 20–50 MW net rated thermal input
PG1/12 (96)	Combustion of fuel manufactured from or comprised of solid waste in appliances between 0.4 and 3 MW net rated thermal input

Waste disposal industry and recycling sector

A2–004	IPR5/9	Regeneration of ion exchange resins
	IPR5/10	Recovery of oil by distillation
	IPR5/11	Sewage sludge incineration
	S2 5.01	Waste incineration: and waste to energy plants for the following wastes: chemical; clinical; municipal; sewage sludge; animal carcasses and drum residues
	S2 5.02	Making solid fuel from waste
	S2 5.03	Cleaning and regeneration of activated carbon
	S2 5.04	Recovery of organic solvents by distillation
	PG5/1 (95)	Clinical waste incineration processes under 1 tonne an hour
	PG5/2 (95)	Crematoria
	PG5/3 (95)	Animal remains incineration processes under 1 tonne an hour
	PG5/4 (95)	General waste incineration processes under 1 tonne an hour
	PG5/5 (95)	Sewage sludge incineration processes under 1 tonne an hour

Non-ferrous

A2–005	PG2/1 (96)	Furnaces for the extraction of non-ferrous metal from scrap

Other guidance notes

A number of other notes have been published, advising on such matters as   **A2–006**
dispersion, monitoring and abatement (D, M and A series) and a wide
range of AQ notes, usually dealing with specific technical, legal and
administrative matters. This last series is produced by the Air Quality
Division of the DoE/DETR/DEFRA, primarily intended for local authority
regulators.

APPENDIX 3

DEPARTMENT OF THE ENVIRONMENT WASTE MANAGEMENT PAPERS

1. Reclamation, Treatment and Disposal of Waste: a Review of the Options (2nd ed., 1992, ISBN 0 11 752644 4)
2. Waste Disposal Surveys (1976, ISBN 0117510033)
3. Guidelines for the Preparation of a Waste Disposal Plan (1976, ISBN 0 11 751124 2)
4. The Licensing of Waste Disposal Sites (3rd ed., 1994, ISBN 0 11 752727 0)
5. The Relationship between Waste Disposal Authorities and Private Industry (1976, ISBN 0 11 750920 5)
6. Polychlorinated Biphenyl (PCB) Wastes—a Technical Memorandum on Reclamation, Treatment and Disposal (1994, BN 0 11 75100 9)
7. Mineral Oil Wastes—a Technical Memorandum on Arisings, Treatment and Disposal (1976, ISBN 0 11 751060 2)
8. Heat Treatment of Cyanide Wastes—a Technical Memorandum on Arisings, Treatment and Disposal (1976, ISBN 0 11 751813 1)
9. Halogenated Hydrocarbon Solvent Wastes from the Cleaning Processes—a Technical Memorandum on Reclamation and Disposal (1976, ISBN 0 11 751103 X)
10. Local Authority Waste Disposal Statistics 1974/75 (1976, ISBN 0 11 751120 X)
11. Metal Finishing Wastes—a Technical Memorandum on Arisings, Treatment and Disposal (1976, ISBN 0 11 751122 6)
12. Mercury Bearing Wastes—a Technical Memorandum on Storage, Handling, Treatment, Disposal and Recovery (1977, ISBN 0 11 751126 9)
13. Tarry and Distillation Wastes and other Chemical Based Wastes— a Technical Memorandum on Arisings, Treatment and Disposal (1977, ISBN 0 11 751127 7)
14. Solvent Wastes (excluding Halogenated Hydrocarbons)—a Technical Memorandum on Reclamation and Disposal (1977, SBN 0 11 751128 5)
15. Halogenated Organic Wastes—a Technical Memorandum on Arisings, Treatment and Disposal (1978, ISBN 0 11 751370 9)
16. Wood Preserving Wastes—a Technical Memorandum on Arisings, Treatment and Disposal (1980, ISBN 0 11 751476 4)

17. Wastes from Tanning, Leather Dressing and Fellmongering—a Technical Memorandum on Recovery, Treatment and Disposal (1978, ISBN 0 11 751320 2)
18. Asbestos Waste—a Technical Memorandum on Arisings and Disposal (1979, ISBN 0 11 751384 9)
19. Wastes from the Manufacturing of Pharmaceuticals, Toiletries and Cosmetics—a Technical Memorandum on Arisings, Treatment and Disposal (1978, ISBN 0 11 751318 0)
20. Arsenic Bearing Wastes—a Technical Memorandum on Recovery, Treatment and Disposal (1980, ISBN 0 11 751472 1)
21. Pesticide Wastes—a Technical Memorandum on Arisings and Disposal (1980, ISBN 0 11 751484 5)
22. Local Authority Waste Disposal Statistics 1974/75 to 1977/78 (1978, ISBN 0 11 751453 5)
23. Special Wastes—a Technical Memorandum Providing Guidance on their Definition (1981, ISBN 0 11 751555 8)
24. Cadmium Bearing Wastes—a Technical Memorandum on Arisings, Treatment and Disposal (1984, ISBN 0 11 751716 X)
25. Clinical Wastes—a Technical Memorandum on Arisings, Treatment and Disposal (1983, ISBN 0 11 751719 4)
26. Landfilling Wastes—a Technical Memorandum for the Disposal of Wastes on Landfill Sites (1986, ISBN 0 11 751891 3)
26A. Landfill Completion—a Technical Memorandum providing Guidance on Assessing Completion of Licensed Landfill Sites (1994, ISBN 0 11 752807 2)
26B. Landfill Design, Construction and Operational Practice (1995, ISBN 0 11 753185 5)
26D. Landfill Monitoring (Consultation Draft)
26E. Landfill Restoration and Post-Closure Management (Consultation Draft)
26F. Landfill Co-disposal (Consultation Draft)
27. Landfill Gas—a Technical Memorandum on the Monitoring and Control of Landfill Gas (2nd ed., 1991, ISBN 0 11 752488 3)
28. Recycling—a Memorandum providing Guidance to Local Authorities on Recycling (1991, ISBN 0 11 752445 X)

WASTE MANAGEMENT ACTIVITIES, INSTALLATIONS AND MOBILE PLANT: CONTROL AND PRESCRIBED DATES

Pollution Prevention and Control (England and Wales) Regulations 2000

[Note: The following descriptions are in general terms. For detailed interpretation see Schedule 1 to the Pollution Prevention and Control (England and Wales) Regulations 2000[1] as amended. For details of Parts A(1), A(2) and B, see para.9–004 above.]

Section 1.1: Combustion activities

- Burning any fuel in an appliance with a rated thermal output of 50 MW or more. (Part A(1); January 1–March 31, 2006).   **A4–001**
- Burning any of the following fuels in an appliance with a rated thermal input of 3 MW or more but less than 50 MW, unless the activity is related to a Part A(2) or B activity, viz waste oil, recovered oil or any fuel manufactured from or comprising any other waste (Part A(1); January 1–March 31, 2006).
- Burning any fuel (other than above) in a boiler or furnace or a gas turbine or compression ignition engine—rated thermal input of 20 MW or more but less than 50 MW (Part B; April 1, 2002).
- Burning of waste oil, recovered oil or a solid fuel which has been manufactured from waste by an activity involving the application of heat, in an appliance with a rated thermal output of less than 3 MW (Part B; April 1, 2002).
- Burning fuel manufactured from or including waste, except as mentioned above, in any appliance with a rated thermal input of less than 3 MW but at least 0.4 MW or which is used together with other appliances which each have a rated thermal output of less

---

[1] SI 2000/1973.

than 3 MW, where the aggregate rated thermal input of all the appliances is at least 0.4 MW (Part B; April 1, 2002).

Section 2.1: Ferrous metals

A4–002
● Heating iron, steel or any ferrous alloy (whether in a furnace or other appliance) to remove grease, oil or any other non-metallic contaminant, including such operations as the removal by heat of plastic or rubber covering of scrap cable unless it is carried out in one or more furnaces or other appliances the primary combustion chambers which have in aggregate a rated thermal input of less than 0.2 MW; it does not involve the removal by heat of plastic or rubber covering from scrap cable or of any asbestos contaminant, and it is not related to any other activity falling within any part of section 2.1 (Part B; April 1, 2003).

Section 2.2: Non-ferrous metals

A4–003
● Unless falling within Part A(2) of this section, producing non-ferrous metals from ore concentrates or secondary raw materials by metallurgical, chemical or electrolytic activities (Part A(1); October 1–December 31, 2001).
● Melting, including making alloys, of non-ferrous metals including recovered products, refining, foundry casting, etc, where the plant has a melting capacity exceeding 4 tonnes per day for lead or cadmium or 20 tonnes per day for all other metals, and no furnace, bath or other holding vessel used in the plant for the melting has a design holding capacity of 5 tonnes or more (Part A(1); October 1–December 31, 2001).
● Melting, including making alloys, of non-ferrous metals (other than tin or any alloy which in molten form contains 50 per cent or more by weight of tin) including recovered products (refining foundry casting, etc) in plant with a melting capacity of 4 tonnes or less per day for lead or cadmium or 20 tonnes or less per day for all other metals (Part B; April 1, 2003).
● The heating of a furnace or any other appliance of any non-ferrous metal or non-ferrous metal alloy for the purpose of removing grease, oil or any other non-metallic contaminant, including such operations as the removal by heat of plastic or rubber covering from scrap cable, if not related to another activity described in section 2.2, but excluding the use of one or more furnaces or other appliances the primary combustion chambers of which have in aggregate a net rated thermal input of less than 0.2 MW and does not involve the removal by heat of plastic or rubber

covering from scrap cable or of any asbestos contaminate (Part B; April 1, 2003).

Section 3.5: Other mineral activities

- Crushing, grinding or other size reduction, with machinery **A4–004** designed for that purpose, of bricks, tiles or concrete, or screening the product of such activity (Part B; April 1, 2002).

Section 5.1: Disposal of waste by incineration

- The incineration of any waste chemical or waste plastic arising **A4–005** from their manufacture (Part A(1); June 1–August 31, 2005).
- Incineration, other than incidentally in the course of burning other waste, of any waste chemical being or comprising elemental or compound form, bromide, cadmium, chlorine, fluorine, iodine, lead, mercury, nitrogen, phosphorus, sulphur or zinc (Part A(1); June 1–August 31, 2005).
- Unless falling within Part B (see below) the incineration of any other hazardous waste in an incineration plant other than of specified hazardous waste* in an exempt incineration plant** (Part A(1); June 1–August 31, 2005).
- Incineration of municipal waste in an incineration plant with a capacity exceeding 3 tonnes per hour (Part A(1); June 1–August 31, 2005).
- Incineration of any waste including animal remains, otherwise than as part of a Part B activity, in an incineration plant with a capacity of one tonne or more per hour (Part A(1); April 1– August 31, 2005).
- The cleaning for reuse of metal containers used for the transport or storage of a chemical by burning out the residual content (Part A(1); April 1–August 31, 2005).
- The incineration of specified hazardous waste* in an incineration plant with a capacity of 10 tonnes or less per day and less than 1 tonne per hour, unless the plant is an exempt incineration plant** (Part B; April 1, 2002).
- The incineration of any non-hazardous waste in an incineration plant, other than an exempt incineration plant, with a capacity of less than 1 tonne per hour (Part B; April 1, 2002).
- The cremation of human remains (Part B; April 1, 2002).
- Specified hazardous waste is defined in the interpretation provisions of s.5.1 in Sch.1 to the 2000 Regulations as including combustible liquid wastes, polychlorinated aromatic hydrocarbons, sewage sludges and infectious clinical waste, all having hazardous characteristics as defined.

- Exempt incineration plant means generally an incinerator with a capacity of not more than 50 kg per hour which does not incinerate clinical waste, sewage sludge, sewage screenings or municipal waste.

Section 5.2: Disposal of waste by landfill

A4–006

- The disposal in a landfill of more than 10 tonnes per day or with a total capacity exceeding 25,000 tonnes, excluding disposals of only inert waste.
- The disposal of waste in any other landfill to which the Landfill (England and Wales) Regulations 2002 apply.

NB: The period of application is specified in a notice served on the operator by the Environment Agency under para.1(9) of Sch.4 to the 2002 Regulations.

Section 5.3: Disposal of waste other than by incineration or landfill

A4–007

- The disposal of hazardous waste in a facility with a capacity exceeding 10 tonnes per day (Part A(1); June 1–August 31, 2005).
- The disposal of waste oils in a facility with a capacity exceeding 10 tonnes per day (Part A(1); June 1–August 31, 2005).
- Disposal of non-hazardous waste in a facility with a capacity exceeding 15 tonnes per day by certain (a) biological or (b) physio-chemical treatments excluded from the Waste Framework Directive 75/442 (Part A(1); January 1–March 31, 2004 (a); June 1–August 31, 2004 (b)).

Section 5.4: Recovery of waste

A4–008

- Recovery by distillation of any oil or organic solvent (Part A(1); January 1–March 31, 2005).
- Cleaning or regenerating carbon, charcoal or ion exchange resins (Part A(1); January 1–March 31, 2005).
- Unless any part of another Part A activity, recovering hazardous waste in a plant with a capacity in excess of 10 tonnes per day, by use of fuel to generate energy, for solvent reclamation or regeneration, for recycling or reclamation of inorganic materials other than metals or metal components, for regeneration of acids or bases, for recovery of components used for pollution abate-ment, for recovery of components from catalysts, for oil re-refining or other reuses of oil (Part A(1); January 1–March 31, 2005).

Section 5.5: Production of fuel from waste

- Making solid fuel (other than charcoal) from waste by a process **A4–009** involving the use of heat (Part A(1); January 1–March 31, 2004).

Section 6.1: Paper, pulp and board manufacturing activities

- Any activity associated with making paper pulp or paper, including **A4–010** activities connected with recycling such as de-inking, if the activity may result in the release into water of certain substances in any 12-month period (Part A(1); December 1, 2000–February 28, 2001).

Section 6.8: The treatment of animal and vegetable matter and food industries

- Disposing of or recycling animal carcasses or animal waste at a **A4–011** plant with a treatment capacity exceeding 10 tonnes per day of animal carcasses or animal waste, or both (Part A(2); June 1– August 31, 2004).

HEALTH AND SAFETY LEGAL AND OTHER GUIDANCE

L5	General COSHH ACOP (Control of Substances Hazardous to Health) and Carcinogens ACOP (Control of Carcinogenic Substances) and Biological agents ACOP (Control of Biological Agents). Control of Substances Hazardous to Health Regulations 1999 (1999, ISBN 0 71 761670 3, £8.50)	**A5–002**
L8	Legionnaires' disease. The control of legionella bacteria in water systems. Approved Code of Practice and guidance	
L9	Safe use of pesticides for non-agricultural purposes. Control of Substances Hazardous to Health Regulations 1994 (1995, ISBN 0 71 760542 6, £6.95)	
L10	A Guide to the Control of Explosives Regulations 1991 (1991, ISBN 0 11 885670 7, £3.00)	
L11	A guide to the Asbestos (Licensing) Regulations 1983 as amended. The Asbestos (Licensing) Regulations 1983. Guidance on Regulations.	
L13	A guide to the Packaging of Explosives for Carriage Regulations 1991 (1991, ISBN 0 11 885728 2, £3.00)	
L21	Management of Health and Safety at Work Management of Health and Safety at Work Regulations 1999 (2000, ISBN 0 71 762488 9, £8.00)	
L22	Safe use of work equipment: Provision and Use of Work Equipment Regulations 1998 (1998, ISBN 0 71 761626 6, £8.00)	
L23	Manual handling: Manual Handling Operations Regulations 1992. Guidance on regulations (1992, ISBN 0 71 769415 2, £5.00)	
L24	Workplace health, safety and welfare: Workplace (Health, Safety and Welfare) Regulations 1992 (as amended by the Quarries Miscellaneous Health and Safety Provisions Regulations 1995) (1996, ISBN 0 71 760413 6, £5.75)	
L25	Personal Protective Equipment at Work Regulations 1992. Guidance on regulations (1992, ISBN 0 71 760415 2, £5.00)	
L26	Display screen equipment work: Health and Safety (Display Screen Equipment Regulations 1992. Guidance on regulations (1992, ISBN 0 71 760420 9, £5.00)	

L27   Control of asbestos at work: Control of Asbestos at Work Regulations 1987 (1999, ISBN 0 71 761673 8, £6.75)

L28   Work with asbestos insulation, asbestos coating and asbestos insulating board: Control of Asbestos at Work Regulations 1987 (1999, ISBN 0 71 761674 6, £6.75)

L31   A guide to the Public Information for Radiation Emergencies Regulations 1992 (1993, ISBN 0 11 886350 0, £5.00)

L43   First aid at mines: Health and Safety (First Aid) Regulations 198 (1993, ISBN 0 71 760617 1, £4.00)

L44   The management and administration of health and safety at mines: Management and Administration of Health and Safety at Mines Regulations 1993 (1993, ISBN 0 71 760618 X, £7.50)

L46   Prevention of inrushes in mines (1993, ISBN 0 71 60620 1, £5.50)

L50   Railway Safety Critical Work in support of Railway (Safety Critical Work) Regulations 1994 (1996, ISBN 0 71 761260 0, £7.50)

L55   Preventing asthma at work. How to control respiratory sensitisers (1994, ISBN 0 7176 0661 9, £6.25).

L56   Safety in the installation and use of gas systems and appliances: Gas Safety Installation and Use Regulations 1998 (1998, ISBN 0 71 761635 5, £10.95)

L62   Safety data sheets for substances and preparations dangerous for supply: Guidance on regulation 6 of the CHIP Regulations 1994 (1995, 2nd ed, ISBN 0 71 760859 X, £3.95)

L67   Control of vinyl chloride at work: Control of Substances Hazardous to Health Regulations 1994 (1995, ISBN 0 71 760894 8, £3.95)

L71   Escape and Rescue from Mines: Escape and Rescue from Mines Regulations 1995 (1995, ISBN 0 17 60939 1, £9.50)

L73   A guide to the Reporting of Injuries, Diseases and Dangerous Occurrences Regulations 1995. Guidance on Regulations (1999, 0 7176 2431 5, £7.95)

L74   First aid at work: The Health and Safety (First Aid) Regulations 1981 (1997, ISBN 0 71 761050 0, £6.75)

L81   The design, construction and installation of gas service pipes: Pipelines Safety Regulations 1996 (1996, ISBN 0 71 761172 8, £6.50)

L82   A guide to the Pipelines Safety Regulations 1996. Guidance on Regulations (1996, ISBN 0 7176 1182 5, £9.00)

L86   Control of Substances Hazardous to Health in fumigation operations: Control of Substances Hazardous to Health Regulations (1996, ISBN 0 71 761195 7, £8.50)

L87   Safety representatives and safety committees (The Brown Book) Approved Code of Practice and guidance on the regulations 1996, ISBN 0 7176 1220 1, £5.75)

L88   Approved requirements and test methods for the classification and packaging of dangerous goods for carriage. Carriage of Dangerous Goods (Classification, Packaging and Labelling) and Use of Transportable Pressure Receptacles Regulations 1996. Approved requirements (1996, ISBN 0 7176 1221 X, £12.75)

L89	Approved Vehicle Requirements. Carriage of Dangerous Goods by Road Regulations 1996. Approved Requirements (1999, ISBN 0 7176 1680 0, £5.50)
L90	Approved Carriage List. Information approved for the carriage of dangerous goods by road and rail other than explosives and radioactive material (1999, ISBN 0 7176 1681 9, £14.75)
L91	Suitability of vehicles and containers and limits on quantities for the carriage of explosives: Carriage of Explosives by Road Regulations 1996 (1996, ISBN 0 71 761224 4, £6.50)
L95	A guide to the Health and Safety (Consultation with Employees) Regulations 1996. Guidance on Regulations (1996, ISBN 0 7176 1120 5, £10.50)
L101	Safe work in confined spaces: Confined Spaces Regulations 1997 (1997, ISBN 0 71 76405 0, £7.50)
L108	Reducing noise at work. Guidance on the Noise at Work Regulations 1989 (1998, ISBN 0 7176 1511 1, £9.75)
L111	A guide to the Control of Major Accident Hazard Regulations. Guidance on Regulations (1999, ISBN 0 7176 1604 5, £14.00)
L113	Safe use of lifting equipment: Lifting Operations and Lifting Equipment Regulations (1998, ISBN 0 71 761628 2, £8.00)
L114	Safe use of wood working machinery: Provision and Use of Work Equipment Regulations 1998 as applied to woodworking machinery (1998, ISBN 0 71 761630 4)
L116	Preventing accidents to children in agriculture (1999, ISBN 0 71 761690 8, £5.50)
L117	Rider operated lift trucks operator training (1999, ISBN 0 71 762455 2, £5.00)
L118	Health and safety at quarries: Quarries Regulations 1999 (1999, ISBN 0 71 762458 7, £9.75)
L119	The control of ground movement in mines: The Mines (Control of Ground Movement) Regulations 1999 (1999, ISBN 0 71 762498 6, £6.00)
L120	Train protection systems and mark 1 rolling stock. Railway Safety Regulations 1999. Guidance on Regulations (1999, ISBN 0 7176 2442 0, £9.95)
L121	Work with ionising radiation: Ionising Radiations Regulations (2000, ISBN 0 71 761746 7, £20.00)
L122	Safety of pressure systems. Pressure Systems Safety Regulations 2000. Approved Code of Practice (2000, ISBN 0 7176 1767 X, £7.50)
HSC 13	Health and Safety Regulations (A short Guide) (1995, Free)
No ref.	Safe disposal of clinical waste no) (1999, ISBN 0 71 762492 7, £10.50)
EH1	Cadmium (1995, ISBN 0 71 760825 5, £4.00)
EH13	Beryllium Health and Safety Precautions (1995, ISBN 0 71 760824 7, £5.50)
EH47	Provision, use and maintenance of hygiene facilities for work with asbestos insulation and coatings (1990, ISBN 0 11 885567 0, £2.50)
EH68	Cobalt: Health and Safety Precautions (1995, ISBN 0 71 760832 9, £4.00)
LOLER	Lifting Operations and Lifting Equipment Regulations (LOLER) 1998 (1999, ISBN 0 71 762464 1, £15.95)

PUWER   Provision and Use of Work Equipment Regulations 1998
         (1999, ISBN 0 71 762459 5, £16.50)
ACL 55   Workplace inspection (1997, Free)

Note also the HSG series, over 200 in number, providing guidance on duties, responsibilities and relevant legislation.

HSC has also issued a brochure, "Waste Industry Safety and Health. Reducing the Risks". Whilst the purpose of the document is not to interpret health and safety law, it provides quite detailed guidance on certain aspects relating to transport, machinery guarding, slips and trips, health protection, welfare facilities and manual handling.

HEALTH AND SAFETY AT WORK

Main Waste Management Regulations

Construction (General Provisions) Regulations 1961 (SI 1961/1580)   **A6–001**

These Regulations impose obligations on every contractor and employer of workmen undertaking any operations or works which are building operations or works of engineering construction as defined in reg.2. They relate to the supervision of safe conduct of work, excavations, shafts and tunnels, safety at coffer dams and caissons, ventilation of unhealthy atmospheres of excavations etc and work on or adjacent to water. They also relate to transport (particularly in relation to rails and rail trucks), precautions in connection with demolition, fencing, lighting and protection from falling materials or collapse of structure. There is also a requirement for the keeping of records. Regulations are amended by virtue of SIs 1988/1657, 1989/635, 1989/682, 1992/2793 (see below), 1994/3140, 1995/2923, 1996/1592, and 1999/3242 (see below). The cumulative effect of these amendments is that the 1961 Regulations are entirely revoked, except for Pt I (regs 1–4), regs 5, 75–79, 85–98 and 100, and regs 1–4 of SI 1952/1584.

Health and Safety Inquiries (Procedure) Regulations 1975 (SI 1975/335)

These Regulations are concerned with the procedure for holding inquiries required by the Health and Safety Commission (HSC) following any accident etc to which s.14 of HSWA 1974 applies. Amended by the Health and Safety Inquiries (Procedure) (Amendment) Regulations 1976.[1]

Fire Certificates (Special Premises) Regulations 1976 (SI 1976/2003)

These Regulations prescribe certain premises for which fire certificates are required because they have special risks attached to them. These premises include manufacturing and other facilities where flammable gas and certain

[1] SI 1976/1246.

flammable materials are stored or used and include buildings temporarily occupied for building operations or engineering construction. These Regulations have been amended by SIs 1985/1333, 1987/37, 1992/1811 and 2001/2795 (see below).

Safety Representatives and Safety Committees Regulations 1977 (SI 1977/500)

The appointment, powers and responsibilities of safety representatives and safety committees are specified in these Regulations. The code of practice and guidance notes are provided, as approved by the HSC. Amended by SI 1992/2051, 1996/1513 (see below), 1997/1840, 1999/860, 1999/2024, 1999/3242 (see below) and s.1(2) of the Employment Rights (Dispute Resolution) Act 1998.

Health and Safety (First Aid) Regulations 1981 (SI 1981/917)

As its name implies, this instrument places a duty on all employees to secure adequate first aid equipment facilities and personnel for employees to deal with accident or illness at work. There is also a requirement to inform employees about arrangements. Health and Safety Bulletin No 241/81 and a code of practice (1997) supplement the Regulations. Amended by SIs 1989/1671, 1993/1897, 1997/2776, 1999/3242 and 2002/2174 (see below).

Notification of Installations Handling Hazardous Substances Regulations 1982 (SI 1982/1357)

Where there is, at any one time, a notifiable quantity of a hazardous substance at any site, notification is required by these Regulations to the HSE. Lists of hazardous substances are indicated in a schedule to the Regulations and include flammable or liquified gases to varying amounts. Notification is also required in connection with certain pipelines but exemption certificates may be obtained in appropriate cases. The notification requirements (mainly to keep the HSE advised) are set out. Amended by the Pipelines Safety Regulations 1996[2] (see below) and 2002/2979.

Asbestos (Licensing) Regulations 1983 (SI 1983/1649)

An employer or self-employed person undertaking work with asbestos insulation or asbestos coating must obtain a licence from the HSE before so doing. An exemption may, however, be granted where health and safety requirements are satisfied. Note that "work" as defined in the Regulations includes removal, repair or disturbance of the asbestos, and includes such

---

[2] SI 1996/825.

work in any supervisory or ancillary capacity. Amended by SIs 1987/2115 and 1998/3233.

Freight Containers (Safety Convention) Regulations 1984 (SI 1984/1890)

Owners and lessees of freight containers at work are required to comply with the International Convention for Safe Containers 1972 as to safety and labelling. A "container" includes an article of transport equipment of a permanent character for repeated use, facilitating the transport of goods by one or more modes of transport without intermediate reloading. The Regulations are essentially type approvals, but there are conditions of use laid down.

Docks Regulations 1988 (SI 1988/1655)

These Regulations are general in nature and apply to dock operations carried out in Great Britain and in certain territorial waters outside Great Britain. A range of responsibilities concerning planning, the provision of fire-fighting, maintenance, fencing and general safety is set out in the Regulations but, having regard to the generality of their requirements, it is important that operators should refer to the approved code of practice, Docks Regulations 1988 Approved Code of Practice and Guidance, issued by the HSC. These Regulations have been amended by SIs 1997/1713 and 1998/2307.

Fire Precautions (Factories, Offices, Shops and Railway Premises) Order 1989 (SI 1989/76)

This Order imposes on certain places of work requirements for a fire certificate and provides an exemption for other premises. The requirements apply to most factory, office, shop and railway premises. See also the Fire Precautions (Application for Certificate) Regulations 1989,[3] the Fire Precautions (Non-certificated Factory, Office, Shop and Railway Premises) (Revocation) Regulations 1989[4] and the Fire Precautions (Workplace) Regulations 1997.[5]

Electricity at Work Regulations 1989 (SI 1989/635)

Duties are imposed by these Regulations upon employers, self-employed persons and employees and relate generally to electrical systems, work activities and protective equipment, the strength of electrical currents and

[3] SI 1989/77.
[4] SI 1989/78.
[5] SI 1997/1840.

other protective requirements. There is an approved code of practice relating to the use of any electricity at quarries, as well as a memorandum of guidance on the Regulations, both of which may be obtained from the Stationery Office. Amended by SIs 1995/2005, 1997/1993, 1996/192, 1999/2024 and 1999/2550.

Health and Safety Information for Employees Regulations 1989 (SI 1989/682)

These Regulations require information relating to health, safety and welfare to be provided to employees by means of posters and leaflets, specimens of which can be obtained from the Stationery Office. Amended by SI 1995/2923.

Noise at Work Regulations 1989 (SI 1989/1790)

These Regulations bring into force the responsibilities set out in Council Directive 86/188/EEC on the protection of workers from the risks related to exposure to noise at work. They impose upon employers various requirements to review and record noise assessments, to secure the reduction of risk of damage to hearing and exposure to noise of employees, to provide personal ear protectors, to identify ear protection zones in the workplace, to monitor the use and maintenance of equipment by employees and employers, and the provision of information. Certain certificates of exemption are provided in circumstances where exposure levels are anticipated to be limited. Amended by SIs 1992/2966, 1996/341, 1997/1993 and 1999/2024.

Construction (Head Protection) Regulations 1989 (SI 1989/2209)

These Regulations contain obligations to provide suitable head protection for use by persons at work on building operations or where engineering construction is required. Amended by SIs 1992/2966 and 1997/2776.

Dangerous Substances (Notification and Marking of Sites) Regulations 1990 (SI 1990/304)

The definition of "dangerous substance" in these Regulations is any substance regarded as dangerous for conveyance under the Carriage of Dangerous Goods (Classification, Packaging and Labelling) and Use of Transportable Pressure Receptacles Regulations 1996,[6] as amended by SIs 1999/2024 and 2000/128. They require that notification be made to the fire and enforcing authorities and, as the name implies, that provision be made for the display of signs warning of dangerous substances. A schedule identifies the matters to be notified.

[6] SI 1996/2092.

Health and Safety (Display Screen Equipment) Regulations 1992 (SI 1992/2792)

These Regulations give effect to provisions of Council Directive 90/270/EEC on the minimum safety and health requirements for work with display screen equipment. Two publications have been issued by the HSE: Display screen equipment work—guidance on regulations and Working with VDUs (both 1992). Amended by SI 2002/2174.

Manual Handling Operations Regulations 1992 (SI 1992/2793)

These Regulations give effect to provisions of Council Directive 90/269/EEC on the minimum health and safety requirements for the manual handling of loads and, in particular, deal with the risk of back injury. The HSE has issued a guide (L23—see Appendix 5) which gives assistance with assessment of risk, its reduction and other matters. Amended by SI 2002/2174.

Personal Protective Equipment at Work Regulations 1992 (SI 1992/2966)

These Regulations contain health and safety requirements concerning the provision and use of personal protective equipment. They give effect to Council Directive 89/656/EEC on the minimum health and safety requirements for the use by workers of personal protective equipment at the workplace. For guidance, see L25 (Appendix 5 above). Amended by SIs 1994/2326, 1994/3017, 1996/3039, 1999/860 and 1999/3232 and 2002/2174.

Workplace (Health, Safety and Welfare) Regulations 1992 (SI 1992/3004)

These Regulations contain requirements as to the health, safety and welfare of persons in a workplace and give effect to Council Directive 89/654/EEC concerning the minimum safety and health requirements for the workplace. Guidance (L24—see Appendix 5 above), being an approved code of practice, has been published by the HSC. Amended by SIs 1995/2036, 1996/1592, 1999/2024 and 2002/2174.

Supply of Machinery (Safety) Regulations 1992 (SI 1992/3073)

These Regulations implement Council Directive 89/392/EEC, as amended by Directive 91/368/EEC (the "Machinery Directive"). They lay down general requirements as to the safety of machinery and marking procedures, as well as essential health and safety requirements. Amended by SI 1994/2063.

Construction (Design and Management) Regulations 1994 (SI 1994/3140)

These Regulations give effect to certain requirements of Council Directive 1992/57/EEC on the implementation of minimum safety and health requirements at temporary or mobile construction sites. Amended by SIs 1996/1592, 1998/494, 1999/3242 and 2000/2380 (see below).

Borehole Sites and Operations Regulations 1995 (SI 1995/2038)

These provisions contain the requirements of Council Directive 92/91/EEC concerning the minimum requirements for improving the safety and health protection of workers in the mineral extracting industries engaged in drilling. Amended by SI 1999/2463 and 1999/3242.

Reporting of Injuries Diseases and Dangerous Occurrences Regulations 1995 (SI 1995/3163)

These Regulations apply to specified serious injuries and diseases arising from or occurring at work. Notification of these matters is required, usually from the person having control of the premises in question, such as the owner of a mine or quarry or pipeline. The requirement to provide a report also arises where there is a dangerous occurrence, as specified in Sch.2. A "dangerous occurrence" includes fire, escape of gas, dangerous failure of plant, flood or failure of safety equipment. Report forms and guidance are available from the HSE. There are significant penalties for failure to report or to keep records. Amended by SIs 1996/2089, 1996/2092, 1997/2776, 1999/437, 1999/2024, 1999/2244, 1999/3232 and 2001/2975.

Health & Safety (Safety Signs and Signals) Regulations 1996 (SI 1996/341)

These Regulations implement Council Directive 92/58/EEC on the minimum requirements for the provision of safety and/or health signs at work. See below for amending regulations, the Carriage of Dangerous Goods (Classification, Packaging and Labelling) and Use of Transportable Pressure Receptacles Regulations 1996[7] and SI 1999/3242.

Pipeline Safety Regulations 1996 (SI 1996/825)

Most pipelines are subject to the requirements of these Regulations which relate mainly to design, safety systems, access for maintenance, type of construction and installation, and arrangements for incidents and emergencies, as well as decommissioning. There is a special section dealing with major accident hazard pipelines.

Health and Safety (Consultation with Employees) Regulations 1996 (SI 1996/1513)

There is a provision in these Regulations for implementation within Great Britain of parts of Council Directive 89/391/EEC on the introduction of

---

[7] SI 1996/2092.

measures to encourage improvements in the health and safety of employees at work. The regulations require employers to consult either their employees directly or representatives elected for that purpose. Amended by SIs 1997/1840 and 1999/3242 (see below), and by virtue of s.1(2) of the Employment Rights (Dispute Resolution) Act 1998.

Confined Spaces Regulations 1997 (SI 1997/1713)

These Regulations contain requirements and prohibitions affecting persons carrying work in confined spaces. Specific prohibitions apply where reasonably practical alternatives exist. Where they do not exist, a safe system of work is required together with provision for rescue. Amended by SI 1997/2776.

Fire Precautions (Workplace) Regulations 1997 (SI 1997/1840)

These important Regulations contain provisions on fire precautions in the workplace, enforcement and offences. They should be read in conjunction with the Management of Health and Safety at Work Regulations 1999 (see below).

Working Time Regulations 1998 (SI 1998/1833)

These extensive Regulations implement in the UK Council Directive 93/104 (the Working Time Directive). They contain rights and obligations relating to working time, exceptions, and provisions for special classes of persons. The schedule deals with workforce agreements. Amended by SI 1999/3242 and the Working Time Regulations 1999[8] and SI 2002/3128.

Provision and Use of Work Equipment Regulations 1998 (SI 1998/2306)

Health and safety requirements relating to the provision and use of work equipment are contained within these Regulations, replacing the 1992 Regulations which in turn mainly implemented Council Directive 89/655/EEC. The new Regulations also implement Council Directive 95/63/EEC. Duties relating to the control of work equipment, inspection and record keeping are placed on employers and employees. Amended by SIs 1999/860 and 1999/2001 and 2002/2174.

Lifting Operations and Lifting Equipment Regulations 1998 (SI 1998/2307)

These Regulations implement Council Directive 89/655/EEC, as amended by Council Directive 95/63/EEC, on the minimum health and safety

---

[8] SI 1999/3372.

requirements for the use of work equipment. Lifting equipment is defined as work equipment for lifting or lowering loads and includes attachments used for anchoring, fixing or support. Amended by SI 2002/2174 (see below)

Control of Major Accident Hazards Regulations 1999 (SI 1999/743)

Requirements relating to the control of major accident hazards involving dangerous substances are the subject of these Regulations. They implement Council Directive 1996/82/EEC on the control of major accident hazards involving dangerous substances. Various duties are imposed upon the operator of an establishment to facilitate the prevention of major accidents and the limitation of consequences. The Regulations require the provision of safety reports, emergency plans together with information to the public, the regulating authority and other persons. Amended by SI 1999/2597 and 2002/2469.

Quarries Regulations 1999 (SI 1999/2024)

It is often the case that landfill and associated operations will be undertaken within active quarries. These Regulations are therefore important to managers. Amended by SI 1999/3242 and 2002/2174.

Management of Health and Safety at Work Regulations 1999 (SI 1999/3242)

These Regulations spell out management responsibilities of employers under HSWA 1974. Obligations include the assessment of health and safety risks to employees and to anyone else with whom the business may come into contact as part of its activities. Provisions to manage these risks are also required.

Pressure Systems Safety Regulations 2000 (SI 2000/128)

These revoke and replace the Pressure Systems and Transportable Gas Containers Regulations 1989 and impose safety requirements on pressure systems and transportable gas containers to be used at work. Amended by SI 2001/1426.

Note also HSG series, over 200 in number, providing guidance on duties, responsibilities and relevant legislation.

Construction (Design & Management) (Amendment) Regulations 2000 (SI 2000/2380)

These regulations amend SI 1994/3140 (see above).

Dangerous Substances and Preparations (Safety) (Consolidation) and Chemicals (Hazard Information and Packaging for Supply) (Amendment) Regulations 2000 (SI 2000/2897)

These regulations implement EU Directive 99/43/EC. They revoke and replace similarly named regulations SI 1991/3193 and SI 1999/3194. As the name implies, the regulations have a consolidating and amending function.

Transportable Pressure Vessels Regulations 2001 (SI 2001/1426)

These Regulations implement Directive 1999/36/EC on transportable pressure equipment including requirements relating to the placing on the market and use at work of transportable pressure vessels.

Health and Safety at Work Etc Act 1974 (Application to Environmentally Hazardous Substances) Regulations 2002 (SI 2002/282)

These regulations extend the reference to dangerous substances in the Health and Safety at Work etc Act 1974 to include environmentally hazardous substances. These regulations revoke regulations SI 1996/2075 and SI 1999/40.

Chemicals (Hazardous Information and Packaging for Supply) Regulation 2002 (SI 2002/1689)

These Regulations revoke and re-enact with amendments the Chemicals (Hazard Information and Packaging for Supply) Regulations 1994, SI 1994/3247. These describe the procedures for classifying dangerous substances and dangerous preparations and the safety data sheets which must be provided when such substances are supplied.

Health and Safety (Miscellaneous Amendments) Regulations 2002 (SI 2002/2174)

These Regulations amend SI 1992/2792 (see above) and the minimum safety and health requirements for work with display screen equipment. They also amend SI 1992/2793 (see above) to include factors which must be considered in determining if manual handling operations involve risk and to give effect to Annex II of Directive 90/269/EEC. They also amend SI 1992/2966 (see above) to give effect to provisions of Directive 89/656/EEC, and SI 1998/2306 to give effect to provisions of Directive 95/63/EC on the minimum health and safety requirements for the use of work equipment.

Control of Asbestos at Work Regulations 2002 (SI 2002/2675)

These Regulations re-enact, with modifications, the Control of Asbestos at Work Regulations 1987 SI 1987/2115 and impose requirements for the protection of employees who might be exposed to asbestos at work and also certain duties on employees concerning their own protection from such exposure.

Control of Substances Hazardous to Health Regulations 2002 (SI 2002/2677)

These Regulations replace the Control of Substances Hazardous to Health Regulations 1999 SI 1999/437 and impose duties on employers to protect employees and others who may be exposed to substances hazardous to health. They also impose certain duties on employees concerning their own protection from such exposure and prohibited the import into the United Kingdom of certain substances and articles. Largely technical changes are made by the Control of Substances Hazardous to Health (Amendment) Regulation 2003 SI 2003/978.

Dangerous Substances and Explosive Atmospheres Regulations 2002 (SI 2002/2776)

These Regulations implement Directive 98/24/EC on the protection of the health and safety of workers from the risks related to chemical agents at work and impose requirements for the purpose of eliminating or reducing risks to safety from fire, explosion or other events arising from the hazardous properties of a "dangerous substance" in connection with work.

Notification of Installations Handling Hazardous Substances (Amendment) Regulation 2002 (SI 2002/2979)

These regulations amend SI 1982/1357 in relation to ammonium nitrate and mixtures containing ammonium nitrate.

The Health and Safety at Work Etc Act 1974 (Application to Environmentally Hazardous Substances) (Amendment) Regulations 2004 (SI 2004/463)

These regulations amend similarly named regulations of 2002 to incorporate references to EU directives 1999/45/EC, 2000/18/EC, 2003/28/EC and 2003/29/EC. It is intended to make further regulations to implement these directives.

INDEX